T0114146

ALSO BY JULIE SALAMON

White Lies

—

The Devil's Candy:
"The Bonfire of the Vanities"
Goes to Hollywood

The Net of Dreams

Julie Salamon

The Net of Dreams

A Family's Search for

a Rightful Place

RANDOM HOUSE

NEW YORK

Copyright © 1996 by Julie Salamon
All rights reserved under International and Pan-American Copyright
Conventions. Published in the United States by Random
House, Inc., New York, and simultaneously in Canada
by Random House of Canada Limited, Toronto.

Library of Congress Cataloging-in-Publication Data
Salamon, Julie.
The net of dreams: a family's search for a rightful place / Julie Salamon.
p. cm.
ISBN 978-0-8129-9169-7
1. Jews—Ukraine—Khust—Social life and customs. 2. Holocaust,
Jewish (1939–1945)—Ukraine—Khust. 3. Holocaust survivors—United
States—Biography. 4. Salamon, Julie. 5. Children of Holocaust
survivors—United States—Biography. I. Title.
DS135.U42K477   1996
940.53'18'092—dc20   95-21829

Book design by J. K. Lambert

146484122

For Roxie and Eli,
Alexandra and David

Oh, I would say, you've never understood me, Harry, that not out of vengeance have I accomplished all my sins but because something has always been close to dying in my soul, and I've sinned only in order to lie down in darkness and find, somewhere in the net of dreams, a new father, a new home.

William Styron,
Lie Down in Darkness

According to the dictionary, "to belong" means to have a rightful place. A rightful place is not one that is granted by the powers that be, not even by parents; this is too shaky a source for a true feeling of belonging. A rightful place is the place we gain for ourselves, first through loving and being loved in the right way, later through one's own efforts. This alone makes the place secure, one's very own.

Bruno Bettelheim,
A Good Enough Parent

Contents

The Net of Dreams

My mother, Lilly Salcman

"Sputnik"

■ Arthur, my stepfather, calls my mother "Sputnik."

Her name is Lilly. She isn't one of those lithe old ladies who fight age with diet and surgery and girlish clothing, though she does color her hair, leaving just enough gray for a certain authenticity. She has always eaten heartily and has widened a little over the years. Her face has some lines, her clothes are comfortable. Though she is past seventy, her vigor and hunger for experience remain primed.

So her response shouldn't have shocked me, I suppose, when I told her I was taking a trip to Auschwitz.

"I want to go with you," she said, as quickly and casually as if she'd said she wanted to go to the grocery store with me.

"What!"

But I meant to say this: "Are you crazy? What about all those avid declarations: 'I never want to go back there!' " *There* encompassed Auschwitz and Huszt, the eastern European town where she'd grown up. *There* encompassed loss so complete that scavenging for scraps of what had existed before seemed not only futile, but unbearable.

Not that the past was a forbidden subject with my mother. She spoke easily about her childhood and her experiences in concentration camp, but only when asked. She rarely brought up either subject herself and, when she did talk about them, was readily distracted. She has preferred to joke, "I have nine lives, like a cat." Whenever she has made that joke, I've laughed nervously; silently I tote up the lives used to figure how many are left. My mother has always contemplated those lives coolly, as if they belonged to somebody else.

My stomach began to hurt. I wish I could say it was only because I was worried that if my mother did join me the demons she's so successfully kept at bay would find new strength on their own wretched turf. But I was anxious for another reason as well. The instant my mother said she wanted to come I felt exhilarated, like a kid so young she still thinks it's exciting, not embarrassing, to have her mother help chaperone a class trip. The excitement set off ancient fears—that she would make all kinds of plans with me, then find something better to do.

I guess I've always understood that it's better not to count on her, just to be glad if she happened to show up. Eventually I came to understand—in theory—that this . . . flexibility may have gotten her through Auschwitz remarkably unscarred, so I must be grateful for it. But I admit that sometimes I have been ungrateful. Sometimes I have wished I could stop measuring my traumas against the impossible standard set by my parents.

Competing with those primal emotions were the rapid calculations of the professional journalist that I am. I wasn't going to Auschwitz to satisfy some general curiosity about human depravity or to fire religious fervor. I didn't need to convince myself that "never again" was a good idea. I would be going to Auschwitz for the reason other people visit family grave sites—not so much for ceremonial reasons but because of the suspicion that spirits may linger in the vicinity of the bodies that once contained them. My grandparents are buried at Auschwitz, and, possibly, probably, some part of my mother must be buried there, too. Who besides my mother could guide me through this family burial ground?

"Juliska?"

I was brought around by her warm voice, with its Hungarian lilt, seducing me with the affectionate nickname that rolled off her tongue like a grace note.

Instead of responding in kind, with warmth and affection, I put on a crisp professional voice. "Do you really want to go?"

I was ashamed. But that cool tone was my armor against the familiar feeling crawling all over me; the thrill of an excursion with Mommy— yes, still Mommy—fighting with the fear that she'd back out at the last minute.

She didn't seem to notice; she'd already set off on her own reverie. "You know, I don't remember much about Auschwitz. Mainly arriving and leaving. When we arrived it was nighttime. The Jewish kapos were helping us off the train onto a platform. While we were standing, there appeared Mengele, like a white god."

Josef Mengele! The Auschwitz celebrity doctor, the man most closely associated with the "selection." Mengele not only decided who would die and who would live. He also determined for what purposes new prisoners would live. Some would be sent to work camps, others might be useful to him and the other Nazi doctors for experiments.

My mother continued, "He started pointing with his finger: 'You go here. You go there.' He had a rather *goyishe* round face, and to me he looked very tall. He was very good looking, though most men look very good in uniform."

I was mesmerized, as I always have been, by my mother's weirdly romantic recapitulation of her history; glamorized, like a feature film, but also, possibly, an accurate reflection of the way, as a young girl, she had seen things then. Dropped into madness, she adjusted to madness. She had that ability, which could be interpreted either as another kind of lunacy or as an astonishing faith in sanity. She could stare evil in the face and make it familiar, thereby reducing it to something manageable. Mengele was good looking, but so what? *Most men look very good in uniform.* Mengele was despicable but ordinary, inhuman but human. His power, therefore, was limited—or so my mother convinced herself.

I wanted to hear more, but as usual she pushed aside the past for what was for her the far more interesting prospect of the unknown.

"But we can talk about that on the trip. When will you hear from Spielberg?"

———

▪ I was, in fact, waiting for a call from Steven Spielberg, the movie director. In the winter of 1993 I'd read that Spielberg was off to Poland to start shooting the film version of *Schindler's List,* the story of a hedonistic German industrialist who found a moment of grace—who became the righteous Gentile—by saving Jews from Nazis during World War II. The film crew would spend some time at Auschwitz.

I wondered whether Spielberg, who had not been too successful when he ventured away from fantasy and adventure films, had it in him to make a film about the Holocaust that wouldn't be embarrassing. I dismissed the thought: That's Spielberg's problem, not mine.

Then I had another thought: Book a ticket to Poland.

Poland? Impossible. Only one story waited for me in Poland and that was Auschwitz, and I was tired of trying to get my arms around it. It hadn't been that long since a cousin of mine devoted to preserving the memory of the Holocaust had encouraged me to join her on a tour of Auschwitz with the director of the new Holocaust Museum in Washington, which was then being planned. The chance of a lifetime, she told me. I told her I felt no need to see the place. I had seen it hundreds of times already—in photographs, in movies, in my dreams.

But now here was Steven Spielberg telling me—I was sure of it—that I had to go to Auschwitz, and I believed him.

Let me explain.

I'd spent the previous months flying back and forth from New York, where I live, to Adams County, the Appalachian outpost of southern Ohio where I grew up. Though I had left there twenty years before, the place continued to pull me back with a nagging persistence that periodically rested but was never put to rest.

I often mention my upbringing in this "colorful" impoverished backwater to let people know I'm not just another Jewish girl from New York. I have watched myself deliberately bring my parents into conversation, often as comic foils for amusing stories about the adventures of eastern European Jews in the American heartland. If the talk went deeper, allowing for the revelation that they were not just immigrants but concentration camp survivors, I dreaded the inevitable expressions of sympathy. I developed a practiced response: "Oh, no, it wasn't like *that* at all. My parents were very unusual, very upbeat. We were very happy."

We were—and we weren't. Like every family, we had our own mythology, and I accepted it, more or less. When my mother told me how lucky she was, how happy we were, I felt I had no choice but to believe her. If she, with her history, was lucky, then I was obliged to be lucky and happy beyond belief.

But when my father died six weeks after I finished high school, I didn't feel lucky at all. I felt unbearably sad. My father's death cracked the notion that my parents were infallible, having been tested in the cruelest of history's laboratories. I came to realize how little I knew of what they had been before, when they had been unlucky and unhappy.

Thus began what has been a lifelong reporting trip, as I tried time and again to write my family's story. The more data I accumulated, the more I found fact and fiction laying equal claim to my imagination. No matter how hard I tried to find the "truth," I found I still didn't know what to make of the happy family portraits sitting in pretty little frames all over my house. Were we—were they—tragic or triumphant?

Maybe things would have become clearer, faster, if I'd stayed in Ohio for a while, instead of dashing back and forth to New York City. But I had a husband and a little girl and a job. After several months all I had to show for my trouble was a big stack of notes and a sizable balance of frequent-flier miles on a bankrupt airline.

My mother had been monitoring my excursions to Ohio like a sports fan. Pursuit of the unknown was her favorite game; perhaps she sensed that, no matter what story I chose to tell, she and my father would figure prominently in it, and she was not averse to immortalization. She had always identified strongly with fictional heroines and was interested to read the story of her life. I had used her once as the model for a character in a novel; later I'd caught her referring to events that had taken place in the book—and only in the book—as though they had actually happened to her.

I wasn't worried that she would disapprove of my going to

Auschwitz. On the contrary, she would applaud my compliance with the dictates of "fate"—or instinct, or whatever it was that was navigating my course. I just hadn't expected her to come along.

———

■ I felt I could call Spielberg; a few years earlier I'd spent a week with him, part of research for a long profile I'd written about him during the decade I was film critic for *The Wall Street Journal*. We'd kept in touch.

I didn't really expect that his interpretation of a Holocaust novel would give me new insight into my parents' past. His parents were American born. What could he know of *my* Holocaust? Yes, he was a great filmmaker, but only so long as he stayed within the realm of fantasy. I questioned his taste—did his houses have to be so big, did he have to spend so much of his creative energy on amassing more wealth?

But seeing Auschwitz as part of a journey to a film set seemed like the only way I could do it. Nothing I would see in the present-day "museum" would reinstate the awful reality of half a century ago. Unreality might be the more appropriate operating mode, and what better place to find unreality than on a movie set where actors would be walking around in the costumes of concentration camp inmates?

Spielberg did call, to try to talk me out of the trip. "You'd be really disappointed in Auschwitz," he said. "It doesn't look like Auschwitz at all. The crematoria have all been knocked down, except for the one ABC built for *War and Remembrance*. It just looks like a park with a museum. We're having to build something that looks like Auschwitz."

How peculiar, I thought. My mother and father, survivors of Auschwitz and Dachau, had come to America to reconstruct themselves because their world was gone. Now Auschwitz, the symbol of what had destroyed that world, was being resurrected by the most American of filmmakers—more specifically, by the man who had created E.T., the friendly alien from outer space, and had then capitalized on his creation by reinventing Hollywood merchandising. What could he possibly know of Auschwitz anyway?

I had no idea then that *Schindler's List* would turn out to be a profoundly moving film, allowing Spielberg to do what he had been trying to do for years—find an "adult" way of expressing the feelings of loss and longing that had given *E.T.* such emotional truth. I wasn't hoping to watch a masterpiece in the making. I confess I really didn't care whether his movie worked or not. I just thought it might help me find my way home.

On the road, in a crummy hotel near the border of Slovakia and Ukraine. *From left:* me; my stepfather, Arthur Salcman; my mother.

1

Nine Lives

■ Our itinerary quickly took shape. We would travel to Huszt, which is now in Ukraine (and is now spelled "Khust"), to Auschwitz, and to Prague. The rest depended on Arthur Salcman, my stepfather. He had recently had a pacemaker installed and couldn't decide whether he felt confident enough to make the trip. He had his own reasons both for wanting to go and for not wanting to go. He had spent the war underground, sometimes fighting with partisans, sometimes working with false papers that identified him as a Gentile.

He'd married my mother in 1975, four years after my father died, two years after his wife died. It didn't take long for Arthur, a quiet, orderly man—an engineer—to realize that he was living with a perpetual-motion machine. She was constantly surprising him with announcements: "Guess who's spending the weekend?"

Or, more unsettling: "Pack your bags. We're going to the airport."

So the nickname he had for her, "Sputnik," carried with it both affection and irritation. Arthur often felt as though he was being dragged in his wife's orbit, an experience that galled him but that he found more pleasurable than he would often admit.

This time the balance was tipped by my mother's nagging and by the free frequent-flier tickets I had to offer. Bratislava was added to the itinerary so Arthur could visit his sister, Zhoffka, and her family. She could have left when he had, forty-five years earlier; they had relatives in America who had provided both of them with visas. But for that generation of European Jews cruel irony was the rule. Zhoffka had survived Auschwitz only to find that her American visa didn't include her husband—even though Arthur's included his wife.

I was slowly coming to understand what should have been obvious from the start. This would be like no other reporting trip I'd ever taken. I would have little control over the agenda. I would be traveling in my mother's wake. She would determine the emotional as well as the geographic landscape.

That became clear not long after our first tentative discussions about the trip. A thick envelope arrived in the mail containing two AAA maps of eastern Europe and a brief note: "Can't wait to leave for our trip. Love, Mommy. P.S. Have you called about renting a car?"

It didn't even occur to me to resist, not even when I heard my sister Suzy's persuasive reason for not coming with us. (How could she leave her two small children for two weeks?) I placed some calls to rental car agencies and taped one of the maps to our kitchen refrigerator, outlining our route with a pink marker so my husband and daughter could follow our travels. I ignored the fact that my three-year-old hadn't yet mastered the connection between our apartment on Sullivan Street and the rest of New York. For her, everywhere we traveled, whether it was Fifty-ninth Street or another country, was simply the place where we stepped off the plane or train. As my guilt over leaving my own child heightened, I began filling the house with mementos of me.

My map knowledge of eastern Europe wasn't much better than my daughter's, even though the war in Bosnia had made that map a front-page staple of my daily newspapers. This came as a shocking revelation one afternoon as I stared at the map I'd taped to the refrigerator (I was saving the other one, in pristine condition, for the trip). Suddenly it struck me. Huszt was *in Ukraine*. The realization should have been no more surprising than the fact that my nose sat in the middle of my face. I knew that after the war my parents had left Czechoslovakia because their hometowns had been annexed by the USSR and Prague was about to fall to the Communists. Why had I never found the locus of these events? I am a reasonably curious person. And I like maps. Whenever I travel, whether on subway or airplane, I always trace my route on a map. It gives me the illusion that I know where I'm going.

Yet I didn't know exactly where the Carpathian Mountains are—Podkarpatská Rus, the foothills of the Carpathian Mountains, to be precise. Was I simply avoiding what I knew? That my family was part of the East (uneducated, impoverished, uncultured), not the West. That my family had lived among the *shtetl* Jews, or awfully close to them. They had always been so proud to be Czech, but it was obvious to me now, staring at the AAA map, that no matter what the political boundaries had become by the time my mother was born in 1922, Podkarpatská Rus was awfully close to the Russian pale. This wasn't the Czechoslovakia of Bohemia or Moravia with its comparatively noble history. This was the land of the *shtetl*—and of Gypsies, Slovaks, Hungarians, and Ukrainians—an ignorant backwater that had been annexed by the USSR after World War II. Now communism was finished and the place where my parents were from had been reshuffled again. Their birthplace had lost the status of affiliation with Czechoslovakia or the former Austro-Hungarian Empire. They were from the Ukraine.

As I stared at the map, I remembered a dinner my husband and I had been invited to at a chic Manhattan restaurant. Our host, a man who liked expensive food and lively conversation, had seated me next to a prominent New Yorker, a Jew who had escaped the Nazis and then returned to Europe as a spy for the Allies. He was a combative man who used his cleverness as a weapon. When he asked about my background I told him my parents were from Czechoslovakia.

"What did they do there?" he asked.

I told him my mother's family owned timberland; my father's owned vineyards.

"Impossible," he said. "*Those Jews* didn't own anything. Where were your parents during the war?"

It's a question I don't like to answer. I hate seeing the pity that follows, the set of assumptions that people attach to "concentration camp survivors," assumptions that don't suit my parents at all.

I found it hard to avoid this direct inquiry, so I told him.

He stared at me coldly.

"Anyone who had anything got out," he said with urbane scorn, the same dismissiveness I'd heard in an editor's voice when I was a new reporter in New York and confessed I was unfamiliar with the city's exclusive private men's clubs.

I wanted to stab him with all three forks at my table setting. Instead I muttered, "They didn't know."

"How could they not know?" he asked with self-righteous disdain. He seemed to be saying, *Those stupid Jews, they deserved what they got, the ones who weren't smart like me.*

Our host noticed the bumps disturbing the smooth flow of conversation. He raised his voice slightly, to engage the entire group in whatever it was he was talking about.

Now, kneeling in front of the map stuck to my refrigerator, I wondered whether I was any different from the man at dinner. I had been proud to be a descendant of prewar Czechoslovakia, always talked about in my home as a kind of Camelot, a place where the ancient rivalries and hatreds of Europe had briefly been laid to rest. It was something else to be part of the *shtetl*—something shameful.

———

▪ The AAA map also reminded me to apply for a visa from the Ukrainian Embassy. I called my mother to remind her to do the same and to ask her whether I should try to rent a car with automatic shift so she could drive. My heart sank when she told me not to worry about renting a car; Arthur's sister knew of a driver who could take us around "for a very good price" and who knew the ropes at the border between Slovakia and Ukraine. We really didn't need to get a visa; the man could arrange everything, my mother assured me. I worried, remembering the last time my family and I had visited my mother and Arthur in Florida, where they spend the winter months.

Before we had made that particular trip, I had begged her not to pick us up at the airport. It's a long drive from the apartment they use in Saint Petersburg. Even though Arthur looks like a trim, hearty man in his sixties and still carries his golf clubs the entire distance of an eighteen-hole course, he is in fact eighty years old. My mother balked at first, unable to bear the thought of us forking over twenty-five dollars unnecessarily to a cab driver. Then she agreed. However, not long before we left, she told us she'd hired a private taxi to pick us up.

"A car service?" I asked dubiously.

"Why do you sound so suspicious?" she asked. "Janet recommended them."

"How much do they charge?" I asked.

Silence. "Don't worry about that. I'll take care of it. You'll just be more comfortable this way."

At the baggage claim in Saint Petersburg we looked around for someone holding up a sign with our names. That someone didn't appear; we collected our bags and were about to look for a taxi when a frail old man who clearly didn't have all his wits about him pressed a crumpled piece of yellow paper into my hand. Being from New York, I automatically reached into my pocket for change. Then I saw that he was pointing at the paper. I glanced at it and saw my name scrawled there, even spelled correctly.

"Oh, nice to see you," I said.

"Shhhh," he said and grabbed my bag, and nodded for us to follow him. If the old man hadn't seemed so pathetic, we might have been afraid; as it was, we didn't want to hurt his feelings by questioning him. So my husband and I took hold of our little girl and our suitcases and followed dutifully, into the bowels of the parking garage. Finally, to our relief, we stopped in front of a car that did indeed have a taxi light on the roof.

Just as the old man opened the trunk and put our suitcases inside, a police car roared up next to us. My husband and daughter and I backed away while the policeman began to ask the old man questions. It was a gentle interrogation.

"Do you have an airport license?"

The old man shrugged and smiled sadly.

My husband and I had been whispering to each other, wondering whether we should cover for the old man and say we were his children. We were spared by the policeman: "Don't worry, I'm just going to give him a warning."

As we began walking back through the parking garage to get a real taxi, the old man waved at us cheerily, as though everything were going according to plan.

———

■ "We aren't going to repeat the Saint Petersburg experience in Hungarian?" I asked.

"Slovak," my mother said.

"What?" I replied.

"Bratislava is now in the Slovak Republic. The driver's first language will be Slovak," said my mother.

"Get a visa," I replied.

———

■ I felt as though I were trekking into the wild for a stay of indeterminate duration, not flying to places where minimum comfort was ensured and for a brief period of time. Feeling a need to set my house in order, I called my sister and my closest friends, and I left elaborate instructions for my husband on how to deliver the postcards I'd left behind for our daughter.

Then I called Hilu, my Uncle Joe. Joseph Rapaport is my mother's older brother and my only living uncle. When I think of him I smell Bain de Soleil suntan cream, the thick orange goop he used to smear on liberally before we sunbathed all day by the ocean at Miami Beach, where we used to spend Christmas vacations together. I feel a pain in my cheek, as if the mere thought of him brings the inevitable pinch. I feel a different pain, the sweet pain of nostalgia, as I remember his valiant efforts to teach me to speak Russian and the way he used to sneak with me into the cafeteria at the corporate headquarters of Merrill Lynch & Company when he came to Manhattan from Queens—his favorite restaurant because the meals were subsidized by the company. Uncle Joe felt entitled to eat there because he was a Merrill Lynch customer, and he was outraged that the company restricted its cafeteria to employees. I believe he was titillated by the excitement of having to duck past the guard, the feeling of getting something for nothing.

I also feel incredibly anxious because we have engaged in many battles over the years—because, my mother tells me, I don't know when to keep my mouth shut. Uncle Joe is short and round and full of opinions, which he dispenses with exclamatory vividness in an emphatic, gravelly voice. It's impossible to predict whether an event will trigger compassion or accusation, whether the roughness in his voice will seem textured or simply cruel. One Yom Kippur, for example, I walked out of the dinner I had prepared to break the fast because he accused my cousin of murdering her parents (in fact, she had been driving the car at the time of the accident and had suffered greatly for her unintended participation in their deaths). Yet when he heard of the financial troubles of a distant cousin in Israel, my frugal uncle immediately asked my mother how big a check he should send.

He is our family eccentric. In his studio apartment in Queens, he kept complete sets of pots and pans hidden under the bed. Blenders, mixers, and other household appliances still in their boxes were crammed into every corner—relics of the 1970s, when banks gave free gifts to new customers. Uncle Joe had accumulated a fair amount of cash "moonlighting" as a refrigerator repairman. He spent much of his spare time moving his money from account to account to collect the goods.

He moved to Saint Petersburg, Florida, from New York a few years ago. These days his biggest pleasure comes from dining out at a local all-you-can-eat buffet.

The rap on Uncle Joe, who has spent most of his life living alone, has always been that he was born cranky. My mother thinks he may have become a curmudgeon later, when he was made to feel guilty for what it is speculated that he did to my grandmother's beautiful legs.

Berthe Rapaport, their mother, was twenty-three when Joe, her fourth child, was born in March 1914. She was still nursing him six months later when rumors swept through Podkarpatská Rus, which was then part of the Austro-Hungarian Empire: The Cossacks are coming. Her husband, my grandfather, wanted to try to salvage a business he'd been dabbling in, so he sent Berthe and the children ahead to what they thought would be safe haven, the town where her mother lived. They had time to pack only the silver candlesticks and a feather pillow so the children could rest en route.

They traveled by horse and wagon south to the town where they could catch a train that would take them where they wanted to go. The station was jammed with refugees on the move. There was no place to sit down. Joe began squalling. His later squally nature allowed legend to transmogrify that natural cry for food into unreasonable impatience. Berthe found a cold stone to sit on so she could nurse him.

It's been said that the cold caused the veins in one leg to pop. Whether or not this conforms to medical knowledge is irrelevant. What matters is that Berthe had one beautiful leg and one swollen one, mottled with varicose veins, and baby Joe was held responsible. It was one of those pieces of family knowledge that seem to float in the air—never mentioned but always known.

Joe has lived a life that has given him many reasons to be crotchety. This legitimacy doesn't make it any easier to call him. You never know what will happen. He might launch into a diatribe about the evening news that cannot be interrupted without risking retribution that can last weeks or years. He might do forty-five minutes on your last breach of etiquette. Or, if you're lucky, he'll spin off into a reverie of days gone by. On these occasions I see that, despite the opposition of their manner and world outlook (Pollyanna versus Cassandra), he really is my mother's brother. They share a storyteller's gift, an ability to find narrative splendor in ordinary events and narrative order in chaos.

"So you're going to Huszt," he said when I called to say good-bye. Anything could follow that opening. I waited cautiously.

"I went back to Huszt after the war," he said, "to see what was there."

I allowed myself to breathe and settled into my chair, fairly secure that a good story would follow.

He didn't disappoint me. "A relative was living in my parents' house," said Joe. "There was some furniture there, but most of the things had been taken out. I went for a walk into town, and a Russian came up to me. I started to talk to him in Hungarian, and he said, 'Talk Russian, this is a Russian town now.'"

" 'What are you doing?' he asked me.

"I said, 'I just came back from concentration camp and I'm looking around.'

" 'Come to work,' he said. 'We're putting up a statue of Stalin in the town square and need workers.'

" 'I told you, I just came back from concentration camp.'

"He looked at me like an idiot. 'You look healthy to me. Come get to work.'

"I didn't say a word, but I thought to myself, 'I just came away from concentration camp. I don't need to do this again.' So I went to the train station. When the first train arrived, I asked the engineer where he was going.

" 'To Bucharest,' he said.

"The trains were free in those days after the war. I climbed on board, thinking I'd never been to Bucharest. I arrived there, found the Jewish relief agency, and they gave me a place to sleep and some food. I stayed in Bucharest a few days, looked around to see what was there. Then I took a train to Prague."

I had heard this story many times before and took comfort in its ritualistic familiarity as well as its symbolism. I imagined my uncle's eyes lighting up as they always do when he tells it, and I felt myself responding as I always do when he talks about boarding the train for Bucharest, not knowing where he was going. At that moment I understand—or think I understand—the thrill of complete freedom.

I can't help it, but being American and of a certain age, I always start humming Janis Joplin when I hear that story: *Freedom's just another word for nothing left to lose.* No job, no family, no home, no nothing, just a free train ride to wherever the trains were going. No schedules either on the War Refugee Tour of Europe.

I realized Uncle Joe was saying good-bye.

"Have fun," he said, without irony.

———

■ The night before we left, a friend told me he had seen a news report about a psychologist who took a group of Holocaust survivors' children from America to Germany to spend a week with children of Nazis.

At first the offspring of victims and victimizers were wary and hostile. But, according to my friend's account, by the end of the week they were all hugging one another, having come to some understanding that they were more similar than different.

"How interesting," I said noncommittally. I didn't find this reconciliation heartwarming. I thought, "There may or may not be a connection between me and them but I don't feel a need to give up my grudge. My children can do that. Maybe then it will be time for the blood to cool. Not yet, though. Not for me. I don't feel I'm okay, they're okay. I don't want to hug."

———

■ On May 16, 1993, I found myself sitting with my mother in the compact but comfortable backseat of Leopold Schragge's bright blue Škoda. My stepfather was up front, and we were all on the way to Cracow from Bratislava, now the capital of the four-month-old Slovak Republic.

We had arrived two days earlier, carrying our small suitcases and two huge boxes. They were filled with booty my mother had picked up during a shopping spree at Sage Allen, a New England clothing store chain that was going out of business. This was a solemn occasion in Old Saybrook, where Sage Allen had been a sturdy mainstay until it was sold as part of a leveraged buyout.

This small example of unfettered capitalism produced hosannas among the relatives in Bratislava. Forty-dollar blouses on sale for two dollars! Sheets and comforters 90 percent off!

Nothing stimulated my mother's generosity better than a going-out-of-business sale combined with a trip to loved ones living in a country without shopping centers. Even as we were turning the boxes over to TWA at the airport, my mother was asking me, "Are you sure you don't need some Laura Ashley sheets?" (Only the bottoms; top sheets weren't included in the bargain.) "How about a comforter, $299 down to $50? Beautiful."

All that seemed far away as the sun beamed in through the Škoda's little sunroof. It was easy to feel part of the cacophony of eastern Europe, with Arthur and Leopold talking Slovak in the front seat, my mother and I speaking English in the back, and my mother and Arthur occasionally using Hungarian to clarify something being translated. We were like archeologists, almost oblivious to the present, forever looking at the landscape for signs of the past. This wasn't as simple as it may sound. Though the past I was seeking was only fifty years removed, the landscape we were traveling across had changed enormously since then and was still in the midst of huge upheaval. Communism had come and gone. To the south, in Bosnia, ancient hatreds had rekindled the instant "freedom" was restored. In Czechoslovakia, nationalism was asserting itself in a more benign way. The state was divided in two: Slovakia to the east, the Czech Republic to the west.

This history eluded the Bratislava I visited with my mother and stepfather. In the home of Arthur's sister, Zhoffka, we ate soup and cakes and cholent—a traditional Jewish casserole made many ways but always with beans. They smelled and tasted like soups and cakes and cholents I'd eaten in my mother's kitchen and all over the world, and that always made me feel at home.

We were given a brief walking tour of Bratislava by Zhoffka's son, Otto, a math professor at the university. My mother examined the streets warily, trying unsuccessfully to recapture some memory of the city she'd visited fifty-six years ago, when her older sister Rozsi had lived there and gave birth to her daughter, Ilana. My mother was the first person to hold the baby and has always been convinced that's why Ilana looks like her, dark and sturdy, instead of like my aunt Rozsi, who was pale and slender.

I can't remember what Bratislava looked like. I only remember the smell of lilac and jasmine near Bratislava Castle, which dominates the city; it was being converted into a residence for the president of the new Slovak Republic. Otto couldn't remember his name. "He's a guy who worked in a bank, spent some time in Switzerland, and four years ago decided to try politics."

He shrugged. "No big deal." It was unclear whether he was referring to the president or to his own inability to remember the president's name.

Otto, a tall, lanky man with appealing puppy dog eyes, speaks the special ironic language of eastern Europe, a language born of double-speak and secrets. He grew up speaking in code and has never lost the habit. "Being a Jew was just another tough secret, something else not to speak about in the house. Like my father listening to radio broadcasts from Vienna, like me checking out the Voice of America." Otto hadn't known he was a Jew until he was thirteen or fourteen, when he found a document identifying his mother as a former Auschwitz inmate. He traveled to Israel to visit relatives when he was a teenager and briefly considered emigrating, yet his own sons didn't find out they were Jewish until recently, when they were teenagers themselves.

The secrecy was necessary under communism, said Otto. "Everyone of a certain class was forced into the hiding of religion," he said. "Religious services never stopped, but the worshippers were people who sweep, low jobs." We visited a Soviet memorial to the World War II dead, still standing but unlit since the "new freedom" of 1989. We passed a restaurant, expensive by local standards, that had once housed the oldest yeshiva in Europe. We watched a Slovakian comedy show. One of the guests was a pretty girl: Miss Slovakia. She would represent Czechoslovakia in the Miss Universe contest that summer, even though the country she would be representing no longer existed.

Otto and his wife, Marcella, had found Leopold Schragge, our driver, through his daughter, a librarian who worked with Marcella. Leopold, a short, stocky man with a broad Slovak face and narrow oriental eyes, had been a trucker. He'd traveled all over Slovakia and twice had been to Moscow—in 1968 to deliver costumes for Holiday on Ice, the American ice show, and again two years later, carrying a more prosaic load of paint for pipes and refrigerators.

The story of how he had begun shuttling Jews around eastern Europe was, like so many stories there, rooted in both the distant and the recent past. Though now maybe 3,500 people of Slovakia's 5 million population admit to being Jewish, Bratislava was once a mecca for Jews from all over the world, or at least eastern Europe. The attraction was the Hassan Sofer, the founder of the yeshiva that was now a restaurant. In 1940 a tunnel was built for a road crossing and the Jewish cemetery by the yeshiva had to be moved. But the Jews didn't want to move the Hassan Sofer's resting place, so his remains were left in a cave behind the tunnel. Legend has it that when the Germans later tried to move the Hassan Sofer, the first German who put his shovel into the ground died on the spot.

When religious people would come to visit the rabbi's remains, they were directed to a woman who possessed the key. She in turn would call on Leopold to drive them to the burial site. More or less conversant in Slovak, Hungarian, German, Czech, and Yiddish, Leopold would chat with these visitors, many of them from America, and discovered many of them wanted to make pilgrimages to the towns they'd come from and weren't sure how to do it. He soon understood there was a market for his services beyond the dead rabbi's grave. He began a little business as guide and chauffeur for expatriate Jews who had come back home.

His little Škoda would carry us across the Tatra Mountains into Poland, then east to Ukraine, then back to Slovakia. I will never forget the hours I spent with my mother in the backseat of that tiny car, learning things I had thought I would never know. The motion of the car seemed to have the effect of a hypnotic trance. Though my mother generally skips from subject to subject, she spoke, into the tiny clip-on microphone I'd brought along, with rigorous concentration and endurance for hours at a stretch about events that had taken place a half century ago or more.

Up front, Arthur and Leopold Schragge continued to chat enthusiastically in Slovakian. Though Arthur's hometown language had been Hungarian, like my mother's, he'd been educated in Kassa (now Košice) and had worked as an engineer at the Škoda plant in Pilsen—both Slovakian cities—before the war. Czech had been his operating language during these fertile periods of his life, as well as during his tenure as a heavy-artillery officer in the Czech Army, and he was glad to have a chance to speak it again.

We had a good time on the road, pausing at rest stops the Slovaks labeled "Nonstops" and eating in the trucker restaurants Leopold liked. The food was densely comforting; I have fond memories of *bryndzo i halušky*, a potato dumpling mixed with a strong, stinky sheep cheese called *bryndza*. Leopold ate it the traditional way, with cracklings—crisp-fried bits of goose or duck fat. We had ours the American way, cholesterol reduced, without cracklings.

The budding of early spring gave a downy beauty to fields littered with ugly prefabricated buildings, remnants of the years of Soviet occupation. As we drove northward the countryside became more mountainous, the houses more charming. However, we were no casual scenery gazers. For us this landscape held many unmarked monuments.

When, for example, we passed a sign for Banská Bystrica, Arthur called back to us, "This is the town where I was captured as a partisan. The exact place was Mount Kislinky." Then he told us a story.

———

■ In 1943 Arthur was doing office work for a tractor factory in Slovakia. The owner was a Zoltán Hazay, a Hungarian whom Arthur described as "a real human being," the highest of compliments, though Mr. Hazay's kindnesses were carried out at a time when one could easily think of describing behavior as "real human" as the worst insult. Mr. Hazay was not a Jew, yet he risked a great deal to save the life of at least one Jew.

In 1943, four years after the German occupation of Czechoslovakia, the invitation Zoltán Hazay extended to Arthur for Christmas dinner would have been enough to make him a fond memory. But Mr. Hazay's kindnesses were more complicated and more dangerous than that. When the Russians began their advance from the east, he moved his factory from one section of Slovakia to another and hired Arthur to be the overseeing engineer, in charge of the redesign and refurbishing of tractors.

It is impossible to imagine the effect of this double life on Arthur, who was working under the Hungarian Christian name of Miklós Szabó (Arthur's private tribute to the real Miklós Szabó, another non-Jew who had previously saved his life). Arthur is an engineer not just by training but in character, a man who takes pleasure in seeing things work the way they are supposed to. He believes in order, not whimsy. Yet the rules of society, as he had so carefully come to understand them, simply weren't in operation in those years. He lived in terror, knowing that every breath he took depended on the success of a lie, on his ability to be Miklós Szabó instead of Arthur Salcman.

The Hazay factory was in Slovakian territory, officially under German occupation. Arthur eased his conscience by telling himself that his factory was doing work not for the Germans but for civilian farmers. But he came to realize in a horribly specific way that there were those who might consider him a traitor. He watched as a young man, a Christian, captured by ten soldiers, was marched to the front of a big church. The soldiers put a mask on him, accused him of spying for the enemy, and shot him. He fell to the ground, writhing and begging for forgiveness. He was shot again.

The soldiers were part of the local underground; the man they shot was accused of working with the Germans. So when two soldiers drove up to the factory in a jeep one day and called him not "Miklós Szabó" but "Lieutenant Salcman," he thought his time was up. After four years of moving, of hiding, the thought was becoming familiar but no less terrifying.

He was taken to the local leader of the Czech Resistance, a man who knew Arthur's military background. He was given a uniform, a rank (lieutenant) and a unit. For the next few months he and his men traveled through western Slovakia, heading toward Bratislava. They would stop in little towns to try to recruit the Slovak soldiers fighting for the Germans. Some joined the partisans, many didn't. Many Slovaks were pleased to have the Germans dispense with the Jews; Slovakian president Monsignor Josef Tiso, impatient for the Final Solution's completion, paid the Germans to ship "his" Jews to concentration camps.

After three months Arthur's troops joined thousands of other partisans on Mount Kislinky, dependent on ammunition and food dropped from the air by the Russians and the British (much of which was found by the Germans). It was a ragtag outfit of Jews, Slovaks, Russians, and Czechs, living in tents, finding relief from the cold only when the snow was heavy enough to serve as insulation. They got so hungry they ate horses killed by gunfire.

Inevitably they were captured, not by the Germans but by the *vlasovci*, Russian soldiers who had defected. Not wanting anything to differentiate him from the group, Arthur pulled off his lieutenant's badge.

They were marched through the forest, down the mountain, where they joined other prisoners under German escort. Cold and hunger briefly created the illusion of camaraderie among the prisoners and their guards.

But it soon became apparent to Arthur that this goodwill born of misery did not extend to Jews. A German officer lay gravely wounded on the ground near his unit. One of the captured soldiers identified himself as a doctor.

"What's your name?" he was asked.

"Spitz," he said.

The officer began yelling. "I don't want a Jew."

Arthur remembered that moment as a turning point. If an officer would rather die than accept help from a Jew, every captured soldier was suspect.

"Who are you? What are you?" they were asked.

They soon learned not to "confess" if they were Jews. Those who did were pulled aside. Their pants were pulled down (to see if they were circumcised), and they were shot as the other soldiers marched by.

The Jews stopped confessing. The interrogators were forced to more devious lines of questioning.

"*Sprechen Sie Deutsch?*" Arthur was asked.

He spoke German very well. But under the circumstances the knowledge was nothing to brag about. It would only mark him as educated and quite likely a Jew. Before he could answer, the soldier next to him, a Slovak, answered for him, in very broken German: "*Er sprecht nicht Deutsch.*"

The German soldier seemed offended. He smacked Arthur on the head with his rifle and snarled, "You dumb bandit." Then he moved on, leaving Arthur to his fate, which, it turned out, wasn't to die at the perimeter of Mount Kislinky.

———

■ Leopold Schragge isn't a religious man, strictly speaking, though he did tell us that he has put on *t'fillin*—leather straps that tie on a box holding prayers on parchment—every day, even during the Communist years. He admitted his devotion to religious observance became more exacting after he went into the business of carting returned Jews around the old country and realized many of his customers were Orthodox. Conspicuously taped to the outside of the Škoda's glove compartment was a piece of paper with Hebrew writing on it.

"What does it say?" I asked Arthur.

He translated the words into richly accented English: "Be the will of our God, the God of our ancestors, to guide us in peace, protect us for our life . . . and return us in peace."

The prayer seemed familiar. I'm sure I've mumbled some variation of it by rote in synagogues over the years. Yet its meaning settled into my heart in the most profound way over the next few days during our passage across what would feel more and more powerfully like unhallowed ground.

Actors on the set of *Schindler's List*

2

Good Color

■ "Tell me what you dreamed and I'll tell you what it meant," sings Golde the milkman's wife to her husband, Tevye, in *Fiddler on the Roof.*

I didn't need Golde to figure out the dream I had the night before I met Steven Spielberg at Skarżysko-Kamienna, a town two hours north of Cracow.

I was walking around a run-down part of town with my daughter, Roxie. At first I didn't know what town, or even what country. Then I realized where I was. My dream was set in one of those wrong-side-of-the-tracks places that used to show up in film noirs.

My daughter was hungry. I took her into a desolate café from another era and a different world. The waitress who came for our order looked the way Bette Davis did in *The Petrified Forest.*

"Don't look over there, honey," she said.

Of course I had to look. Someone was lying on the floor, drunk or dead, in a puddle of vomit. I felt sick, unable to stomach what I was seeing, unable to look away.

When I finally broke my gaze I realized that Roxie had disappeared. I ran out onto the street. There she was, being pulled into an X-rated video store by a woman dressed as a Gypsy. As I ran up the street I thought, "No one dresses like that anymore, do they?"

My mouth was dry as I gasped for air. My exertions seemed useless. The door to the video store seemed to be moving as fast as I was running.

Just when I thought I would collapse, my little daughter emerged from the shop. She was running toward me. "What a resourceful kid!" I thought proudly, instantly forgetting that the situation was dangerous until I saw that the Gypsy was just a few steps behind her.

Invigorated by Roxie's spirit, I began running again, now with a comforting sense of building momentum. I felt my hand lift involuntarily as I closed in on the Gypsy. I watched in amazement as my index finger and pinky went up in the air and I began to hiss: *I curse you. Keep away from my daughter.*

———

▪ I couldn't go back to sleep for a long time after the dream. When I did, finally, I slept so deeply I didn't hear my alarm go off at 6 A.M. Instead I was awakened by the phone ringing at five minutes to seven.

I dimly heard my mother's voice. "Are you ready?"

"Five minutes," I mumbled.

So much for preparing myself for the day with a shower and a leisurely shampoo. I would meet Steven Spielberg with dirty hair.

Six weeks earlier I'd gotten a call from Poland, from Anne-Marie Stein, the publicist working on *Schindler's List*. Her job was to herd press people onto the set of *Schindler's List* and to give them the illusion that they had managed, in just a few hours, to become privy to the "real story" behind the film.

"Steven said you can come." Her voice was faint. The phone connections to Cracow were also a throwback to another time, crackling and faint.

"Great!" I said. "Auschwitz?"

"No," she said. "We're done with Auschwitz. We filmed there for two days and finished. Oh, it was amazing. They wouldn't let us build inside, so we put up five barracks in the parking lot at Birkenau."

I interrupted. "Can I see those?"

"No," she said. "They tore those down after they were done."

Ever reassuring, she said, "But don't worry. You can still visit Auschwitz. There's nothing as complete as what we built, but it's amazing. And when you visit the set—I'll let you know what we'll be filming when you get here—I can promise you all the locations are amazing. Really authentic."

"Well, thanks," I said, trying not to sound as ungracious as I felt. "Could you send me hotel recommendations and information on visiting Auschwitz?"

"No problem," said Anne-Marie. She followed through on April 10 with a cheery fax. "You do not need any reservation, and there is no charge to visit either Auschwitz or Birkenau," she wrote, with assurances that "getting there really isn't very difficult."

I thought, "That may be. It's getting *away* from it that really is very difficult."

———

▪ The Cracovia was my choice, picked blindly from guide books after I found the more charming hotels Anne-Marie had suggested were filled. Listed among the luxury hotels, the Cracovia sounded fine. "Recently renovated . . . the furniture is a bit heavy but it's quite comfortable" was the description in one book.

The description wasn't inaccurate. The hotel's exterior blurs in my mind with much of the Communist-era architecture: big and bland, like an all-white Holiday Inn. But I remember my little room distinctly—more or less the size of a prison cell with dark, heavy, sparse furniture: a bed, a desk, a closet. The bathroom was clean and the price acceptable: sixty dollars a night. For eighty dollars my mother and Arthur got a "suite"—two cells joined together. Leopold Schragge offered no opinion, but he seemed pleased with his accommodations. Indeed, he seemed reluctant to emerge from his room, where he occupied himself with the television and a nice spread of sausages and bread and schnapps he'd brought with him from home. When we asked him if he'd like to come with us to meet Steven Spielberg, he laughed.

"I'm happy here," he told us.

The call from my mother gave me five minutes to get ready. Anne-Marie had said she would pick us up downstairs in front of the hotel at 7 A.M. I stumbled out of bed and knocked against the desk. There was no room in this hotel for partial wakefulness; all senses were required just to maneuver between the furniture and the walls. In five minutes I was dressed in the khaki shirt and black linen pants I had decided was the uniform of the foreign correspondent (though more suitable for Cairo than Cracow).

I met Arthur and my mother downstairs. Shivering in the cool morning air, my mother complained that the early call had forced us to miss breakfast, a huge buffet that was included in the price.

This simple and legitimate complaint set off a complicated barrage of thoughts. I was annoyed at her simply for giving voice to my own desire for coffee, then angry at myself. Why shouldn't she complain? She, after all, was entitled to complain. Unlike me, she didn't have to measure petty discomfort against Auschwitz. She'd endured, she'd survived. She didn't have to be stoic about anything.

We waited for nearly half an hour. Anne-Marie apparently wasn't struck by the same sense of urgency that had propelled us out of bed. Finally, at 7:25, a large white van rolled up and she rumbled out, winning forgiveness with a profusion of apologies.

We settled into the middle seat of the van, with Anne-Marie up front with the handsome young driver, Itek, and began our trip to Skarżysko. This had been the site of a munitions plant used by the Germans during World War II. It had, in fact, been one of the forty so-called satellite camps for Auschwitz; Jews had been brought in, 1,200 at a time, to handle phosphorus and sulfur—toxic materials—without protection. Every week or two, a new transport would bring replacements for the dead. Between 1941 and 1945, 35,000 Jews worked and died at Skarżysko. There is no mention of this history at the Skarżysko plant, which is still in operation, though it no longer makes deadly weapons. For a few days the factory, which still contains some fifty-year-old machinery, would be used as a movie set, Oskar Schindler's shell-casing factory.

Our drive took us through the verdant Polish farmland, which looked a little like southern Ohio, only grander, more sweeping. We seemed to be moving backward in time. The few tractors we saw were tiny by American standards; other signs of modernity were relatively few—the occasional International Harvester bin. Men and women were bent over potato plants; the fields were worked by oxen and horses pulling wagons and plows.

We arrived at the set, a cluster of nondescript old and new buildings, at around nine-thirty that morning. The grassy stretches between the buildings were filled with vans and campers; people wearing jeans and baseball caps were walking around, many holding walkie-talkies, many sitting in folding chairs looking numb. In other words, it looked just like any other film set. Breakfast had been laid out on a folding table: steam trays filled with eggs and sausages, brown bread, tea, and coffee. Someone complained that the plastic cups melted when hot water was poured into them. Four months in Poland, and the L.A. contingent was longing for Styrofoam.

Then I saw a group of women who sent a chill up my back. Their hair was tucked into scarves, they wore heavy boots and frayed dresses with yellow Stars of David sewn at the breast. They were horrifyingly familiar; I have seen hundreds of pictures of women who looked like that. I knew these ghosts come to life must be actresses, but it was shocking to see them anyway.

I noticed my mother staring at them and walked over to her, worried that she was being overtaken by some unbearable memory. She pulled me close to her and whispered, "We never wore that kind of dress."

I looked at the actresses to see what they were wearing—sagging housedresses, the kind farm women in Adams County used to wear when I was a girl.

Then I saw my mother was upset only by the idea that I might think she hadn't known how to dress properly when she was young. "We were different from those Poles," she said.

There they were, the ancient divisions bursting with life. The Hungarian Jews feel superior to the Polish Jews, who feel superior to the Litvaks, the Lithuanian Jews. Again I remember feeling so proud as a child that my parents were from Czechoslovakia, not Russia, and having no idea why except that my parents must have made it obvious that one was better than the other. Now my mother's hometown is in Ukraine, worse than Russia, maybe even worse than Poland on the Jewish snob scale. The social gradations stay alive no matter how the borders may shift. Governments may come and go, but the ancient hostilities and suspicions survive.

We left the actresses behind and continued onward. We were, after all, tourists on a movie set. Our own Universal Pictures tour. My mother and Arthur were examining everything, collecting anecdotes to take home, like any other sightseers. I had slipped into the comfortable anxiety of work, my antennae up.

Anne-Marie had instructed an assistant to take us inside, into a cavernous room filled with large machines and hundreds of people, some wearing the costume of World War II prisoners and Nazi guards, some wearing jeans and jackets, the uniform of contemporary filmmakers. This was an international crew: Israelis, Poles, Americans. Though cameras are prohibited on movie sets, cameras were clicking all over the place. Everyone wanted a souvenir. Jonathan Segall, a movie star in his native Israel, was nearby, videotaping the scene. The Israeli actors fawned on him; otherwise he was anonymous.

Liam Neeson, dashing in a smartly cut 1940s suit (despite the waxy gloss of movie makeup), was standing on a platform overlooking the crowd, reading pages of script. In the corner of the room, sitting on a canvas director's chair, was Steven Spielberg, talking to Ben Kingsley, who plays the Jewish accountant, Schindler's conscience and confidant.

Anne-Marie warned us not to talk to Ben Kingsley.

"He's—" She paused and grimaced. "Difficult" was the word this nice woman finally settled on to finish the sentence.

We waited at a respectful distance. Even with a resolutely friendly director like Spielberg, a man who likes to be liked, who eats lunch with the crew, the rigid code of movie set conduct was evident. No one approaches the chief until the right signal is made. However, when Spielberg glanced up and saw us, he jumped out of his chair and gave me a big hug. I was unnerved by the intimacy of the gesture, even though I knew it was a standard Hollywood greeting. I introduced Spielberg to my parents.

"This is great!" he said in his boyishly disarming way. "My dad's going to be here today, too."

Ben Kingsley appeared at Spielberg's side. We were introduced. Having been warned by Anne-Marie, I was shy of Kingsley, though he made it obvious that we had been cleared by Spielberg's friendly greeting.

My mother, happily oblivious of movie set politics, chatted congenially with the star.

"We just saw you in *Dave*," she said. "You were quite good." In that movie, just released in theaters, Kingsley played vice president to the amiable presidential look-alike, a *shlemiel,* who takes over at the White House when the real president goes into a coma.

"I haven't had a chance to see it yet," Kingsley said.

My mother looked shocked. *Dave* had been the big hit of the spring. "Well," she said, "did you see *Gandhi?*"

Gandhi was the movie that a decade earlier had made Kingsley famous, in the role of Mohandas Gandhi.

That's it, I thought. We're going to be evicted.

Kingsley stared at her a minute, trying to decide what she was up to, if anything. Then he assured her that he had indeed seen *Gandhi.*

"For *Dave*," he said with nice theatrical slowness, "I was here."

Just then an assistant pulled Spielberg away, and Kingsley drifted off. The three of us began doing what most people do on movie sets: We waited.

It didn't take long for my mother to begin talking to the woman standing near her. She was Miri Fabian, a forty-nine-year-old Israeli actress with the fine-boned exoticism of a ballerina. She was wearing clunky boots, a limp housedress, and a kerchief, a babushka scarf around her head. Within minutes they discovered that they had mutual acquaintances in Israel, that they were both of Czech origin, and that they both had the same sense of *distinction.* "I tied my scarf the way my mother did," Miri confided, turning her head to show a knot at the base of her neck, "not like the Poles."

She told us she had been born in a Slovakian work camp in 1944 and she was playing one of the women saved by Schindler.

"My niece was the manager of the Dalia Hotel," my mother was telling Miri Fabian when I joined them.

"I *know* the Dalia Hotel," said the actress. "That's where my father-in-law used to stay."

They began talking as though they had known each other forever. In many ways they had. I automatically reached into my bag for a notebook and began writing down what they were saying.

"When I auditioned in Israel I didn't know what I was auditioning for, just that it was for Spielberg. I do films there, but mainly the stage. It was just a reading, tell a little about yourself. I didn't know it had anything to do with the Holocaust. I knew Spielberg. I had seen *The Color Purple* and *Empire of the Sun.*

"Then I found out I got the part and what it was. I was happy but very sad. Here was something my mother saved me from—Auschwitz—and here I am going of my own free will. I didn't know why I was chosen. I never met Spielberg before, just auditioned on videotape. Finally, at the Seder he gave for us here, he told me that he knew watching my audition that this face either had experienced pain or knew what pain is."

The crowd of extras milled around us. Fabian pointed to a young man. "That's Jonathan Segall. He's a big movie star in Israel. All the young Israeli girls couldn't believe he was next to them when they first came."

Segall was walking around with his camera, pausing to drink mineral water. He smiled at us when he saw Fabian pointing at him.

Fabian's pale green eyes lit up as she talked excitedly, eager to tell her story. "I didn't know about Schindler. I was so surprised because I read a lot my whole life, the literature of the Holocaust. Yet after I got the part I visited a close friend of mine for Succoth and I was telling her this story and there was a dead silence. She said, 'My sister-in-law was a survivor because of Schindler.' "

As she talked I sensed an ancient rite being activated; the spirit of *b'shert*—of fatalism—was asserting itself.

" 'Please, please let me talk to her,' I said. My friend told me she didn't know, the sister-in-law was angry all the time, she had only talked about this for the first time five years before.

"So then I phoned the daughter of the character I'm playing and said, 'I'm playing your mother. Can I visit you?' I did, and she showed me photographs of her parents as they were then, then new photographs of them as old people. I said to her, 'I know those people! They live opposite me. I see them every day on the street.'"

As we talked, Liam Neeson kept repeating the speech Schindler gives to his workers at the end of the movie, as the war is ending. He is saying that at midnight they will be free and he will be a fugitive. He asks the SS guards to go in peace. The speech echoed hollowly in the cavernous factory. Though everyone was very still, you could barely hear him. Neeson was reading the lines off giant cue cards being held by assistants off to the side. As I stared at the cue cards, Anne-Marie Stein suddenly materialized at my side.

"Liam just got those lines this morning. Usually he doesn't use cue cards, never," she assured me emphatically. This is the publicist's lot, worrying that a movie will be "destroyed" by the "revelation" that the star *read his lines off a cue card.* I had no doubt that Neeson could manage a few lines of dialogue. He had made his way through *Anna Christie* on stage, after all.

I turned back to Fabian, who was saying, "My whole family survived. I was born in a concentration camp, Lager Novaky, a Slovakian camp, in 1944. My mother was a very beautiful woman. When they were shipping people out from the work camp to Auschwitz, she went with the baby—my brother—to the commandant and said, 'Please let him stay.' He looked at my brother, he was a beautiful baby, and said, 'Okay.' Probably thinking, 'Who cares, this transport or the next transport.' But that was the last transport!"

An assistant director announced that shooting was about to begin. Fabian finished her story in a whispered rush: "After the war my mother had another son. The brother I told you about, the one who saved our lives in a way, was killed in 1967, in the Israeli war. This is the tragedy of the Jewish people."

I mumbled something sympathetic. Fabian shrugged. "My whole family survived. My mother is dead. My father is alive. My father was a merchant in Topolcany. Nothing special. Nothing interesting. When I told him I wanted to go to the town where we were from, he said, 'Don't go to Topolcany. There's nothing to see there.'

"We had the first three days of May for vacation. I went to Zakopane, a Polish resort in the Tatra Mountains, just across the Czech, now Slovak, border. I got up in the morning and decided to go to Topolcany. It took seven hours, two hundred kilometers. On bus. On train.

"When I got there, I couldn't remember anything. Nothing was familiar. Then I saw a house I thought was our house, but I couldn't be sure. I knew if I could just go into the backyard, a courtyard really, I would know. I knocked on the door and spoke to the woman who lived there. I told her I just wanted to take a look, but she was not willing at first.

"They think the Jews are coming back to claim their property. I told her, 'If you let me go to the backyard, I will remember. I know it's not my property. I just want to see it. I am Jewish.'

"The woman said, 'No, no, you don't look Jewish.' "

Miri Fabian repeated this idea several times, that people never think she looks Jewish. Even though she expresses indignation at the idea that someone thinks there is such a thing as "looking Jewish," that it is a ridiculous idea, she also seems proud to be the object of this confusion, to "not look Jewish." Indignation, shame, all mixed up together.

"When they did let me in, everything was where I said it would be. Then I remembered Topolcany, the street, the girls. I had this connection to some past of mine that I never had. It isn't emotional. Suddenly I saw myself as this little girl I didn't remember.

"I had my camera with me. Fully automatic. It started to flash and flash, and I thought, 'Oh God, the camera is dead.' I put it away and went out without a picture. When I came back, I pulled the camera out and found it was only the film was not loaded properly. I'm not stupid. I can mend things, do things by hand."

Then she paused. "I realized why this had happened. If I had come with a camera, no one would have let me in the house," said Fabian, who, like my mother, clearly believed in fate. "But now I'm thinking I should get in a taxi and go there. Boom! In one day, take some pictures, come back.

"But my father was right, of course. There was nothing to see in Topolcany."

As Fabian talked, I found myself staring across the room at Spielberg, in his baseball cap and letter jacket, and began to wonder if there was any point in trying to understand how it was that he had been the force that had drawn Fabian and me there, to Poland, on our separate but parallel journeys.

Fabian noticed where my gaze had wandered. "He's really great," she said. "He really feels for the actors. He respects actors. He feels for them."

Then, as if she had tuned into my thoughts, she told me what Spielberg's decision to make this movie meant for her. "We were never taught about the war by our parents. They never said a word about it. I remember in 1950 we got a book called *Tragedy of the Jewish People,* with photos. We were children, small, and we asked our parents, 'What's that?'

" 'Nothing, nothing,' they said.

"Here we filmed it. Two hundred, three hundred naked ladies in the shower. And I was there, and suddenly I lost recollection of the fact that this was a movie. I just wanted to get away. I was dead, dead, dead.

"My mother wouldn't like me to go back, to do anything with the Holocaust. She never talked about it ever, ever, never. She died fifteen years ago. I was a mother with two children. I wore the wedding ring my mother bought after the war to replace the one taken from her in camp. We were married really." She laughed, but it didn't seem to be a joke, this marriage of souls.

"I am not unique in Israel. I am unique here. In Israel, everybody has a story."

We exchanged addresses and parted ways; I went to look for my mother, who had drifted off to the sidelines, where Arthur was sitting. I bumped into Anne-Marie, who asked me what I'd been doing. When I told her I'd been talking with Miri Fabian, she nodded approvingly. "Good color," she said.

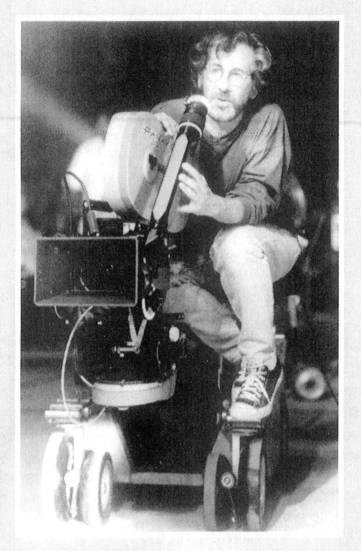

Director Steven Spielberg

3

Fievel's Grandson

■ By the time I arrived in Poland, Spielberg had opened his set to fifteen journalists; he had already developed a way of talking about his reasons for making *Schindler* that seemed rehearsed. The stories he told were vivid, almost perfectly constructed, like scenes from a movie, complete with narrative arc and dialogue. I didn't think the stories were fake; they just felt enhanced, larger than life. That wasn't surprising. Spielberg has been talking about himself into tape recorders for most of his adulthood. He wasn't yet thirty when *Jaws* made him as familiar to the public as a movie star. He gives the impression of being remarkably revealing yet manages to remain unknowable, hiding behind the myth he keeps reconstructing for himself as he reevaluates what that entity—Steven Spielberg—should be.

This didn't make me doubt his sincerity. However, I realized quickly after we began talking that his Holocaust was different from mine. This may sound absurd, this talk of "his" Holocaust and "my" Holocaust. But I had to accept the fact that both of us, each in our own way, were trying to lay some claim to the tragedy that neither of us had experienced.

In between shots, while my parents patiently waited, I listened to Spielberg talk about how being Jewish had affected him as a child. Spielberg's spiritual odyssey was becoming the engine that would drive the giant publicity mill for the movie. He was a compelling spokesman for himself, talking with a born showman's instinct for the telling anecdote. His was a variation on a classic American story: how the nerd assaulted by the golden boys in high school had survived. Now the story had been modified: Spielberg told of being the Jewish boy besieged by the *goyim* for being Jewish. In both cases the unstated ending is the same: The nerdy boy, the beleaguered Jew, grows up to become richer and more famous than all of his former tormenters put together.

My favorite of these stories was the kind of story I am especially susceptible to: A child, for reasons that are entirely understandable, tries to separate himself from his parents or grandparents, not because he doesn't love them but because his association with them, because of who they are, is too complicated to explain to the friends whose approval he so desperately wants. In this particular kind of story, love and shame are bound up together, impossible to disentangle.

"When I was seven or eight years old my shame about being a Jew was because my dad moved in these circles of computer specialists, no other Jews," said Spielberg in a rush of words. It was impossible to "read" him because he was wearing sunglasses as he always has, even indoors, even in dim light. He has said he needs the glasses because his eyes are sensitive to light.

"My dad was becoming successful quickly, we were in a nice neighborhood of all Gentiles. I was always different. My mother and father were very proud of being Jewish. We celebrated all the holidays. We were Orthodox then. They grew up in kosher homes in an Orthodox neighborhood with kosher preparation of food, in Avondale [Cincinnati], on Reading Road.

"My grandfather wrapped *t'fillin* every morning. We shared a bedroom, so I watched him *davin* every morning. My grandfather was in the sundry business. He would bring me up to the attic of his house. There would be a hundred belts, three hundred belt buckles, fifty pairs of shoes, a hundred sports jackets, a thousand cuff links and tie clips, five hundred ties, shoelaces—thousands of shoelaces—for sale, socks.

"That was my mother's father, my grandfather Fievel. He would go out in the town to sell. I remember playing with all the merchandise. My dad's father was a salesman, too, kind of a Willy Loman. He sold anything he could sell. I never met him."

Spielberg is almost always referred to as a boyish man, and I think the impression comes more from the way he tells a story than from the boyish way he dresses (jeans, sneakers, T-shirts, and letter jackets). He blurts out anecdotes with a kind of amazement and pride that kids seem to take naturally in the recollection of even ordinary incidents. This ability eludes most adults until they are very old and their unself-consciousness is restored. Like a child, Spielberg loves the stories he has to tell, no matter how many times he tells them. In the end this may be the true source of his genius.

"My grandfather with the yarmulke all the time, Fievel," he continued. "I was seven, eight years old, playing football outside with my friends and my grandfather would come out and he would only call me by my Hebrew name, 'Shmuel.'

"I'm having trouble enough because I was never very coordinated, so my playing football in itself is a contradiction in terms. I'm trying to block the best I can and suddenly my grandfather comes out of our house, two houses down, and starts yelling, 'Shmuel, Shmuel, Shmuel!'

"And I'm denying that name. I'm not answering him. I'm pretending I don't know him. My friend is saying, 'He's looking your way. Does he mean you?' And they're pointing my way. And I'm denying the existence of my own grandfather, saying, 'No. It's not me.' "

———

▪ As he continued talking, it struck me that this *Yiddishe* gloss on the Spielberg mythology was something new. The family's sometime Orthodoxy, which in the past had been played for laughs, now became semitragic, the source of a young boy's shame. In his interviews as in his movies, Spielberg's Jewishness had never been more than a footnote. I remembered reading an essay he had written once for *Time* magazine, which included a cute anecdote about the time he and his mother had bought some lobsters for dinner just before the rabbi dropped by for a surprise visit. Again, the anecdote, as Spielberg told it, had the feel of a movie scene; he and his mother had hidden the lobsters under Steven's bed. The minute the rabbi had left, they had thrown the lobsters into a pot of boiling water.

After Mrs. Spielberg divorced Steven's father, she returned to the Orthodoxy of her youth. She married Bernie Adler, a follower of the Lubavitcher sect, a man so religious that, in accordance with the Orthodox laws, he won't shake hands with women because they might be "unclean." I knew this because I had once interviewed the Adlers at the Milky Way, the kosher dairy restaurant they run in West Hollywood. It was Bernie Adler who had hung *mezuzahs*—the tiny prayer scrolls observant Jews hang on door frames—at Amblin Entertainment, Spielberg's ministudio on the Universal lot. Amblin was designed in the Santa Fe style popular in Hollywood in the early 1980s; to match the decor the carved wooden *mezuzahs* looked as though Hopi Indians might have made them.

The Adlers had come to Poland to visit, a kosher chef in tow to prepare their meals. They had already left by the time I arrived. But Spielberg had told us that his father was around, and sure enough, not long after I'd arrived on the set, I saw a tall, white-haired man wearing a blue sweater and gray slacks following Spielberg around with a small video camera. I'd asked Anne-Marie Stein, the publicist, who the man was.

"That's Steven's father," she whispered.

A few minutes later Spielberg glanced up and noticed me watching his father videotaping him. He shrugged his shoulders and rolled his eyes, for a moment just another exasperated son indulging his father.

I had interviewed Arnold Spielberg a few years before as well, on the telephone, and wasn't expecting much by way of introspection from him. My impression had been of a blunt man who took pains to let me know that he was not his son's sycophant. (His father told me, for publication, "I didn't care for *Indiana Jones,* and I hated *1941.* When I told Steven, he said, 'Don't talk to me, Dad.' ") It had been Spielberg's mother who doted, profusely, on her oldest child and only son. Leah Adler adored Spielberg's celebrity, showing up on talk shows to do her

Jewish mom *shtick,* happily telling reporters about how the late Steven Ross, the legendary Time Warner chairman and her son's surrogate father, had had the cabin ceiling of the Warner corporate jet covered with Milky Way wrappers in honor of Mrs. Adler's restaurant, the Milky Way, to welcome her aboard. Spielberg's father was the heavy, the absentee workaholic who was constantly disappointed at his son's lack of interest in the traditional pursuits of upwardly mobile Jewish-American boys, like law or medicine or computer science. I had heard many stories from Spielberg about being forced awake before dawn to study math with his father, then feeling like a dunderhead for not comprehending any of it.

They had more or less settled their differences, though Spielberg could still do a nonstop twenty-minute riff on the various ways he did not welcome criticism from his father.

Before I had a chance to talk to Mr. Spielberg, Sr., I was wandering around the set interviewing people, most recently Branko Lustig, one of the producers of *Schindler's List.* He was a tall man with thinning white hair, who was born in Yugoslavia, lives in Los Angeles, and corrects anyone who calls him a Yugoslavian ("I am a Croat," he says). This shrewdly pragmatic man had begun his education in the special art of making movies in eastern Europe thirty-eight years before, in Zagreb. His job was to make sure everything a director needs is available, and he found it difficult to do so on *Schindler's List.*

"Everything was much better before, under the communism," he told me in a Slavic accent that gave a slightly mysterious overtone to everything he said. "You bribed only one, and he gave the orders. Now you must bribe everybody!"

I met with Lustig in one of the trailers parked outside the factory; some contained dressing rooms, some toilets, some served as offices. Lustig was shouting his story at me until he asked me if I minded doing without the noisy air-conditioning, which I didn't.

Lustig had many credentials for *Schindler's List,* perhaps most significant the seven years he had spent on *War and Remembrance* and *The Winds of War,* the television miniseries versions of the Herman Wouk novels. But nothing he had done was more persuasive than the tattooed number on his arm. When he was ten years old he had been taken from his home in Yugoslavia and shipped off to Auschwitz. Most of the young Jewish boys had been killed immediately, but he was very tall for his age and had been spared to work in a coal mine near Auschwitz. He had been transferred to another concentration camp, Bergen-Belsen, where he was reunited with his mother, from whom he'd been separated at Auschwitz. They had both survived the war; Lustig's father, who had joined the partisans, hadn't.

There is an urbane coolness about Lustig, especially when he is given a chance to complain about the pressures of life in Los Angeles. "My wife spends all her time driving our daughter to lessons, tennis lessons, swimming lessons." His wife is Catholic, and, in the ecumenical American style, the family celebrates all holidays, Christian and Jewish.

Lustig said he keeps an apartment in Zagreb and plans to retire there, then went on to describe the place in a way that made his ambition seem insane. "You should say in what you are writing that the problem here is nationalism," Lustig said. "If you change the names in Bosnia and Croatia and put instead Auschwitz and the Germans, you will have the same story. The faces are the same, the suffering is the same."

Why, exactly, did he want to return to live among the Croats, Nazi collaborators and anti-Semites? Lustig waved away the question. "I am very popular there. Yes, there was big anti-Semitism during the war. Now they try to make connections with Israel. I have a lot of friends, and what's more important, I have a lot of enemies. I make movies there for thirty years. When I go to the café and sit down the waiters know my name. Now they are very objective to the Jews because there are only four hundred, five hundred Jews left. They killed all the Jews, so now they can be friendly."

Rather than try to unravel Lustig's psychology, I fell back on journalistic routine and asked him what it was like for him, with his memories, to work on this movie, with this subject. "The first time I made a Holocaust movie it was in Yugoslavia. Then sometimes I had nightmares. You cannot remember everything. So many things happen and you forget. Then when you see something similar you start to remember. The spirit of the concentration camp is in books and films like this. They are the documents."

He continued, "You know, the Polish extras on this film don't know much about what they are filming. They heard about it. But the Poles don't want to know about the Holocaust so much. Our assistant director explains the scene in Polish. Everybody knows they just don't want to know. In this town where thirty-five thousand Jews died, there is no monument, not anywhere in this town and in this factory."

Lustig returned to Auschwitz for the first time in 1984, for the filming of the television miniseries *War and Remembrance*. "I was very hungry, I remember," he said with a grim smile. "Every time, still now, when I come to Auschwitz I start to feel hungry."

I asked him what he thought of Spielberg's approach, his decision to make the film in black and white, in the style of a documentary, without any of the special effects that have become part of his trademark. "This film was very different for me," said Lustig. "He came here only three days, he saw the locations—approved some of them, some of them not. Then he went away for *Jurassic Park* and came back three days before shooting. With other directors, they are telling you who, what, where, how. Here I brought everything to him, like to a painter, canvas, brushes, paint. He just came in and shoot it, like cinema verité. He is working like the Italian neorealists. Like De Sica."

When I returned to the set, I found Spielberg replaying a shot on a video monitor for his father. I told him that Branko Lustig had compared him to the Italian neorealists.

"*Oy,*" said Spielberg.

"What does 'Italian neorealist' mean?" asked his father.

"It means 'not commercial,' " said Spielberg with a laugh, but the dark glasses hiding his eyes made it hard to decipher the laughter.

Spielberg nodded at me, a signal to follow him to the corner of the room where his canvas director's chair had been set up. Just as I sat on Ben Kingsley's chair, Spielberg glanced up at the movable scaffolding next to us. He looked around, spotted a production assistant.

"Could you move these chairs?" he asked, explaining to me, "Those things are dangerous. Things can fall off."

He picked up on our conversation exactly where we had left off; I had asked him about how his family had reacted to living in Poland. His family had grown considerably since I had first met him almost seven years before. At that time he had been married to Amy Irving and they had one son, Max, who was then eighteen months old. He and Irving had since divorced and he'd married another actress, Kate Capshaw, the female star of the second *Indiana Jones* movie. Capshaw had been pregnant with their second child when they had married; she also had a teenage daughter from a previous marriage and was caring for a black child, whom she and Spielberg had adopted. Capshaw, who had grown up Methodist in Florissant, a largely Catholic suburb of Saint Louis, had never met a Jew until she went to college.

Strangely enough, Capshaw, this pretty *shiksa*, could be seen as a crucial part of Spielberg's metamorphosis into Jewish family man. Amy Irving, half Jewish by birth, brought up as a Christian Scientist, wanted to raise Max "with options." Spielberg, however, wanted to see his son become a bar mitzvah. Capshaw demonstrated that no such conflict would arise with her. While she was pregnant with Sawyer, her second child with Spielberg, she undertook a conversion to Judaism by Orthodox instruction, including a trip to the *mikvah*, the ritual bath observant Jewish women are required to take monthly. She would refer to the excursion as a "triple dip." She took with her not only Sawyer *in utero* but the infant Sasha, who had to be converted even though Spielberg was her father because Capshaw wasn't Jewish when she was born. Then Capshaw undertook the circumcision of the black child, Theo, who was three.

She and Spielberg would always insist that the conversion wasn't a marriage requirement; however, marriage did follow the conversion (and Spielberg's mother did remind him that her husband, Bernie Adler, as a devout Orthodox Jew, wouldn't be able to attend the ceremony if the marriage was mixed).

"All five children are here," Spielberg said. "Max is here part of the time—he goes back and forth. Jessica [Kate's elder daughter] brought three sixteen-year-old friends; they're all taking second semester of their junior year of high school here. They're taking biology and math and history, all the usual subjects. It's harder than in the States because it's more focused and . . . harder. But it's easier because they don't have the malls to escape to, the boyfriends, the weekends at the movies.

They are focused on school. If they were this focused in America they'd be getting straight A's."

I listened to this earnest recitation, which might have been coming from the mouth of any suburban dad.

"At first they were very depressed. They got here and said, 'Oh, my God, we're stuck here for three and a half *months*.' And after about two weeks they fell in love with it, and now they're actually teary eyed to be leaving."

A pretty young woman walked up to us with a curly-haired moppet in tow.

"Hello, Jessica, hello, Max," said Spielberg, pulling Max up onto his lap. Jessica wandered off, leaving Spielberg to talk to his son in a cooing voice.

A second child materialized next to Spielberg, little Theo. Spielberg moved Max to one knee and placed Theo on the other, whereupon Max shoved Theo.

"I want to sit on your lap," said Max to his father, crankily.

"I have two laps," said Spielberg.

I asked him if the children will be raised with religion. "Theo, Sasha, and Sawyer, they're going to be brought up Jewish. They'll go to Hebrew school. Max is pretty much going to make up his mind when he gets older. Amy is not in agreement . . . we have our own ides about how our kids are going to be brought up. Amy and I both feel that Max is smart enough to make a choice about what he'd like to study. He's exposed to Judaism when he stays with us."

He glanced over at Jessica Capshaw, his blond sixteen-year-old stepdaughter. "Jessica's our resident *shiksa*."

———

■ Later, after Spielberg had gone back to work, I saw that he was standing next to a tall, slender woman wearing blue jeans, heavy black shoes, and a white T-shirt. Though her hair, which usually has been blond in movies, was now reddish brown, it was obviously Kate Capshaw, his wife. She moved with that combination of self-confidence and self-consciousness common in movie stars as well as the wives of rich and powerful men, and she was both. She had learned to transcend ordinariness even while projecting it. Her T-shirt, for example, seemed extraordinarily white. Like her husband, she kept her sunglasses on indoors.

When Spielberg left her to talk to the actors, I made my way through the crowd of extras to the video monitor, curious to hear her impression of this experience.

Capshaw greeted me warmly. When she began to talk, I could see that she was a strong match for Spielberg. There was a more complicated dynamic between them in operation than the obvious connection between director and actress, between Jew and *shiksa*, between multimillionaire and ambitious woman. Like her husband, she had a shrewd control of her anecdotal material that gave her impassioned conversation an unnerving polish.

"I've been taking the girls on field trips, and we went to Auschwitz," she began. "There were the four girls, myself, their teacher, and our American teacher and a guide. I kept probing, the girls kept probing, the question you would logically ask: How did it happen?

"By the way," she interrupted herself. "The president of the United States knew what was going on, the pope knew what was going on, the Church knew what was going on. Everybody knew what was going on. But it *was* happening here, in the country that was closest to Germany."

She continued with her story. "And the tour guide wouldn't at all give in to any kind of admission that there might be any racism in Poland that would at least be a good petri dish for the death camps.

"I realize that some of that was cultural, nationalistic. But she was an adult, a woman in her forties, who was at the university.

"The girls went to the rug with this woman. They kept asking, 'Weren't there perhaps some Polish people who are racist? You have racist people all over the world. You have racist people in America.'

"But her resistance was real strong."

Capshaw paused and pulled off her sunglasses. I was startled by the purity of her light blue eyes—and distracted by them. Suddenly the whole scene seemed too strange. The crowding and noise of the set, the actors dressed in Nazi uniforms and refugee rags, my mother and stepfather somewhere in the back of the room—I hadn't seen them for a couple of hours—the flashbulbs popping here and there. What was I doing here?

Capshaw had begun to talk again, explaining that she wasn't "judging" the Poles or even the guide whose behavior she found offensive. Her tone implied that grudge holding and rage were not appropriate forms of emotional expenditure, and she wanted to correct any misimpression I might have gotten from her outrage at the guide's resistance.

Her tone had become politic. "However, on behalf of the Poles, one of the things that has become clear to me is that had I been Polish, with my five children, if I were old enough—which I am—to make a decision to harbor a Jew, would I risk my entire family, my five babies?

"The Germans didn't like Poles, either. I've heard the Poles laugh about how they're the easiest, most conquerable country in the world. There was even a period of time when there was no Poland. And there were Jews who volunteered to become kapos. The worst! The worst! Then I've met Jews who say, 'My family line was saved because my grandpa chose to be that hideous, evil person.' How do you point fingers?"

I was mesmerized. I wondered why her movie career hadn't taken off; she was very persuasive.

I asked her when she had learned about the Holocaust. "The thing that really brought it home was the television film *The Holocaust*, in 1976. Before that it was just an event that happened. It didn't have names and faces. I had learned about it in college, in history at the University of Missouri at Columbia. Our professor showed us *Night and Fog.**

"But here, here is where it came home to me. A friend of mine who collects antiques came to visit, and we went looking for things in Cracow. She saw I wasn't into it and said, 'This is boring you.'

"I said, 'No, I'm not actually bored as . . . it's eerie to me. I look at a piece of jewelry and I wonder: Where is it from? Is that a piece of jewelry that was taken from a Jew? Is that a piece of jewelry that was worn by any member of the Nazi party? Is that a piece of jewelry that was made from stones that were taken from a Jew?

"Every place you walk you wonder: Who walked here? Which alley

---

*A 1955 short film about Auschwitz directed by Alain Resnais.

did the Jews run down? Where was blood washed off the sidewalks? As you walk around, it becomes part of your consciousness. I think it's partly because we're making this movie, the images I'm looking at."

One of the assistants shouted, "Quiet on the set!"

Capshaw whispered, "Being here reminds me of France, after the German occupation. The joke is, when you talk to people anytime you're at a dinner party and World War II is brought up, everybody's family was part of the Resistance."

Then she stopped talking as Liam Neeson began reciting his speech once again so the camera could catch him at yet another angle.

When the take was finished, Capshaw left to take the children home. Arnold Spielberg took her place by the video monitor. We began talking. Unlike his voluble son and daughter-in-law, Mr. Spielberg answered my questions matter of factly and compactly.

Periodically glancing at the video monitor, as though he was afraid his son might make a mistake if he stopped watching, Mr. Spielberg summed up his recollection of his family's connection to the Holocaust. "I lost fifteen to twenty relatives in the Holocaust, but I didn't talk to Steven much about it. Our family, I guess, was living in today. We really didn't talk about it that much, even though Steve's mother and I for a while were Orthodox. We were off and on Orthodox, Conservative, Reform, you name it. In and out of being religious. Our kids were not especially religious. Steven went through Hebrew school and became bar mitzvah, but we didn't really dwell on the Holocaust. It just wasn't in our family. We were too much into having fun. Steven wanted to make movies. He was making movies ever since he was a Boy Scout.

"Most of that kind of information came from his mother's side. My parents were immigrants from Russia and told us about their experience in Russia, especially during the pogroms, but my parents died before the kids were born. My father was in the Russian army. He was a sharpshooter and of course I became a sharpshooter and then I taught Steve to become a sharpshooter when he was a Boy Scout.

"But the closest I ever came to the stories relating to the Holocaust were actually letters we got from relatives in Russia. They would say, 'We're living so comfortably, only sixteen to a room.' But during the war I was in India and didn't hear a thing about it, the Holocaust, until after the war."

Then Mr. Spielberg's voice changed. He seemed less distracted, more engaged in his subject. I realized he'd changed subjects. The Spielberg he was talking about now was not Steven but himself.

"Ever since I retired, they say to me, 'With the name Spielberg, you've got to be able to make movies. So they got me making movies at my company. I've made two, and we're working on a third one. It's commercial stuff for the company . . ."

I nodded politely but found my mind wandering. It was time to move on.

Our Auschwitz tour guide, Dorothea Cieplinska (left), talking to Arthur, my mother, and our driver, Leopold Schragge

4

The Lucky One

■ I am looking at a photograph. There is a tall, slender young woman wearing a black skirt decorated with a pattern of brightly colored musical notes. The skirt has suspenders. She is wearing flat walking shoes with laces and a short-sleeved white shirt. Her straight black hair is pulled back into a long ponytail, and she wears glasses. Two people looking at her might describe her very differently. One might say she is "cute." Another could just as easily say she is "dorky." She is a Polish woman named Dorothea Cieplinska, and she reminds me of the way I looked when I was her age, in her early twenties, or slightly younger. I may have even had a skirt like that.

Dorothea is standing stiffly, like a soldier at attention. She is speaking to a handsome couple, elderly but full of life. Their vigor is evident even in a still photo. The man, deeply tanned, his white hair blowing in a breeze, is standing at attention like Dorothea, only his posture is better. He is wearing a deep purple sport shirt, navy blue pants, comfortable shoes. The woman next to him is listening to Dorothea with what appears to be great interest. Her feet are slightly apart, her hands are in her pants pockets. She, too, is wearing a short-sleeved white shirt and sunglasses. Standing slightly to one side is a third man, wearing a baseball cap and a turquoise sport shirt. There is a camera around his neck.

They are standing on an unpaved road lined on both sides with tall, thin trees. Set back from the trees are rows of solid two-story brick buildings. There is grass around the buildings. It is a bright, sunny day; that is obvious from the glare on the road and the sharp contrast of the shadows cast by the people. The setting might be a college campus, a military base, or a kibbutz.

I took this photograph of my mother, Arthur, Dorothea, and Leopold Schragge shortly after we began our tour of Auschwitz.

Why am I describing this photograph? I am describing this photograph because I need it. I need it to see what Auschwitz looked like when we visited it because I can't remember. I need the photograph, because as we walked around the campuslike *Stammlager*, Auschwitz I, and even later, at the ruins of Birkenau, I felt disconnected from my surroundings as they stood. I was too conscious at Auschwitz of its former incarnation. So I looked without real comprehension at the display cases of human hair and clothing and eyeglasses. These objects, contained in glass, put even more of a distance between me and the horror they represented. I had no objection to them. I understood why they were there, to "personalize" what had happened in this place, to convince doubters. I didn't need this kind of evidence.

Only one exhibit broke through my detachment. A broken doll, taken from a child, was on display. Its body was intact, its porcelain face was shattered.

I felt a burning grief as I stared at the doll and listened to Dorothea, who had guided my parents and Leopold to the case.

"Children had no ability to live here," Dorothea said. "Also pregnant mothers. If a baby was born, both mother and child were killed by lethal injection. This was at first. Later a new commander who replaced Rudolf Hoess changed this rule. He allowed 'Aryan' children to live, the ones with the blue eyes and blond hair."

▪ On our way to Auschwitz from Cracow that morning, my mother had remarked on how close we had come to celebrating the forty-ninth anniversary of her first visit there. "It is May 18, 1993," she mused. "When I arrived in Auschwitz in 1944, I believe it was May 24."

She recalled that it had been a nice day then, as it was now. The temperature had been in the high seventies, the countryside green and welcoming.

Not long after we left Cracow, she reached into her bag and pulled out a sandwich wrapped in a napkin.

"Are you hungry?" she asked me. We had just eaten a substantial breakfast from the Cracovia buffet table. The food had been a little greasy and nondescript, except for the glassfuls of luscious plum jam. But it had been plentiful, and so we had pronounced it "delicious."

"Did you take those from the buffet?" I asked, laughing. I remembered as a child reaching into my mother's purse and coming up with petrified fragments of pecan pie wrapped in napkins, pats of butter melting in aluminum foil, or packets of jelly with the plastic lids crushed in.

"No," she said with a guilty grin. "They were passing them out yesterday at the movie set while you were talking to someone. Arthur ate his, but I wasn't hungry and I thought we might need it later."

After Arthur and Leopold declined, she returned the sandwich to her bag.

A few minutes later my mother spoke again.

"I feel bad for the way I looked at those poor Polish girls," she said.

"Which Polish girls?" I asked.

"The girls at the movie set. The way they were dressed. I remember when we came to Auschwitz, girls like that had been there for years already and they were so mad at us. They said, 'What are you complaining about? I don't want to hear it. You should have been here like us. We were here suffering and working while you were there. Don't you complain to us.'

"I was so mad at them. Now I see I would have felt probably the same way. It's the way I feel about those hostages who were kept for a year or ten months and complaining about what it did to them. You see them on television, talking, talking, talking. And they came home to their families. I came home to nothing. I had nothing."

Her voice had been rising in passion and then stopped. I started to lean toward her—to comfort her, I suppose. Before I could put my arms around her, I could hear her voice again, now bright.

"Oh, look how beautiful it is."

"What?"

"Look, Juliska, out the window, it's gorgeous."

As she gazed serenely at the landscape, I marveled at her ability to behave according to the aphorisms she liked to hang on the wall or send to me or my sister: "When God shuts the door, open a window." "Smile and the world smiles with you, cry and you cry alone." "It's better to remain silent and be thought a fool than to speak up and remove all doubt." Sometimes it seems as though her emotions have a built in circuit breaker to stop her feelings from gaining too much momentum.

There was a shout from the front seat.

"Museum Auschwitz!" Arthur called out, pointing to a road sign.

Leopold spoke rapidly to Arthur in Slovak.

"What's he saying?" I asked my mother.

Leopold hadn't realized Auschwitz was on our itinerary until after we'd set out from Bratislava. He'd told Arthur that he had spent three days at Auschwitz when he was sixteen years old, then he was sent off to work in a mine. Of Auschwitz he remembered nothing except the sound of dogs barking and the sound of music.

"He's saying he has mixed emotions about going in there," said my mother. "He had never wanted to go back there, but he has never come this close. He's only coming there because he's taking us. He will see when we gets there."

We were approaching the outskirts of Oświęcim; we passed by the Scorpion Nightclub. For the first time since we'd left Cracow no one was talking, in any language.

My mother broke the silence with a pronouncement. "I'm really glad I came, now that I'm here. This was a big part of my life, the turning point for my life."

Then we saw the signs: Auschwitz. Birkenau. Parking. As we pulled into the lot, I had the strange sensation of being back at Spielberg's movie set. The chirping birds, the kids playing on the grass surrounding the asphalt, the souvenir kiosk, the tour buses all seemed familiar. We might be at Pompeii or some rustic version of Disneyland.

I saw my mother eyeing the tour buses. They were empty. She grimaced and began opening her door before Leopold stopped the car. I had seen this impatience before and thought I had it figured out: The empty buses implied that a large number of people were already inside and she was being left behind. My suspicion was confirmed by the way she jumped out of the car the instant it stopped and began marching across the parking lot, assuming that we would catch up with her—or not.

I saw her glancing back at us with a familiar look: *What's taking you so long?* I watched her head for the museum entrance, then stop.

"What's wrong?" I asked, breathless from my trot across the parking lot.

She explained: She'd forgotten to bring film. Back at the hotel were twelve rolls of film she'd bought for a very good price before she'd left Connecticut, at Caldor—on a Wednesday so she could avail herself of the 10 percent senior citizen discount.

Scowling, she took a deep breath, then set off toward the souvenir kiosk. I followed. As we got closer, I could read the bold sign, printed in English: "books, postcards, stamps, film, videocassettes, cigarettes, drinks (cool!)."

All these things were, indeed, available, and the film was only moderately overpriced. While we waited for the salesclerk we examined the postcard display on the counter: There were straightforward snapshots of familiar Auschwitz landmarks, like the "Arbeit Macht Frei" gate, as well as more creative inventions like the card with fake flames superimposed on the train tracks leading into Birkenau.

My mother decided postcards could wait until after our tour, but she did buy a guidebook. "Look at this," she said. "The English version costs fifteen thousand złotys and the Polish guide is only ten." She seemed pleased by the discrepancy, as though she liked the superiority, in this particular place, of being the prosperous American tourist ripped off by the locals.

As we left the kiosk and headed toward the museum entrance, she said, "You know, if I hadn't gone through this place I probably wouldn't have led such an interesting life."

I raised my eyebrows and waited for her to elaborate.

She correctly interpreted my wordless response as skepticism. "You know what I mean," she said impatiently.

I did and I didn't. I envied her ability to look at her Auschwitz experience with such detachment, though I didn't understand it. As we entered the museum I was overcome by fear. Was this a horrible mistake?

The thought began to overwhelm me as I excused myself to stop at the bathroom, just down the stairs near the entrance. It was a huge public restroom, impeccably clean. As I looked around, the thought struck me: I'm at Auschwitz, and look how clean the toilets are—far cleaner than most public toilets at home. This antiseptic purity magnified my doubts. Why had I allowed my mother—no, encouraged her—to come back here? What would this "museum" tell me about what had happened to her? More important, more frightening, what would this experience mean for her?

"Are you all right?" my mother asked me when I came upstairs.

"Fine," I said with false brightness. "Too much coffee. That free breakfast."

She smiled at my weak joke, as though reassuring me.

There was no line at the ticket booth, despite the tour buses outside. Apparently this wasn't the busy season. We decided to hire a private guide.

After a minute Dorothea appeared and introduced herself. She began speaking in the universal monotone of the professional guide. "Hello, I am your guide. We will begin the tour here in Auschwitz I. Then, if you like, we can go to Auschwitz II, which is Birkenau, about two kilometers away. It will take a few hours. There is a movie playing in a few minutes that is good to see before we begin. First, come with me."

We followed her into the sunlight, and she stopped. We could see barbed wire and the barracks in the distance. Dorothea recited her introduction.

She told us that the first camp, Auschwitz, had been "built"—actually, converted from a military barracks—in 1940; that Birkenau had been added a year later and that there was a third camp and forty subcamps called "satellites." She told us that Auschwitz had first been used mainly for political prisoners and then as a men's camp. She told us that the first crematorium had been built in 1940, the first gas chamber in 1941, and that the first victims of experimental killings had been Russians. Then had come the Jews of Upper Silesia, then all the Jews. She told us that for the first two years Auschwitz had been "an ordinary camp, with slow death from work." In 1942 it had become a camp whose specific purpose was death.

"Dorothea," my mother interrupted, "when I came here in 1944 I remember a fire. That's my only memory. But I don't understand why I remember a fire when I should remember smoke."

Dorothea nodded. "At Birkenau bodies were burned outside in piles because the crematoria couldn't keep up with the gas chambers by 1944; the gas did its work in ten minutes, but it took the crematoria thirty minutes to turn the bodies into ashes."

My mother looked pleased to have her memory confirmed.

Dorothea then told us that tourism had fallen to less than half the one million annual rate of a few years ago. "We used to get tourists from Yugoslavia and the Soviet Union, but now a war in Yugoslavia, the Soviet Union has its troubles," she said.

She led us a short distance to the infamous "Arbeit Macht Frei" gate that led to the barracks.

"Excuse me, Dorothea," my mother said. "Is there another gate like this at Birkenau?"

Dorothea shook her head.

"I'm sure I remember this sign. I remember they brought us once for disinfection to this camp. I think that's when I saw this sign." My mother seemed upset but not in the way I expected. I saw no signs of a rush of memory. Rather, she seemed annoyed at her inability to put the pieces together accurately. "That must be it."

Dorothea nodded, still impassive. Perhaps this kind of piecing together had become familiar to her. I wondered about her, a Polish woman leading Jews around Auschwitz. What did she think of them? Of us? Was she an anti-Semite taking secret pleasure in this dark past? Or had Branko Lustig been right when he said, "The Poles don't want to know about the Holocaust so much." Had history been erased for Dorothea? Was this just a job?

My mother asked again, "Are you sure there wasn't a sign like this at Birkenau?"

"Only here," said Dorothea.

My mother shrugged. "I must remember it from the movies," she said. This theme would be repeated throughout the day, the way her real memories had been altered by subsequent information provided by books and movies.

Leopold asked Arthur to ask Dorothea about the music he'd heard. Dorothea told us there had been an orchestra at Auschwitz, which we Americans knew about from the television movie *Playing for Time*. Standing there in front of the "Arbeit Macht Frei" gate, I thought about Vanessa Redgrave and the "scandal" about her starring in the film because she was a PLO sympathizer. "The Germans had orchestras play at the working camps and satellite camps mainly. The prisoners had to march to the music. It made it easier for the SS to count them."

We had been walking back toward the main building, where the introductory film was about to start. We'd stopped by a long, low building that Dorothea told us had been the kitchen. On the side of the building was a blowup of a photo of one of the Auschwitz orchestras.

Again my mother looked worried. "I don't remember hearing any music."

Dorothea asked her where she'd come from and when. "Ah," said Dorothea, nodding. "There was no orchestra at the transitory Hungarian Jewesses camp."

This term would come up again and again: "transitory Hungarian Jewesses." There was something insidious about that word: Jewess. Again a flashback, to my second or third year at *The Wall Street Journal*, when I was a young reporter covering the banking industry. My editor had received a nasty letter condemning the paper for leaving its financial coverage in the hands of Jews. The writer had included a list of offenders, with my name at the top: "That cunning little Jewess . . ." The letter had been dismissed as the work of just another crank; the writer's Jewish cabal had included Tim Carrington and other reporters with solidly non-Jewish names. But even that small display of anti-Semitism had unnerved me.

It was time for the film. We had to pay 5,000 złotys in addition to the fee for our tour.

"Highway robbers," muttered Arthur. "Making money out of tragedy. The Germans should pay for this!"

Dorothea said gently, "Last year the German government gave about ten million marks, about six million dollars."

She left us to watch the film in the comfortable modern theater. The documentary footage was horribly familiar. A narrator described what we were seeing, though most of the images were self-explanatory, at least to us. Refugees wearing yellow stars stared blankly at the camera. Gaunt women crowded together in what appeared to be horse stables. Skeletons wearing pajamas wandering around in a daze—the *Mussulmen*. We watched this degeneration from human to barely human to piles of bones. There was footage of children, the subjects of Nazi medical experiments. We saw them waiting for surgery, sitting calmly on examination tables, then afterward, cruelly deformed. The camera scanned piles of hair, of toothbrushes, of teeth. The narrator intoned, "Every inch of soil is proof of horrible crimes."

One thought went through my head repeatedly: *My father and mother were good people, decent people.* I felt desperate, as though I were trying to believe what my parents had taught me despite what I was seeing—that decency was possible and they were proof. I heard Arthur and Leopold weeping. My mother held my hand tightly, but she didn't cry.

Dorothea was waiting for us outside. Her noncommittal expression was comforting, like a cool cloth on a fever.

"Do you want to tour the exhibits?" she asked.

We nodded and followed her toward the barracks that housed the exhibits, beyond the main gate.

Recalling my conversation with Kate Capshaw, I said to Dorothea, "Someone I know was told by a guide here that no one knew what was happening at the camps." I think I was deliberately provoking her, to see what lay behind that dispassionate face.

She looked at me and began to speak in the same calm tone with which she had previously dispensed statistics.

"My grandparents lived not far from here. They remember seeing the trains coming with the people. You could smell it for many kilometers. My mother was a child, seven, eight years old. She remembers seeing the trains, the people at the windows, asking for water. But there were the dogs, the soldiers, they couldn't help."

She turned to my mother. "My parents remembered seeing the flames as children, and they lived twelve or thirteen kilometers away. At night the sky was light from the bodies burning in piles outside the crematoria."

My mother nodded. "That's what I remember. The flames."

We walked silently for a few minutes. Then Dorothea spoke again. "My uncle was killed in Auschwitz. He was a partisan fighting the Nazis."

Dorothea's status had shifted dramatically. Now she was one of "us."

I asked her, "How can you stand working here?"

She shrugged. The gesture, so familiar in eastern Europe, wasn't all that different from the resignation of the *shtetl*. "It's depressing sometimes, especially at the beginning."

I pressed on: "But why do you work here?"

She smiled indulgently. "I studied ecology at Jagiellonian University in Cracow. After I finished my degree I found there were no jobs for ecologists. We were a luxury. For a year I tried to find a job in my chosen field."

The shrug again.

"Then my sister—she was working here—told me to come here to become a guide. I knew about this place from the time I am a child, from my parents. It wasn't discussed in school under the communism."

The tour continued. Dorothea mentioned that there was a record-gathering operation at Auschwitz; perhaps my mother and Leopold would like to stop by the office? If so, we had to make sure to be there by 2 P.M., when the office closed.

"Yes, I want to go there," said my mother. "Okay, Dorothea, show us what there is to see here. Then we'll visit the office and then go to Birkenau because that was really where I was."

The barracks in the *Stammlager* that had been converted into museums seemed remarkably benign. We walked through the exhibits reading the explanations, which were supplemented by Dorothea. Though I have a reasonably good memory, I remember very little of the museum. I do remember the room with the blown-up black-and-white photographs taken by a camera-happy SS man. He was a talented photographer, or maybe he simply had a surefire subject in the doomed Hungarian Jews stepping off trains.

"See how they're dressed," my mother said, pointing to a man wearing a handsome coat, a woman in a stylish hat. "That's the way we looked. We brought our best things."

We read documents connected with the selection process, the accounting of who had been chosen to die: "Too weak." "Too young."

We spent a few minutes in a room staring at a surreal diorama: Piles of hair cut from inmates as they entered the camp preserved behind glass. Dorothea explained why the hair was grayish. "It was treated with a chemical to keep away the insects, and over the years it has had this effect."

It was the vast miniature model of Birkenau, however, that proved to be the catalyst for my mother. This elaborate re-creation gave her the overview she had lacked, architectural logic and constraint for her free-floating memories. She couldn't stop asking questions.

The model vividly laid out the physical scope of Birkenau, which was thirty times the size of the *Stammlager* at Auschwitz I. We could see the rows and rows of barracks of this vast complex and the four crematoria near the woods in the back. This overhead view allowed us to see the completeness of the organization, the orderliness.

I was reminded of Spielberg's reaction to Birkenau: his angry appreciation of the finite detail and his peculiarly American way of describing it. "Nothing had been overlooked. It was a factory where the only product was corpses. You looked around, and you saw a factory with the same kind of mind to efficiency and detail a slaughterhouse might have, where Jack-in-the-Box and McDonald's hamburgers might come from."

The barracks were divided into *Lager*, subcamps labeled with letters and numbers. The prisoners gave the *Lager* nicknames. Inmates in the "Mexico camp" didn't have clothes, just blankets, so they were thought to resemble Mexican Indians. The buildings holding looted Jewish property were called the "Canada barracks" because U.S. immigration restrictions had made Canada, not America, the rich new world for Poles.

"I was in 'C' Lager," said my mother, pointing to the model. "There were thirty-four stables in them, each stable held a thousand people. There were three rows of planks, like bunk beds, each for twelve people. I was in number eight. I know on the other side was number three."

Then Dorothea asked, "Do you want to see the exhibit of the clothing?"

My mother looked at her watch. "I think we should go to the records office. It's getting late. Do you want to see the clothing?"

She looked at the rest of us in a way that encouraged us to say "No." As we left the building my mother said, "My feet were so cold. I saved some bread until I was able to trade it for some boots."

The records room was light and airy, a bright, cheerful room with highly polished floors and red geraniums by the window. There was a small waiting area and a desk separating the waiting area from the archives. The women behind the counter were familiar types—busy, earnest clerks trying to be helpful even though you could sense that people were more interesting to them in catalogue form.

Dorothea warned my mother, "Don't expect that they will be able to find you. The Hungarian Jews were not registered at the camp. They were given clothes and numbers of those already killed. The young ones weren't even given numbers, they were going to be sent on."

An explanation, at last, for the absence of a number on my mother's arm. My father didn't have one either, but he had been interned at

Dachau, not Auschwitz. I had always been thankful they hadn't been branded. Neither of them had ever seemed like victims to me. But my mother wanted some tangible evidence of her stay at Auschwitz. Now that she had let down her resistance to memory, she wanted it to come in clearly.

"I think my number was 84,000," she told one of the women. "I had a number on my dress when I was leaving, actually, not when I was coming in. When they sent me to the work camp, they gave me the striped dress."

The woman didn't comment. She just disappeared and returned a few minutes later with a giant ledger. No luck. She tried again using Rapaport, my mother's original last name. My mother then tried to find Baba, my father's niece, who had been twelve years old when she had come to Auschwitz and who had lived with my parents for a time after the war. Again, no luck. Arthur and Leopold couldn't find the names they were looking for either.

As we left I asked my mother why she wanted to know about the number now. "I was very glad before I didn't have it tattooed on me," she said. "I didn't want to dwell on it. Baba may have been in the last transport that came in that had the tattoos. The transports of Hungarian Jews were coming so fast and so many, there wasn't room for them. They had to make room for them. I don't know. The Polish Jews . . .

"I know you try to dwell on it, but I remember, like I told you, watching those hostages from Iran on the television. The hostages told what was so, that they just lived from day to day. That wasn't enough for the press. They built it up into such a big story."

She looked at me. "Like you."

I persisted. "But we don't understand if we haven't lived through something."

"Okay." Her voice had the mild exasperation of a parent caving into a whining child—which, I suppose, was what she was doing. "You want to know why I want to find my number? I read later on what good records the Germans kept. I wondered if anywhere there was a sign that I was there or if I was just a nothing, without a name, without an identity."

A guide to Auschwitz-Birkenau, as it was

■ My stepfather, Arthur Salcman, is a handsome, muscular man who bronzes easily in the sun. The year he turned seventy, he climbed the Pyramids. When he turned eighty, he still carried his own golf clubs and walked the course with my mother. He is also a worrier, a fastidious person with an eye for the floorboard that might be slightly out of kilter. At the American Machine & Foundry Company, where he worked as an engineer for twenty-six years, he was known as "Mr. Lowerator." He invented the mechanism that pops up plates in cafeterias—the Lowerator—and was rewarded with a model of his invention and a dollar. He likes to understand the way things work and is deeply disturbed when he doesn't. Unlike his wife, Lilly—my mother—he doesn't trust fate.

While we were walking around Birkenau, he had his own memories to contend with. Arthur had spent most of the war in and out of hiding, in and out of the partisan army. At roughly the same time my mother was taken to Auschwitz, in 1944, he had made his way to Bratislava, where he worked with false papers for a Czech factory owner. During the weeks he worked there, Bratislava was under constant attack by the Allies. Every time the airplanes flew overhead the workers had to run outside in case the factory was bombed.

On our way to see the latrines he told me about what it was like to experience those air raids. "I was really praying to God that I should be killed. Every day there was fear, fear, fear. I was always afraid they would recognize me. I didn't want to live this way."

I touched his arm. His skin, warmed by the sun, felt hot against my icy fingertips.

"Oh, you're so cold," he said, grabbing my fingers and rubbing them chivalrously.

I could think of nothing to say but the obvious. "It must have been so awful for you."

Arthur looked up and saw a group of schoolchildren coming toward us. They looked about eleven or twelve years old. They were chattering and shoving one another playfully.

"What do you think they make of this?" Arthur asked me.

I was distracted by a distant figure in the background. My mother was far ahead of us, with Dorothea and Leopold. Unconsciously I picked up the pace, still the child waiting to be scolded for lagging behind.

"Do you think Mommy ever wanted to die?" I asked Arthur. I wasn't changing the subject. This was the subject. My first reaction to Arthur's story had been horror—not just at what he'd endured but at his desire to die. Yet as I thought about it his reaction made a lot of sense. After so many years of a torturous existence death would be a relief.

"Your mommy?" Arthur asked. "Your mommy has a different way of looking at things."

A few minutes later, overhearing my mother, Arthur caught my eye while nodding toward her, as if to say *See what I mean?*

"I was so lucky," she was saying as we walked on floors of hardened dirt in barracks carved from stone.

Rats had been a problem here, in this women's camp, Dorothea said. We were separated by railroad tracks from the camp for "transitory Hungarian Jewesses," where my mother had lived during the spring, summer, and fall of 1944. It seemed strange to think of the seasons passing at Birkenau.

Yet my mother was sitting on a "bed" carved into the hardened mud of the wall and telling us how lucky she had been in the barracks across the tracks. Her barracks had been built from wood in the style of a horse stable. "Ours had high ceilings, and we were free to move around," she said, like a real estate agent trying to force a condo on a reluctant buyer. "We didn't have rats."

Here is a photograph of the "lucky" barracks: a wooden barn with dirt-packed floors, filled with rows and rows of what my mother described as "bunk beds." These "bunk beds" were three-tiered open boxes, built to accommodate six people per tier. By the time my mother arrived in 1944, Birkenau was flooded with "transitory Hungarians," as well as Gypsies and men and women described simply as being of "various nationalities." Twelve women were jammed into each shelf of this "bunk bed" designed by their oppressors to accommodate only six. They managed by dividing into two groups of six, sleeping with feet touching, heads out.

I took many photographs at Birkenau. There is Arthur, wearing a yarmulke and a Polo sport shirt, saying the Kaddish, the prayer for the dead, in front of the guard tower that leads into Birkenau. There is Leopold Schragge, taking his own photos of the vast field of grass, mostly empty now except for a few structures that were rebuilt, the railroad tracks leading to the unloading dock, and rows and rows of chimney stumps, the remains of the barracks. The barracks themselves were ripped down after the war by the Polish farmers whose land and homes had been expropriated by the Germans to build the death camps. At one time Birkenau had been just a village, called Brzezinka in Polish.

It was a long, hot walk across Birkenau's vast acreage. My mother was pumped up, collecting details like a journalist who fears there will be no chance for follow-up. It was as though she was hoping Dorothea would provide some logical way of putting in order the discombobulated images in her memory. Bit by bit she pieced it together: This is where she was deloused (stripped, showered, shaved). This is where her bunker was, the C Lager. This is where Baba might have lived, on the other side of the tracks—Baba, her niece by marriage, who at age twelve had been assigned the job of emptying the suitcases of incoming prisoners and separating the contents into piles: shoes, food, jewelry.

One by one she got the answers to questions she'd never asked before. Why hadn't she heard the legendary Auschwitz orchestra play? Why hadn't she had to work at Auschwitz? (The transitory Hungarians had been kept on hold, to be sent out to work camps as weakened Jews died.)

I saw my mother's head jerk around suddenly. I knew she was looking for Arthur, to make sure he was keeping himself occupied while she was talking to Dorothea. When she located him, walking next to Leopold, she turned back to Dorothea, satisfied she wasn't needed.

I knew this gesture well. My mother felt that everything and everybody would fall apart if she didn't keep an eye on them. Yet when she was distracted from her watch—and she was easily distracted—she became oblivious to everything but the object of her attention. Thus she can provoke irritation in exactly opposite ways, by seeming smothering one minute, lackadaisical the next.

I was relieved to see that jerk of the head. It assured me that this visit, instigated by me, hadn't yet triggered a transformation in her. Her defenses seemed intact.

This was the ignoble thought I was having as I trailed behind my mother and Dorothea at Birkenau. I gazed across the chimney stumps and the barbed wire and the expanse of green, trying to conjure what had been there before.

Nothing.

I took some more pictures, hoping when we got home they would show me what I'd missed. Maybe life was an afterthought, something to think about later, in a safe place.

Finally we arrived at the blackened remains of a large structure, bordered by cypress trees. Next to it was a large hole in the ground that might have been the imprint of an ancient swimming pool.

"This was one of the gas chambers and crematoria," Dorothea told us, matter-of-fact as always.

The ruins of a crematorium at Birkenau. Is this my family's grave site?

It was so very quiet—strangely peaceful. Silently we found comfortable perches on the stone remains of the gas chamber. For several minutes we rested there, basking in the pleasant spring sun. Dorothea stood to one side, waiting for a cue.

So this was it, wasn't it? The grave site I had been looking for—or maybe not. Maybe my grandmother had been burned in the crematorium on the far side of the woods.

My mother broke the silence. "Are those the tracks?" she asked, pointing to lengths of iron sunk into the ground behind the gas chamber.

Dorothea nodded. "Wagons could come there to take the things away from here."

She indicated we should follow her to a large shallow dip in the ground. "This is the pit where the ashes were dumped after the burning," she said. She leaned over and picked up a tiny pebble. She handed it to me.

"This is ash," she said. "Human bone."

Staring at the pebble in my hand, I realized how naïve I had been, thinking I could reconstruct Auschwitz as my family's burial plot. What spirit would linger in this place, where the disrespect for the dead had been redefined for the ages?

I stared at the pebble in my hand. Should I shriek or say the Kaddish for my grandparents? I glanced at my mother, who had tilted her face toward the sun and was smiling faintly, like a contented bather at the beach. I knelt down and returned the pebble to the ground.

My mother as a little girl. She's sitting on the rocking horse, surrounded by the other Rapaport children. *From left:* Hilu, Erzsi, Gyula, and Rozsi (sitting).

5

The Genius

■ To understand what my mother meant when she spoke those words—"I was not a nothing"—at the age of seventy you must know what those words might have meant to her at age twenty-one, when she first arrived at Birkenau.

This is what she meant to say: "I was really something." Her parents were thought to be finished with child making when she came along: Berthe was thirty-three and Nathan was forty-three when she was born in 1922. It's fair to say this fifth child was considered both a gift from God and an embarrassment. Her arrival upset the family's fragile equilibrium. Eight years had passed since baby Joe, known as Hilu, had been born and the Cossacks had driven the Rapaports from Nathan's hometown of Volove. Poor Nathan, the son of Gedalya Rapaport, a man who could make money without even trying, had a gift only for failure. When World War I was breaking out he traveled to Hungary to buy flour, anticipating a boom in flour prices. The Cossacks interfered with his plans: His flour went up in flames with the rest of Volove. He and his family moved in with his mother-in-law, who was then living in Satu-Mare.

They all soon tired of one another, and Nathan decided to take his family to Huszt, the town where Berthe had been born. Falling back on his inheritance, as he always did, he bought a house on the courtyard that Berthe's family had once owned. Her mother, Julia Weiss, was a shrewd businesswoman, a grocery wholesaler. Julia's husband was a *Torah chacham,* a scholar, of whom it was said, "He studied and made children." It was Julia, of course, who gave birth to their ten children and of whom it was said, "She had the babies and went right back to work."

Living in eastern Europe, she might as well have been a *shlemazel*—luckless—like her son-in-law Nathan. She'd sold the three houses she'd owned in Huszt and left in 1910 to settle in Satu-Mare for reasons no one can remember. Maybe it was only that Satu-Mare was a pretty town, though there probably was more to it than that. She had taken her profits and invested in state bonds. By the end of World War I, the Austro-Hungarian monarchy had collapsed and Julia Weiss was living in Romania with a trunk full of worthless banknotes. The loss wouldn't ruin her, though: She saved money as naturally as Nathan lost it.

Huszt would remind Nathan of his financial ineptness in many ways. He lived just down the street from the Koruna Hotel. Occupying an entire block, it loomed almost as big in life as it did in the Rapaport family mythology. Nathan's father, Gedalya, was an impulsive, expansive man. His legacy included three wives, thirteen children, and the story of how he had bought the Koruna Hotel. According to the legend, one day Gedalya traveled from Volove to Huszt on market day. It was only about twenty-five miles but far enough by horse and wagon. He had been trying to buy the Koruna for some time, but the owner didn't want to sell. On this market day, he disguised himself as a beggar and went to the restaurant on the main floor of the Koruna, where yesterday's rolls could be bought for a good price. He stood outside of the restaurant gnawing on one of the rolls, which was stale. As he tried to tear off a bite with his hand, his arm slammed backward into the window and it shattered.

He immediately began to scream, "Get me the owner!"

The owner came outside. Before he could say anything, Gedalya, who appeared to be a beggar, said indignantly, "These rolls are like rocks!"

The owner replied, "How will you pay for the window, you *shnorrer* [bum]?"

Gedalya said, "How much do you want for the whole hotel?"

The owner laughed and called out to the crowd that was gathering. "Look who wants to buy my hotel! Sure, wise guy. You can buy my hotel if you can come up with the money." He named his price.

In front of the witnesses Gedalya opened his money belt and counted out the asking price.

Who knows if the story is true? But that's how Nathan remembered it. By the time he moved to Huszt, however, his father was long dead and the Koruna had fallen on hard times. Huszt became part of Czechoslovakia, a beneficent new country in some ways, a nightmare to property holders who had to pay for its socialist policies. Taxes were prohibitive. It was no longer simple to sell off a few acres of forest when Nathan needed money. Nathan bought a store next to the house in Huszt and tried his hand at the hardware business. This time there were no Cossacks to blame for his failure.

Still the family found ways to maintain the illusion of prosperity. They kept the children in good clothes ("You don't need *many* things, just *good* ones," Berthe would say). Berthe refreshed herself every year by visiting her mother in Satu-Mare and by spending a few weeks at the spa in Biksad. The Rapaports always had a maid.

Berthe financed these luxuries by renting the spare room off the courtyard. When the second daughter, Rozsi, and the first daughter, Erzsi, finished school—neither of them went to *Gymnasium,* high school—they asked their father if they could use the store next door, since no one else was. They opened a little coffee shop, where they sold sandwiches and ice cream. Their younger brothers, Gyula and Joe, were in school.

All in all, the Rapaports could tell themselves with some conviction: *Life is good.*

Things were so good that when Berthe became pregnant her teenage daughters could afford the luxury of mortification. They no longer worried about the Cossacks but about what the neighbors would think. They could indulge themselves in the self-centeredness of youth. How could their parents impose this humiliation on *them*? Berthe went to the spa as usual that year, even though she was in her ninth month of pregnancy. She hoped the girls would be happier about the new baby by the time she returned.

They weren't. They were dispatched to relatives in Beregszaz before the baby's birth. Berthe didn't want her new child to find its first breath contaminated by their agitation.

When the girls returned home they refused to look at their little sister, Lilly. *Simchah,* blessing, was her Yiddish name, and she was already being called "Szimi" by their parents. Some blessing, they thought.

Their brother Gyula, the designated good son, the boy who only wanted everyone to get along, came to his sisters and coaxed them with his gentle charm.

"Come and see that little girl," he wheedled. "Come see that beautiful girl."

They did and were instantly captivated by the little darling. Or so they told her.

She was a funny child with huge dark eyes and remarkable self-assurance. When she was four years old it was discovered that she could multiply big numbers instantaneously.

She was a genius.

This talent gave Rozsi and Erzsi a practical reason to love their little sister. She drew customers to their coffee shop. When Hungarian lumber merchants would come to town to talk business with their father, they would set Szimi up on the table and throw her numbers: 555 times 432; 1,296 times 347.

She never missed. Soon she started performing for money: "Come on, mister, throw me some numbers."

Szimi wasn't sure if God had given her this gift or not, but she wasn't taking any chances. She became very devout. She memorized the Hebrew prayers as easily as she multiplied 692 times 345 and refused to touch money on the Sabbath.

Her faith was tested at the height of her fame, when she was almost five. It was a Saturday, Shabbat, and she was roaming on the main street, as she often did. She wandered into the bank where her Uncle Adolf worked as a cashier.

"You want to see something?" Uncle Adolf asked some lumbermen from Budapest as he lifted his niece up onto the teller's counter. "Ask her to multiply any numbers you want."

"Impossible," they said.

They gave her two numbers, and she gave them the answer. The bank's secretary worked out the answer on a piece of paper.

"The *genius* is wrong," she said.

"Count it over," Uncle Adolf replied.

The secretary counted it over and found her error. The lumbermen laughed and gave the little girl fifty crowns.

She handed the money to her uncle as though it were flaming hot. "I can't take this money. It's Shabbat," she said with horror.

Uncle Adolf looked at her a minute, trying not to laugh, then he went behind the cashier's counter. He came out and stuffed an envelope into the ruffles on the bodice of Szimi's dress. "There," he said, "you're not touching it."

Szimi ran home and told Rozsi what had happened. Rozsi put the money into a drawer and told Szimi to buy whatever she liked. The next day she bought something she had been dreaming about, bright red sandals from Dr. Popper Shoes.

The gift for numbers would eventually fade into a more ordinary talent for mathematics. But Szimi remained a singular child, convinced she could solve any problem as unconsciously and easily as she once had found answers in multiplication.

———

▪ It was the summer of 1939. Szimi Rapaport was sixteen years old. She was living in the epicenter of international geopolitics.

Britain's prime minister, Neville Chamberlain, had sold out Czechoslovakia to the Germans in September 1938, agreeing to hand over the western territory, the Sudetenland, to the Germans in exchange for "peace for a century." Eastern Czechoslovakia—including Huszt and the entire Carpathian Mountain region—became Hungarian again as Germany solidified its alliances.

The country where she was born no longer existed. Yet Szimi didn't see this overnight change in borders as especially abnormal. After all,

My mother as a
teenager, in her Girl
Scout uniform

she and her mother had been born in houses that overlooked the same
courtyard but were in different countries. One day it would occur to
her that she had spent her entire life speaking with an accent. When she
spoke Hungarian, she had a Russian accent; her Russian sounded
Czech; her English would be Hungarian flavored. Her grammar might
be impeccable, but she would never be mistaken for a native wherever
she might go.

The shifts were abstract to her in a way they were not to Jews in Germany, who had lost all civil rights, or to opponents of the Nazis who
were being herded into concentration camps. Political prisoners at
Dachau had been ordered to sew Stars of David on uniforms to prepare
for a mass influx of Jews.

Szimi, however, was dreaming about Scarlett O'Hara. She read *Gone
with the Wind* that summer, and that was all she and her friends
could talk about. They followed news of the movie version closely and
couldn't wait until it came to Huszt. She loved movies, especially
American movies, especially romantic ones.

The year before, she had been dreaming about China, and she and
her best friend, Nadia Heinrich, had learned all they thought there was
to know about it. They knew every river, every mountain. When Szimi

closed her eyes, she could see the map of China in her head. She and Nadia had plans to become doctors and travel to China or someplace—the Pacific islands would do. They would save lives and see the world. That's what they saw in their future. A prestigious occupation, good work—"good" in the sense of noble, not well-paying. They were young enough and privileged enough to be motivated by a sense of *noblesse oblige.*

Her sisters had already taken to the road. Both of them had married men who had sought their fortune in Palestine. Rozsi, the beautiful sister, was especially conscientious about sending pictures home. How exotic! Rozsi, dressed in mock Chanel and high heels, ankle deep in sand.

Very few of Huszt's five thousand Jewish children continued their education past middle school. Orthodox children didn't attend the public schools, which held classes on Saturday—the Sabbath. But Nadia and Szimi were modern girls. They went to school on Saturdays but were excused from writing, a modernist interpretation of

My glamorous Aunt Rozsi and her husband, Franz Winkelsberg, on a street in Tel Aviv, circa 1935

the Talmudic prohibition against working on the Sabbath. They were also relatively wealthy. Nadia's stepfather was a pharmacist. Szimi's father, Nathan, was the son of a rich man, Gedalya Rapaport, owner of ten thousand acres of forest.

When Szimi thought about what her father did, she had to admit to herself: He didn't do much. Nathan Rapaport would occasionally travel to his woodlands to have a few trees chopped down, to pay the large taxes collected by the Czech government. He spent most of his time playing chess with his friend, the liquor store owner. Occasionally, once in a great while, he would play chess with Szimi. She assumed he was proud of her for being so smart, but she always knew it was an assumption, since he spoke to her but rarely. Nathan became a blur in her memory, a shadowy figure surrounded by cigarette smoke.

Nathan was reluctant to part with his trees, so the family's wealth always seemed hypothetical to his children. The family's cash still came from Berthe, who continued to invent new ways to turn her home into a profit center. She began operating a lunchroom out of the family dining room, charging six or eight crowns for a meal. The children were embarrassed by the strangers who came to lunch. Berthe wasn't ashamed. Her children always had *good* things, and that was what mattered.

Parents and their inexplicable ways weren't high in Szimi's mind in the summer of 1939. She had been a genius child, but she wasn't a genius student. She was determined, though. In the spring term of her next-to-last year in *Gymnasium* she became friendly with the literature teacher, who gave her assignments for the summer. That fall she would be studying Dostoevsky and Tolstoy in Russian.

It was while Szimi was memorizing *Anna Karenina* that Germany was dismembering Czechoslovakia. Podkarpatská Rus was Czech no more. Huszt's Czechs became foreign nationals and had to leave. By 1939 there was no more Czech school. Nadia and Szimi would have to finish *Gymnasium* in Huszt's other high school, where Ukrainian was spoken. Szimi had learned phrases of the language when she was young, from her Ukrainian nanny. Nadia didn't know a word. They would have to study a lot that summer to prepare for this important final year, the year that would determine whether they would be admitted to medical school and go to China or the Pacific islands.

Later Szimi would say, "That summer we lived a normal life." Her mother sent photos of Szimi wearing a two-piece bathing suit to Rozsi in Palestine. For the first time in her life Szimi was slim, not that she'd ever been obese. But she was always struggling to lose weight. Every morning she would walk a couple of kilometers to the hill at the end of the main street, and climb nine hundred feet up to the ruins of a castle. She found she could accomplish two things at once on these daily hikes—think about Anna Karenina and keep her weight down. She had climbed the hill from the time she was a little girl, when she would stop and rest on the benches in the Hungarian Reform Cemetery. She felt peaceful there, surrounded by the dead, whose pictures were imprinted on the headstones. She especially liked sitting by the grave carrying the wedding picture of a young bride, so tragically romantic.

Later she would say, "We really had a very nice life." Every night she and her friends would "make the promenade," walk up and down the main street. On Sundays there were tea dances in the park. Twice a week—at least—she went to the movies. Oblivious to the terror gathering around her, she sought terror in the gangsters played by Edward G. Robinson. Mainly she was dazzled by Fred Astaire and Eleanor Powell and Ginger Rogers and hordes of girls tap dancing and sashaying in movies like *Broadway Melody* and *The Great Ziegfield*. Later she would say, "Isn't it something I remember all those people even today, and these new actresses just disappear as you watch them."

The illusion of normalcy was maintained by the adults as well. Throughout the 1930s Berthe's letters to her daughters in Palestine barely hinted at the political situation in Europe.

She wrote newsy dispatches about everyday life: who was marrying, how Szimi was doing in school, who was gaining weight and who was losing it. She reported a surprising number of suicides.

The letters contained an undercurrent of worry, not about Adolf Hitler but about how her daughters were faring so far away from home in a primitive land. Mainly she stayed close to the events of the day, of the days in Huszt: a storm blew off the synagogue roof; the tailor's son eloped with the daughter of a Christian minister and moved to America; a local man was arrested for tax evasion and hanged himself in jail with his *t'fillin*.

She sent dried mushrooms and vanilla sticks and pictures of Gyula, Hilu, and Szimi. She took pains to praise her daughters, to tell them how very beautiful they looked in the pictures they sent her. She paid Erzsi the highest compliment: "In this picture you look like Rozsi." She seemed to understand Erzsi's need for reassurance; she flattered her frequently. When she reported an illness of her own, she minimized her suffering by recalling a pain one of her daughters had once had. She asked her daughters to tell her that the disturbing rumors she'd heard weren't true: that in Palestine, 90 percent of the people broke the prohibition against smoking and eating on Yom Kippur.

How could Berthe be mindful of politics at large when life at home was becoming so chaotic? Rozsi and her husband, Franz, had returned to Czechoslovakia after a devastating failure in Palestine. Franz was a talented engineer but a hopeless businessman. He'd lost all his money and had come home to the family engineering firm. In 1937, when Berthe was forty-seven years old, her first grandchild was born. Rozsi, Franz, and the baby moved in with Rozsi's parents until they could afford their own place.

Berthe wrote to Erzsi, who was still in Palestine, "We are fine, only I am very tired. The family is expanding instead of getting smaller."

———

■ Franz worked steadily, and soon he and his family set up housekeeping in Užhorod, a few hours from Huszt. After the partition of Czechoslovakia, they moved to Brno, which remained on the Czech side of the border, so Szimi was sent there to take classes while the fate of her own *Gymnasium* was being decided. She stayed with Rozsi's family for five months, occupied with her studies and with her baby niece, Ilana. *Life was going on.*

In August 1938 Berthe wrote a letter to Erzsi and her husband, Laci.

My dear children:
    Please forgive me that I am just now answering your letter but I have been without a maid for four weeks and Szimi is at Rozsi's. I got myself into a big mess. The floor in the big room was wob-

bly. I thought just the middle would have to be fixed, but it turned out the whole floor underneath was rotten. They had to remove all the sand from underneath, bring fresh dirt and sand, and replace the whole floor. We will not be able to paint for another two weeks, until the wall dries all around the new floor. We are all fine, only I am tired. I should go to a spa, but by the time this mess is finished I will have to get ready for the holidays.

Gyongy is still going out with Neufeld, but he still did not ask her to marry him.

Grandma sent a letter with Mr. Glick and asked you to write to her. Also when you sent her the coffee she thanked you for it and you did not answer her. If you knew how she is looking forward to your letter you would have written her right away. Please write. *Umberufen* she is in her 81st year and feels fine. She would like to go to Palestine now that she is all by herself because Aunt Eva and Uncle Aladar were expelled from Romania as Czech citizens. They are now here and would like to go to Palestine with what money they have—if there were some opportunity to go into business or to become partners in your store. They don't want to stay here. Everything is very unsure.

Szimi cannot write enough how sweet Pupa is. She walks already holding on to her hand.

How is business? How does your apartment look?

Aunt Berta is very unhappy that Gyula is going out with Bozsi Landau. Mrs. Goldstine says he'll marry her.

Again, please don't be angry that I just now answered. God be with you. Expecting your early reply.

With all my love, your devoted Mother.

The only hint of worry: "Everything is very unsure."
A brief letter followed a month later.

My dear children:

Our dear Rozsi and her sweet little girl were here. They came Sunday and went back Monday noon. We would all be fine if there were peace. Accept our best wishes in the coming New Year.

May the Almighty bring fulfillment of all your wishes. Have an easy fast.

With all our love and kisses
Your devoted Mother

Franz and Rozsi, more worldly, had no illusions about what was going on. They had been trying frantically for months to get papers for Palestine, even though Franz was doing well. He'd been in charge of the construction of an airport for the Czech military near Bratislava, and when that was finished he moved to Užhorod to join the engineering firm run by his sister and brother-in-law. But the instant the Germans marched into Austria he insisted they leave Czechoslovakia.

Rozsi's letters to Erzsi sounded notes of panic. In September 1938 she wrote:

I got all upset that Laci wants to send money *here*. Today it is not worthwhile to buy anything here because we don't know what will happen. You probably heard that a week ago today evening they mobilized. František came home at seven, and at 10 P.M. they announced on the radio that everybody has to report to his division. František left Saturday morning, you can imagine what our state of mind is. Who knows what will be with us!

I already ordered the two easy chairs for you and Gyula shopped for shirts for Laci, very beautiful, but who knows when they will be there. Nobody can travel anywhere. I would love to go to you with Pupa, but we can't. We had to take in the radio to the government. There is complete blackout. If you listen to the radio you will know what is happening here. Your letter was censored.

We wish you a Happy New Year, may the Almighty help us, that everything should turn out well and we can see each other.

I have no patience to write more. The three Frischmann boys [cousins] are in the Army and many more in the family were mobilized.

Kisses with love, Rozsi

While Franz worked to get exit visas, Rozsi and Szimi went on a buying spree: china and crystal, bedding and towels, furniture, cloth.

They packed a giant container full of things and shipped it off to Palestine, hoping to follow soon. Rozsi urged her parents to go with them—or at least to send Szimi if they didn't want to leave. However, by December it became clear that she, Franz, and their baby would be the only ones to leave. On December 26, 1938, she wrote again to Erzsi:

> I received your letter and am glad you got the money we sent. Probably the money from Gyula will arrive also.
>
> I was in Prague twice this week. I did a lot of shopping. Everything is very expensive. Your friend is leaving for Switzerland Thursday. She praised you, said what a wonderful businesswoman you are. We have problems with the visas to Palestine. I hope Olga will be able to help me and that we can get approval to take out the money. We cannot take Szimi with us. One can only take his own child up to the age of 18. She is still here, but maybe she'll go home soon because classes are starting in Huszt. She is sorry she cannot come with us, but when we are there I will start right away to apply for her permit.
>
> Our friends advised us that it is not worthwhile to buy silver and china here. One can get it there very cheap. You should inquire.
>
> As for our parents, it is very hard today to sell anything. Money has very little value. In my opinion if they stay here they will be okay because the peasants there cannot get along very well without the Jews. And you know how hard it is for older people in Palestine. The situation is not easy.
>
> Let me know what you really want me to bring.
>
> Kisses to you and Laci. Rozsi.

On March 15, 1939, Szimi was awakened by the sound of loud voices screaming through megaphones on the street: "The German Army of Occupation has entered Prague. Stay in your houses! Don't do anything until further notice!"

Yet she remembers no sense of alarm, no panic. Rozsi's family was leaving for Palestine, and she was going home to Huszt. Franz's was the only voice she heard saying, "This cannot have a happy end."

My mother in 1939, finished with high school and ready to conquer the world

6

Passover

■ "Western man, by and large, is the most natural man, a mental bourgeois, and he cherishes his mental comfort. It is almost impossible to
admit disturbing evidence."

The writer Joseph Brodsky laid out this theory of "mental self-
preservation" in 1994, during a conversation he had with a *New Yorker*
writer about the Western press's refusal to believe in the Stalinist mas-
sacre of millions of people. Brodsky talked about a "mental fence," a
protection against the idea of such brutality, and said he believed it was
the special creation of intellectuals, the educated classes.

Fifty years earlier, the Rapaport family hadn't exactly been Western,
not in the sense Brodsky was talking about. Nor could they easily have
been considered intellectuals. But they had become masters of "mental self-preservation."

War was devastating Europe, but Szimi would remember the spring
of 1940 for her graduation from the Ukrainian *Gymnasium* in Huszt.
She danced at her graduation ball and took a trip to Budapest with her

brother Gyula, her friend Olga Mermelstein, and Olga's father. Szimi suspected the trip was really to arrange a match between Olga and Gyula, but she wasn't sure. She didn't care. This was her first taste of the world beyond, and it was all she'd hoped for. It helped that Mr. Mermelstein had no trouble parting with money. They drove to Budapest *in a car*, stayed at the Royale Hotel, went to the theater, had their pictures taken by a professional photographer. Szimi was elegant in her new gray dress with the white collar. It didn't even bother her when she would tell people she was from Huszt and they would say, "Ah, Felvidék"—ah, the upper region. She knew what the *ah* meant. They thought she was low class, a peasant. The Carpathian people were the hillbillies of eastern Europe.

The most fantastic part of the trip came near the end, when Mr. Mermelstein took his group to a restaurant in a suburb of Budapest. Szimi found it most glamorous, this big expensive restaurant where the waiters wore the bright, traditional clothing of Hungary. The fish they would eat that night had been raised in the carp pond on the grounds. No matter how the carp was prepared—and you could have it prepared any way you wanted—it was guaranteed to have no bones. Find a bone and eat for free.

From Budapest Szimi continued her graduation trip alone. She traveled to Kiskörös, where her widowed aunt lived. The aunt was prosperous. She owned forty hectares of vineyards and a winery. But after the excitement of Budapest her aunt's dark house felt like a tomb. Szimi was bored by the strictures of this Orthodox household. Two days into the week she was supposed to stay there, she was ready to go home.

Yet she didn't want to cut short her graduation holiday. She was supposed to be celebrating.

She proposed the following to her aunt: Could she spend the rest of the week out in the vineyards? The shack the workers used during harvesttime was empty. The caretaker's house wasn't far, if she needed anything.

Her aunt said weakly, "A young girl . . ."

Szimi replied, "There's a two-burner. I'll be fine."

From Monday until Friday Szimi lived in the vineyard. She walked. She ate peaches. She read. She walked to the caretaker's house for fresh

The Germans had invaded Czechoslovakia, but life was going on.

milk from their cow. She enjoyed the solitude as much as she had enjoyed the frenzy of Budapest. Even then she was a chameleon, adapting to her environment or finding an environment to which she could adapt. When she left Kiskörös, she felt settled on where she would go next, if not when. As soon as the Germans pulled out of Prague, she would start her studies. China would soon be near.

———

■ She had her first major crush that summer, just after she left the vineyard. She stopped back in Budapest on the way home to stay with another aunt. There she met a lumberman who was doing business with her father. She was invited to his home. When she arrived, the man wasn't there but his son was. The son was handsome and a doctor, in the middle of his internship. They went rowing on the Danube and for coffee, more than once. When Szimi returned to Huszt, he showed up at her house one day, spent a few hours, and then left.

Szimi wasn't yet eighteen and wasn't interested in marriage. (Neither was he; she never saw him again.) She and Nadia, her best friend, had their plans and didn't understand their friends who didn't. One of their good friends was a girl named Hedy, a beautiful young woman with a finely chiseled face. Later Szimi would see Vanessa Redgrave in the movies and think of Hedy. That bone structure. Hedy was older than Nadia and Szimi, but only twenty, when she married a man her friends considered "a nothing." They didn't express their objections very clearly, or maybe they did. "He was very nice, sweet, but such . . . she was *taller* than him." There could be only one explanation, they decided. Hedy's mother had a brain tumor, and Hedy wanted to be settled so her mother could go in peace. That must be it.

Nadia and Szimi were waiting for the Germans to leave Prague so they could go to medical school. Their parents urged them to fill the time learning a craft.

The girls decided to learn how to sew. They thought the seamstress they chose to teach them was a whore because she would go to bed with anybody who would go to bed with her. These nice middle-class girls may have disapproved of her social life (just as they were titillated by it), but they had to admit she was a talented seamstress. She said she would take them on as apprentices if they paid her.

Right away she taught them how to baste and hem. She would cut out the material, and the girls would baste and hem. A few weeks went by, and it occurred to the girls that they had mastered basting and hemming. They asked the woman: When will you teach us to sew on the machine?

"Don't worry," she said.

Two weeks later they asked again.

"What's your rush?" she asked.

"I know how to baste, inside out," said Szimi. "I'm not in a rush, but I don't want to baste all the time."

Maybe the woman's answer wasn't satisfactory, or maybe Szimi and Nadia had come to the conclusion that the life of a seamstress wasn't for them, even temporarily. They left, telling each other that the seamstress was really very low class.

———

▪ In 1941 and 1942 the letters Rozsi and Franz sent from Palestine were no longer chatty. The language was guarded—for the censors—

but the message was clear and emphatic: "Sell everything! Come out! Sell everything!"

Berthe and Nathan could have gone. Rozsi and Franz were prospering the second time around. The hotel they were operating in Netanya was being used by the British military as local headquarters. They had connections.

It must be said. Greed killed Nathan Rapaport. Maybe it wasn't greed for money. Maybe it was greed for something more ephemeral, the satisfaction of having an accomplishment beyond being a rich man's son.

It doesn't matter. What matters is that the replacement of the Czech government by the Hungarians caused the lumber business to boom. The boom was amplified by the war. Everyone was building. Nathan was no longer a dilettante lumberman. Now, instead of cutting down trees only to pay taxes, he was cutting down the trees to make money. Finally, already past his sixtieth birthday, he was operating a flourishing business. The war was turning out to be a blessing for him. He could now be, truly, *paterfamilias.*

The dire warnings from beyond couldn't penetrate this bubble of prosperity, this unique situation. How bad could things be in a world that allowed Nathan Rapaport to offer his sons a livelihood? Gyula, who had been working as a bookkeeper for other people, now worked for his father as well. He was a big shot, traveling to Budapest to meet with the lumbermen, perhaps becoming a regular at the restaurant so fine it would give you a free meal if one carp bone was inflicted on a customer. He traveled to Volove with Nathan to supervise the cutting of the timber. What a thrill it was, watching the logs float down the Tisza River, en route to the Danube and Budapest. Sell everything? Leave that? This is what Nathan had been waiting for since he could remember. What should he do? Go back to days of chess and cigarettes?

"Nothing will happen to us," he told Berthe, when she would read the letters from Palestine.

It would be easier to understand Nathan's "mental self-preservation" if one fact could be omitted from the story. If only what happened to Hilu didn't have to be reported.

He had gone to medical school in Prague in 1936. His studies were cut short by the German invasion. Students were offered the chance to go to London or Washington. Hilu chose to go home, to Huszt. He'd heard the rumors that Hitler wanted to eliminate the Jews. But possibly the rumors were exaggerated. Besides, who did he know in London or Washington?

Back in Huszt, the rumors were rarely discussed. Even the war was rarely discussed. The Rapaports were existentialists. Each day was a separate day, disconnected from the past and the future. They would talk of each day as a *found day,* meaning a fortuitous happenstance. It was an age of low expectations.

In 1940, as the family timber business began to prosper, Hilu received the equivalent of a draft notice from the Hungarian Army. It was a highly specialized draft. Only Jews were called. He and his cousin reported to Jasine, a Carpathian town not far from the Russian border. He found this a relief—better near the Russians than near the Germans. There he was assigned to the trenches. For eighteen months he dug.

Life at Jasine wasn't pleasant, but it wasn't bad either. It was wartime, after all. The men lived in military barracks, ate well, and periodically were given furloughs home.

In the middle of 1941 the men at Jasine heard they were being transferred to the Hungarian town of Jutas. They were terrified. Jutas was known in two ways, as a lovely lakeside resort and as the training ground for the vicious Hungarian gendarmes. When you heard a policeman came from Jutas you shook. The Jews at Jasine sensed they weren't being sent to Jutas to take the sun.

They arrived in the late morning. The captain came out and looked them over.

Then he began to talk. *Munkaszolgálatos,* he said.

Hilu's cousin whispered, "My ears must be deaf. He called us *munkaszolgálatos.*"

Munkaszolgálatos means "Hungarian labor camp workers." As if he'd overheard Hilu's cousin, the captain explained.

"We are not going to call you *büdös zsidó*—dirty Jew—here. We are going to call you labor camp workers."

With this bit of semantics the captain altered the way Hilu would think about Jutas forever. He would always describe it as a beautiful resort town, and he would laugh at the trick he felt he'd played on fate, though all he'd done was show up.

His luck—he would think of it as luck—held out at Jutas. His commanding officer there was a Carpathian man, from the same town where Berthe's sister and brother-in-law lived. One day he and Hilu were playing Carpathian geography, and the commander learned that Hilu was the nephew of Mr. Frischmann. When he learned Hilu had completed two years of medical school, he found an excuse to give him a cushy job. He was made camp medic and given a Red Cross band to wear around his arm. He was a *Liebling,* a darling, given passes home whenever he wanted them.

When he would describe the time he spent at Jutas, he would express no bitterness toward the Hungarians who had put him there. Indeed, he felt kindly toward them for failing to be cruel. His anger was reserved for his cousin, who never resisted the opportunity to belittle the Red Cross band Hilu wore so proudly on his arm.

"Some doctor!" the cousin would sneer.

Hilu never failed to take the bait. "I didn't tell them I was a doctor. I showed them my university certificate. Two and a half years completed."

When he talked about Jutas, he would redden only when he mentioned his cousin's name, the traitor who doubted his sincerity.

———

▪ Later, Szimi would try to explain: "We lived as normal. We didn't know what was happening."

She would amplify: "We knew Hitler was anti-Jewish, but we had nothing to do with Hitler."

They knew a great deal, in fact. They listened to the radio and heard about the *Blitzkrieg* attack on Poland. They took in tenants who could offer firsthand testimony about what was going on. A Polish professor, a non-Jew, brought his family to live in the spare room. They weren't the only Poles to show up in Huszt in the autumn of 1939. They came by buggy, by foot.

"Oh, that," Szimi would say. "Well, he is Poland and we are Hungary and Hungary was neutral at that time. Life was going on. They wouldn't come down south."

What about what had happened in 1941, when the Hungarians had announced their presence in Podkarpatská Rus in a way that was not "normal"? They had begun gathering up Jews who were "foreigners"—a term vaguely defined—and pushing them over the border to Kamenets-Podolski in German-held Ukraine.

Szimi's best friend, Flora—her religious best friend, that is, not to slight Nadia—fell into this category because her mother was from Bratislava and considered a Slovak. Whenever Szimi would speak of Flora, she would say, "A very smart girl, Flora. She was . . . God shouldn't punish me . . . very ugly. She had some kind of eye disease. She was very smart, but her parents wouldn't let her go to *Gymnasium* because you had to go on Saturday even if you didn't have to write."

Flora's family had been taken to Kamenets-Podolski. They returned to Huszt eventually and would say nothing of what had happened to them, only that it was horrible. (In fact, the Hungarians used a few thousand of these stateless Jews for slave labor and the Germans massacred most of the rest.)

"That's true," Szimi would say. "But you don't understand. Life was going on."

There was cause for hope. In 1943 the Germans had to retreat from Stalingrad. The BBC reported an assassination attempt against Hitler. The Allies were bombing Germany regularly. The Americans were in the war in full force, with men and airplanes and ammunition.

Still, the Rapaports understood that they had stretched the idea of "a normal life" to its utmost possibility. They finally had to admit that one might argue that the omens were not good. One by one the poles holding up the "mental fence" protecting them from the unimaginable had been torn down. They could no longer dismiss Hitler as a clown. They could no longer look to America for salvation. America! A sitting duck at Pearl Harbor for Japanese bombs! The Japanese had done the unimaginable—sent airplanes thousands of miles across the ocean. They could no longer convince themselves that they would be overlooked.

They could no longer turn Hilu's experience into a source of comfort. They could no longer say, "See, Hilu has been in labor camps on and off for two years and he isn't having it so bad."

Everything changed when Gyula was ordered to join the Hungarian military in Poland, where he and other Jews were forced to clear minefields.

For almost three years Gyula had smooth-talked his way out of the service. Everyone who knew him liked him, and he made a point of knowing everyone he needed to know. The draft notices would come, and he would explain that his services were indispensable to the businesses whose books he kept. But there came a time when personal relationships had to be set aside. Gyula had to go.

That may have been the moment when Berthe understood that her son-in-law František was right: "This cannot have a happy end." She would never say such a thing, but she couldn't hide her fear. That year her hair turned from black to gray.

Gyula had always been lucky, but now it seemed he'd used up all his luck. Every day he marched out to face death on an empty stomach. Like all the Rapaports, he believed strongly in fate yet never was willing to accept it. He found a Hungarian sergeant who could be seen as humanitarian or profiteer—his motives didn't interest Gyula. The sergeant distributed food on credit to ten of the Jews under his watch. He kept records of the transactions in a notebook.

The notebook was found, and the ten young men were charged with bribery. They were sent to Kassa (now Košice), a town in Hungary, where they were to be court-martialed by the military. Now they were considered soldiers.

Berthe thanked God that Gyula was safe in jail, not tempting fate every day in a minefield. She and Nathan agreed that Szimi, who was twenty that summer, should travel to Kassa by train and hire a lawyer to get Gyula out. They managed not to consider exactly why he had gotten *in*. Instead they proceeded as though they were ordinary Hungarian citizens demanding the justice they deserved under Hungarian law. This wasn't unreasonable. The new prime minister, Miklós Kállay, had stopped the deportation of Jews and refused to require the wearing of yellow badges. Hungary had become a haven for Jews from Austria, Slovakia, and Poland. Kállay wasn't a son of a bitch like the Slovak prime minister, Monsignor Josef Tiso, a Catholic priest who hated Jews so much he was happy to comply with the mass deportations.

Szimi took food to Gyula in jail and discussed strategy. Two of the young men awaiting trial with him were rich boys from Kassa. Their families invited Szimi to stay with them until the trial.

It all happened quickly. They were tried and sentenced to thirteen months in the prison near Szeged in southern Hungary. Szimi began traveling back and forth to Szeged, taking Berthe's cakes for Gyula and tobacco for the guards—apparently not worried about repeating the crime that had landed Gyula in jail. "He looks great," Szimi would report to her mother and father.

On December 6, St. Nicholas' Day, the Hungarian regent, Nicholas Horthy, declared amnesty for all military prisoners with sentences of under a year. Gyula and his fellow bribers had all received sentences of one month more than a year. Szimi didn't know if this was merely coincidence, but she assumed the worst. She decided she would show those no-goods! If she could only get Gyula out of prison on a month-long furlough, she had faith that he would find a way to make the amnesty apply to him.

Now the genius of her childhood would reemerge in a new form. She had outgrown her talent for instantaneous multiplication. But she felt it had been replaced by a different magical skill—an ability to make something happen if she wanted it to happen.

She packed her nicest dresses and went down to Budapest to see the marshal, the top man of the military court. His only superior was a man Szimi knew as the one who wore a gold leaf. She had no idea what she would say to him, but she knew she would figure it out. Gyula had told her to try to appeal and so she would, without a lawyer, in the highest military court of Hungary.

So she returned to Budapest for the first time since she'd graduated from high school. She stayed with her Aunt Freda on the Pest side of the Danube. Freda lived in a lovely section on the outskirts of the city, near the Jewish Hospital, where Freda's husband was the administrator. Szimi would always think of it as an enchanted place. Freda lived on America Boulevard, and close by was English Park, where Szimi would go with a young man she met while she was in Budapest. Budapest seemed to have a ready supply of young men available to escort visiting girls from the hinterlands. They walked and talked and rode the ferris wheel and the roller coaster, always twice, because Szimi loved the roller coaster.

This wasn't a vacation, however, though her aunt and uncle didn't take her mission seriously. What could a young girl say to convince the Hungarian government? Szimi told them not to worry. She put on her best dress and took the trolley to the other side of the Danube to Buda, where most of the government buildings were. She paused to admire how grand they were, then found her way to Budapest's Pentagon, to the office of a dear chubby gentleman with a gray mustache, the *tábornok*, a high-ranking Hungarian general. She herself didn't know exactly how she found him but she did.

She must have looked engaging in her gray dress with the white collar, those round shiny cheeks, not all that different from the little girl standing on the counter at the bank wowing the lumbermen with her numbers tricks. Without hesitation she laid out her case. "We are trying to appeal, but my mother is so sick. My mother went gray within a year when my brother went out there in Poland. She is so sick now, and her only wish is to see her son. Just let him come home for four weeks."

The nice plump *tábornok* was sympathetic. "Let's see what we can do."

Szimi went back to Huszt for two weeks. When she returned to Budapest, the *tábornok* assured her that he had no objection to giving Gyula four weeks' parole. However, the request had to be approved by the attorney general of the military.

Now it was the beginning of February 1944. The attorney general was a little man, very trim, very stern. He invited Szimi into his office and offered her a cigarette.

"I don't smoke," she said, wondering if her reply could be categorized as truth since she smoked only in secret.

He urged her to speak.

Her eyes teared up almost before she began to repeat the story she had now perfected: "My mother is sick and her only wish is to see her son."

She felt at first as though she were playing a role. She could see her eyes welling with tears, she could hear her voice saying words that were, she supposed, not true. Yet she didn't feel as though she were lying. Her mother wasn't sick, technically—but don't we all know about cases where heartsickness can kill someone?

By the time she began to cry she no longer felt as though she were acting at all. When she said, "My mother's only wish is to see her son," she knew she was telling the truth.

The attorney general nodded again and put out his cigarette. She wouldn't forget that, watching him neatly snuff out the flame, no wasted motion.

"I'll see what I can do," he said and stood up.

Szimi went home that Friday afternoon, triumphant. She told her aunt and uncle that on Monday the decision would be made and Gyula would come home. It was a double celebration—for Gyula and for her. She could see how impressed they were with what she'd done. She called her mother to tell her that everything was looking good, that after she received the official decision she would travel to Szeged and let Gyula know.

On Monday she ran up to the office of the *tábornok,* glad that she would receive the papers from such a kind man. When she saw his face, she knew the celebration had been premature.

"I have bad news," he said. "He refused it."

Even if she had dared to ask why, Szimi was physically unable. Her tears this time were quite unrehearsed. In fact, she sobbed hysterically. "I can't go home."

The *tábornok,* who seemed quite elderly to her, patted her on the shoulder. "Don't cry," he said.

Szimi was now heaving with sobs. "It will kill my mother. I told her he's coming home."

The *tábornok* said, "Please don't cry. I'm going in to my superior officer."

He left her weeping in his office. She was overcome with humiliation. She had called her mother and told her everything would be fine, and now she would have to tell her she had failed.

She couldn't stop crying even when the *tábornok* returned and said, "My dear, don't cry. Your brother is going home. They gave him a four-week furlough."

A friend of the family drove Szimi to Szeged, where she told her brother that everything was arranged. His furlough would come through in four weeks or so. Szimi planned a triumphant return to Huszt that March of 1944 in time to celebrate Gyula's homecoming with her parents as preparations for Passover were just beginning.

Instead, however, she returned home to find two German soldiers living in the spare room of her parents' home. The German Army had just arrived in Huszt. For the first time since the war began the city's Jews were ordered to wear Stars of David outside their homes.

Even then the Rapaports were assuring themselves: "Maybe it won't be so bad." The Germans asked for what they needed politely, and they didn't need much. Their room was separated from the rest of the house by a corridor, and they kept to themselves.

Berthe diligently adhered to routine, to the spring cleaning rites ordained by the laws of Pesach. On that Friday, March 17, the cleaning was almost finished when there was a knock at the door. Szimi and the maid were in the courtyard scrubbing the kitchen chairs; Berthe was in the kitchen rearranging dishes, inspecting the cupboards to make sure that every crumb had been swept out, every potential speck of forbidden leavening. They were hurrying to finish before nightfall, when both the Sabbath and Passover would begin. Szimi's father, Nathan, was taking a nap in the small room in the back of the house.

Szimi opened the door. Two giant feathers waved in the air. If she had allowed herself to experience fear, she surely would have been afraid. The feathers were the mark of the Hungarian gendarmes, a police force with the dubious distinction of being more vicious than Nazis, at least by reputation. The feathers reminded Szimi of the little beard on her father's face, another dubious mark of distinction in the Podkarpatská Rus of 1944. The beard was the sign of a Jew. The gendarmes were famous for yanking on Jewish beards.

"Are you Rapaport?" a gendarme asked.

"Yes," said Szimi, knowing that acknowledging her name was a confession. Rapaport was a Jewish name.

"Where's your father?"

This time she lied without hesitation. "He's not here."

"Where's your mother?"

Now the truth. "She's in the kitchen."

During the war years Szimi had honed the shrewdness she'd been born with. This was her genius now. She knew when to tell the truth and when to lie. She knew they might have seen her mother in the courtyard.

The gendarmes ordered the two women to go with them to the police station. This was no furtive capturing in the middle of the night. The Rapaport women traveled in an open carriage down the main street in full view of their neighbors. The trip was short, about a kilometer. Szimi felt calm. They hadn't done anything. But she could see her mother was worried.

At the station they were taken to separate rooms for questioning. The gendarmes were scrupulously polite as they explained the problem. The police had been monitoring the post office for "suspicious" correspondence. That morning a telegram had arrived for the Rapaport family from a Gyula Rapaport. He was trying to come home to Huszt but Huszt had become a military zone. He was writing his family to send him proof of residence.

None of this was news to Berthe or to Szimi. They had received the telegram. Szimi had gone to city hall for the papers. They were in the mail, en route to the aunt's house in Kiskörös, where Gyula was waiting.

For an hour the questions were repeated, firmly but politely.

"Who is this Gyula Rapaport? Why does he need these papers? What does he mean by this telegram?"

Neither Szimi nor Berthe was touched or threatened. They remained calm. Despite the wartime change in boundaries, they hadn't stopped thinking of themselves as Czech. They still held on to the increasingly quaint idea that the person who had done no wrong had nothing to fear. Their responses were consistent.

Over and over they explained: Who. What. Why. "He's the third Rapaport child. He needs the papers so he can come home. The telegram means that he wants us to send him papers so he can come home."

They were released. No carriage was provided for the return trip.

That evening Passover began. Ordinarily this was a splendid family occasion as the entire family gathered to repeat the story of how the Jews had escaped slavery in Egypt. That evening, however, only Szimi and her parents sat at the table. Nathan blurted out the service for this celebration of freedom in a rapid mumble of Hebrew. He went even faster the next night, as if trying to preclude an opening for wistfulness. That second Seder would become a rushed, unhappy marker for the end of Szimi's first life.

A week later the gendarmes returned, at seven on Sunday morning. This time they wouldn't leave without Nathan. Berthe asked them to wait a few minutes so she could send along some breakfast for her husband. There was no food in the house. The cupboards had been emptied for Passover, which had just ended the day before. There were only a few pieces of matzoh left, and they were specifically for Passover use. Berthe sent Szimi across the street to ask their Christian neighbors for bread.

What kind of reaction was this? "Would you mind waiting just a minute, sirs, while my daughter gets a bite of breakfast for my husband?" It seems like an astonishing belief in human civility under the circumstances. Berthe remained a believer: in Jewish ritual, in middle-class propriety, in human kindness. Indecency continued to shock her, no matter how often she was exposed to it. Though increasingly she lived in a world where reports of indecency were outweighing goodness, she still believed evil was an aberration. She still believed that she could send her husband to the police station with a piece of bread, and he would return home exonerated and not too hungry. Hadn't she and Szimi done just that a week before?

As soon as the gendarmes took Nathan away, Berthe and Szimi were out on the street. The five thousand Jews of Huszt, then a city of about twenty-five thousand, lived throughout the city. It was a heterogeneous city, populated by Czechs, Jews, Hungarians, and Gypsies, as well as the so-called *Russkys*, the native people of Podkarpatská Rus. The Catholic church was right across the street from the Rapaports. The Gypsies lived apart, in tents and shacks on the outskirts of town. The Russkys were illiterate, and the religious Jews were secular illiterates. In Cheder, they studied in Yiddish, which they could read and write.

Under the Czech regime, Huszt was a civilized place. Everyone knew Szimi, or so she felt, and she knew everyone. From the time she had been a small child, she had roamed the streets alone. She had been raised among the modern Jews of Huszt, who felt more threatened by assimilation than by anti-Semitism.

Much of Huszt was new, built during the years of the Czech Republic. Szimi's high school, for example, was a spacious Art Deco building. The main street was a large, bustling boulevard, with clothing stores, a *chocolatier*, grocery stores, two butcher shops, one kosher and one nonkosher, a jewelry store, fabric stores, a post office, a courthouse, pharmacy, a Catholic church. There were the *Konditoreien*, little cafés that served pastries and ice cream and espresso coffee with whipped cream. These were the gathering spots for the nightly promenade. On Sunday afternoons there were dances in Slovak Hall, just off the main street. Summers the dances moved outdoors, to the park around the outdoor gazebo where the bands would play. The grand synagogue, with its lavish murals, was the centerpiece of the old Jewish quarter, which also contained a *mikvah*, a kosher butcher shop, and an open-air produce market. There were two smaller synagogues on the other side of town—a small Hasidic congregation and another "modern" temple.

The Rapaports lived on the main street, though their house, which opened onto an interior courtyard, wasn't readily apparent from the street.

After the gendarmes took her father, Szimi went to the Jewish community center, just two houses down. Glancing up the street, she saw nothing different. Everything appeared the way it always had.

She quickly realized that appearances were, in fact, deceiving. Her little haven no longer existed. In a daze she heard someone telling her that Nathan and nine other "prominent citizens" were being held hostage in the synagogue across town.

Szimi ran over to her friend Flora, the Orthodox girl. She was one of the religious girls Szimi referred to as her "home friends." Szimi had been closer to them when she was younger, before she became more skeptical about God.

Her doubts had begun when she had stayed with Rozsi and Franz after Ilana was born. Delivering the baby had left Rozsi with a thrombosis in her leg, and she couldn't walk. When Friday night came, she had told Szimi to put on the light.

"But it's Shabbes," Szimi replied. In Huszt, the maid acted as *Shabbat goy*, the non-Jew on call to carry out chores Jews were prohibited from doing by religious law.

Rozsi, now a sophisticated architect's wife, laughed. "Your hand won't fall off."

Szimi turned on the light, and indeed her hand didn't fall off. That summer, when she returned to Huszt, she continued to experiment with the breaking of Jewish Orthodoxy. When she went swimming with a group of friends, also Jewish, she allowed herself to be coaxed into trying a bread and butter and salami sandwich, a brazen violation of the prohibition against mixing milk and meat. At home, however, she stuck to the laws, thereby managing to rebel without upsetting her mother. Flora belonged to that part of Szimi who wanted to be a good Jewish girl, not the girl dreaming about China and Scarlett O'Hara.

"I'm going to my uncle's house in the ghetto," said Flora.

Ghetto? Szimi didn't understand. There was no ghetto in Huszt. Impatiently, she left Flora, continuing to move through the crowd that had filled the hall. She stopped when she found Nadia, her best friend, the girl she'd finished *Gymnasium* with, her fellow dreamer.

Nadia filled her in: "The thing is, they say you have to find somebody to move in with. They are moving all the Jews into two streets. The Jewish community has to arrange for it. All the Jews who live on those streets have to take in the other Jews. You have one week to find someone to move in with. Your father and nine other men are being held hostage in the other synagogue to make sure everything goes smoothly."

Did Szimi feel terror? She couldn't remember. What did she do next? She couldn't remember.

On Monday Berthe and Szimi received a letter from Gyula, who was still waiting at the border. He told them he'd received the papers they'd sent, but he wasn't coming home. He knew about the ghetto and that the ghetto was the beginning of something ominous, though he made no mention of Auschwitz. He said he wasn't coming home because he might be able to help better from a distance. He asked them to send him a suit, clean underwear, socks, and shoes. He signed the letter the way his mother had taught him, with love and kisses.

Szimi packed a bag for him, everything he asked for and more. Before she closed the suitcase she slipped in a small blue leather photo album filled with pictures of her. She'd bought the album on her high school graduation trip to Budapest, four years earlier. She'd gone to a professional photographer, who produced twelve lovely pictures of a round-cheeked girl in a pretty dress with a white lace collar. Szimi wanted her photographs saved from the ghetto.

Berthe and Szimi went to work. They had been told to take only one or two suitcases because space would be tight. They expected to return home; they spent a week figuring out the best place to hide the family's small treasures while they were gone.

There wasn't much: a few pieces of cut glass, the Shabbes candlesticks, the silverware. Perhaps the memory of the last pogrom tempered Berthe's acquisitiveness. Or, more likely, the family's modesty had more to do with Nathan's inability to convert the Rapaports' paper wealth into tangible goods. He remained land rich and cash poor until the end, when it no longer mattered whether he was good in business or not.

Berthe wanted to save what she had. She sent the maid home, then she and Szimi filled a huge trunk with clothes, photographs, the glass, the silver. They dragged the trunk into the courtyard they shared with their neighbors. A stable separated the two families' outhouses. In the stable lived a buffalo the Rapaports milked every morning. Berthe always said to Szimi, "Drink a glass of buffalo milk every day, and you'll never be sick"—and she never was. The two women buried the trunk in a hole in the wall. They hid their cash in the chimney.

Under the new rules, Jewish homes were opened up to local Hungarians. This was the final stage of Huszt's return to its "rightful" occupants, descendants of the Austro-Hungarian Empire. Even before Berthe and Szimi moved out, their house's new "owners" moved in. The beneficiaries of this change seemed embarrassed by their good fortune. They were a butcher and his wife, people Berthe and Szimi passed on the street every day.

"Don't worry," they told Berthe. "We'll take good care of the house while you're gone."

Berthe may or may not have thanked them for their thoughtfulness, but there's no reason to think she didn't. Civility hadn't yet become a relic of the past.

Berthe and Szimi had been invited by family friends, the Goldsteins, to move into their house, situated on one of the ghetto-designated streets. They had decided to go there—what other choice did they have? When Szimi's friend Nadia dropped by, she told Szimi she could come with her to the home of Dr. Lakatos, a Jew turned Catholic. He had been friendly with a priest, who'd helped the doctor carry through a suspiciously abrupt decision to convert a couple of years earlier, when the doctor had been almost eighty years old.

Dr. Lakatos's house became a kind of mini-Switzerland. He lived in the middle of the ghetto, but he was allowed to come and go freely. He told Nadia to bring along some friends and he would tell the Hungarians the girls were household help.

The seriousness of the situation eluded the three girls kept by the Lakatoses. Mrs. Lakatos was a wonderful cook, and food was plentiful. Szimi didn't see her father or her mother for the four weeks she lived with the doctor and his wife, but she got reports from the young Jewish men patrolling the streets. They were doing well under the circumstances; the Jewish community was taking care of the hostages, Mrs. Goldstein was providing for her mother.

The priest dropped by every morning to pray with the Lakatoses. The girls kept their distance, though Szimi knew the priest well. She used to go to the churchyard, next to her house, to drink from the well, which was said to be the best water in Huszt. In her extreme youth, as a child genius, the priest would stop Szimi and quiz her: What's 334 times 546?

The truth was, Szimi enjoyed her stay at the Lakatoses. The elderly couple catered to her and her girlfriends. Though like all the Jews the girls had been told to stay indoors, their confinement was very comfortable. The Lakatoses had a bathroom and spacious rooms. At home Szimi still used an outhouse, even though her parents had recently installed running water.

At the end of the fourth week Szimi was working in the garden when the Jewish patrol came by.

"What's new?" Szimi asked, as she always did.

There was no snappy answer this time.

The silence was alarming. She looked up.

One of the men said, "We've been told the Hungarians are taking us to work camps. There will be three transports, and the first transport is leaving tomorrow."

Another silence.

"I think your mother is going to be taken tomorrow."

Szimi didn't hesitate. "Wait for me. I want to go with my mother."

She went inside to collect her things and to say good-bye.

When she arrived at the Goldsteins' house she realized how protected she'd been at the Lakatoses'. Somebody gave her a yellow Star of David to sew onto her dress; she hadn't worn one at the Lakatoses'. She saw that her mother had been sleeping on the floor in a room with eight other people, though Berthe assured her that there had been enough food. Once again they were packing, now consolidating their things into the one small suitcase allowed per family.

That night Nathan was released. There would soon be no need for hostages.

The Rapaports had a quiet reunion. No one speculated on what would happen the next day. It had become evident, perhaps, that speculation was fruitless because no one had experience that could help predict the future. This was not like a pogrom—no warning hoofbeats. There was no noise at all. Whatever was happening to them was happening quietly.

Early the next morning the gendarmes came. The people staying at the Goldsteins' joined their neighbors on the street. Everyone looked heavier than usual, and hot, because the solution to the one-suitcase rule had been to pile on clothing, layer upon layer.

Szimi didn't realize that she was being humiliated until she was patted down by the gendarmes. This vague feeling of humiliation solidified when the procession turned onto the main street, the street where she lived. How many Sundays had she promenaded up and down this street, giggling with her girlfriends, strutting a little, knowing that she was part of an elite by virtue of youth and education and lineage? How often, as a child, had she popped into and out of stores, proudly displaying her genius?

Now the streets were lined with people she'd known all her life, all of them non-Jews. They watched the parade of Jews as the Rapaports and about fifteen hundred others moved silently across town. Nobody talked, neither the watchers nor the marchers, during the two-kilometer walk to the train station.

Szimi was furious. How could they stand there and watch? Why weren't they doing anything?

Of course, the same question might have been asked of her: Why did she and her parents so obediently fall into line, not knowing their destination?

Later, much later, there would be endless discussion of this phenomenon: Why didn't they rebel? Some of the Jews who had paid attention to the warning signs and left would sneer at the Jews who stayed behind: *shtetl* Jews. Bruno Bettelheim, the child psychologist who had himself spent a year in concentration camp, would introduce the notion of a self-defeating "ghetto mentality."

But isn't it also possible to think that the Jews didn't rebel that day for the same reason the non-Jews didn't intercede? The citizens of Huszt were accustomed to rapid changes in governments and populations. Szimi had been born in Czechoslovakia; when her mother had been born, the same place had been part of the Austro-Hungarian Empire. Huszt was a polyglot town, a Babel, where there was no universal agreement on what was a "native tongue." The poor Jews spoke Yiddish, the wealthy ones spoke Hungarian. The *Russkys*—the "local locals" spoke Ukrainian, the Czechs spoke Czech. It didn't take too much self-delusion to think this movement of people was part of a continuum, another shift in the political landscape.

We can't comprehend it now, even those of us who have seen the indisputable evidence of the Final Solution—the films, the records that were kept, the correspondence. Why is it impossible to believe that those Jews in Huszt didn't anticipate what would happen to them, even those who had heard the rumors of mass extermination? It was 1944, and they were alive after five years of war. Were they willing victims or were they simply unimaginative, unable to conjure up the insane mechanism that had been designed to obliterate them?

My mother would say how lucky she was that her Birkenau barracks didn't have a leaky roof.

7

The Gypsy Woman

■ "You see," my mother said when we were back on the road, traveling toward Ukraine, "there was a Gypsy woman. Not a Gypsy, really,
but a nice Jewish woman who had learned from a Gypsy."

My mother would always have this inner battle between her desire
to tell a good story—*there was a Gypsy woman*—and her compunction
for truth—*not a Gypsy, really*. She was not opposed to altering the facts
to make them fit her vision of the universe. She realized there were
many ways to construe the facts of her life. They could be interpreted
as tragic or absurdist—not that she would think of them in those terms.
She preferred to think of her life as a romance, with herself as the
dauntless heroine, carried through the maelstrom by a combination of
fortitude and luck.

Still, she respected historical accuracy—*not a Gypsy, really*. But in her
mind she would always see that nice Jewish woman as a Gypsy, a seer
with magic in her hands.

She continued, factually, "We were supposed to be in the children's barracks, and she was the one with a little girl. But there were only three children with us. The rest of us were between eighteen and twenty-five, all in very good physical condition."

Then her voice changed. She spoke with the quick, light excitement of a child reporting back some marvel. "This woman was very small, very pretty, and she came from Hungary. She was reading my palm, just as she'd learned from a Gypsy woman, and she said, 'You'll come out. You'll survive. As a matter of fact, you will be very happy. You will be very lucky in marriage and in life."

"I just believed it, that nothing could happen to me, that I'll come out. I just didn't know how and when and what."

I pressed her for details. I wanted to know how and when and what. She hadn't yet told me what she'd thought of our excursion the day before. Once again I put myself into the position of the journalist at the fire, asking the sobbing woman whose house has just burned down, "How do you feel?"

"How do I feel?" my mother repeated. "Your question is, did I feel anything at Auschwitz now? I'll tell you. I'm very glad we went. I really had no idea how Auschwitz and Birkenau were laid out. I had no idea about where the crematoria were because from where I was you could see one smokestack and nothing else. I was never taken out from my Lager C. I didn't know about anything. Maybe I didn't want to know."

I shook my head.

"I understand what you're saying," my mother said. "I'm saying I know my attitude isn't normal. But it's what I am. I never worry about the past or the future, I worry about today. I think that's why I survived it better than other people. Sometimes I feel ashamed of it, but that's how it is."

I felt a tightness in my chest from the pressure of holding back my desire to cry. Crying would violate the unspoken agreement between us—that we would not spare each other these details, the way we had always done before. But my mother couldn't stop herself from relieving the tension, at least for the moment.

"I'm *meshugge* [crazy]," she said, with a false lightness. "But I'm a harmless *meshugge*."

Then she laughed, a big laugh, in full appreciation of the beauty of this craziness and the peace it had allowed her.

She wasn't trying to get off my hook. Having relieved herself with this little joke, she went back to considering where we had been— where *she* had been. She pulled the map up from the floor and had her finger on Auschwitz.

"I just now realize where Auschwitz is," she said. "Until now I never looked for it. On the train there were just these high windows with bars letting in a little light. Some of the young men got up there to look out to see where we are. Once they said we were at Užhorod. I can't believe Auschwitz is so close, with the car we could make it in a day or two from Huszt. When we left that day, it was late in the afternoon by the time they put us on the wagons. The train would go and then stop. I read just now that while the trains were going and stopping there was really no room for the Germans to take their military equipment through. But this had precedence. The Jewish wagons had to go."

Inspired by her visit to Spielberg's set, my mother had just started to read *Schindler's List*. She seemed to realize that while her memory of the period was in same ways vividly acute, it was also microscopic. She seemed determined now to get the macro view, to put her experience in context. This meant separating the facts of her life from the facts she had absorbed over the years, mainly from popular novels like *Exodus* and from movies and television. She has a habit of talking about characters in movies as though they are real. Sometimes I think she has carried on so well because she sees her life in cinematic terms, as a "story." She responded best to questions that advanced the "plot," providing remarkably detailed descriptions of events she hadn't discussed at length since they had happened. It was only on points of emotional detail that she became sketchy and discursive.

For example, when I asked her how she had felt, packed into a cattle car, she said she couldn't remember.

"I'm sure we were thinking, Well, a few months and it will all be over. When you arrive you're numb from being on that train and you're glad to be able to stretch and everything goes so fast. That's why the whole German invasion, the *Blitzkrieg*, worked, as it says, like a lightning. They describe it in many books, that it was organized this way so it would be a surprise, they didn't give you time really to think."

She saw that I wasn't satisfied. Like her, I may not give voice to my emotions, but my face betrays me.

"In that train you just sit and go and wait and snooze and eat, you always get hungry, so you eat some bread."

She paused.

"Weren't you afraid?" I knew that I was probably being too direct, but I couldn't stop myself.

"The only thing I felt was I hoped it will finish soon, that we will arrive soon. Just to get out of the train. We thought no matter where we'll go we'll be together and be working and the war will come to an end. It was already '44, and the Allies were bombing Germany day and night. We had a radio in the ghetto at Dr. Lakatos's, and we listened to it every day. We heard the Allies are bombing and they are hoping the war will be finished soon."

She stopped again and I asked her again. "But don't you remember what you were feeling?"

My sturdy mother seemed very fragile at that moment, sitting with her hands folded on her lap, the tape-recorder microphone clipped to her shirt. I realized this was the first time I could remember talking to her for this long. She is easily distracted—by phone calls, by chores. Her attention comes in short, intense bursts. I see it with her grand-children. She will roll around on the floor with them in a brief happy frenzy of giggling and tickling rather than sit with them and read. The only time I remember having a prolonged audience with her as a child was when I would cry out for her in the middle of the night; she would show up at my bedside and crawl in beside me and wrap her legs around me. Even then, now that I think of it, she would immediately fall asleep. I realized that this telling of my family's grievous history was perversely giving me the pleasure of my mother's company without in-terference.

"Yes, yes, I remember what I'm feeling," said my mother, who had clearly been upset by her inability to answer my question.

"What I'm feeling, and this was all through the concentration camp and all through my life really, I felt so sorry for my parents and especially for my mother. To me she was an older woman—she was fifty-four—and she had gone through so much and she had to sit there. I tried to make her comfortable and at the same time I tried to take the corset off of her to take the money out that was sewn into it so she wouldn't be killed. And then you discover it was all for nothing. That it didn't make any difference whether she had it there or not.

"I was rushing to take that money out, and it was a hard thing, inside those narrow openings. She had this strong girdle with whalebone stays and we pulled them out and stuffed the money in there. We could hear the Hungarian gendarmes yelling that if anyone was found with jewelry or money on them they would be killed. They yelled it in through those small windows. Everybody tried to throw out whatever they could through the window rather than give it to them."

She held up her hand. "You know, I did look outside of the window one time. I saw these boys walking along the track and I remember thinking, Maybe they'll find a lot of jewelry and money if the wind or the rain doesn't take it away.

"When we arrived, it was nighttime. It must have been nine o'clock because it was dark and there was no daylight savings time. As we stepped out, the Jewish kapos were helping us off the train, and then while we were standing there Mengele appeared."

Then she repeated, more or less, what she had said to me on the phone the day I'd called to tell her about Spielberg.

"He was standing there like a white God. To us he was very good looking, and to me he looked very tall. Like most men, he looked very good in the uniform. Or maybe he just looked good standing there under the lights, compared with us who arrived in not the best condition after two nights and three days traveling in a cattle car. I was wearing a decent dress—two decent dresses so I didn't have to pack it—and I always wore nice shoes, slip-ons or sandals, not heels.

"When we got out, I realized it was the most horrible trip you could imagine. My mother and father and me and a hundred people in one car with just enough space to sit. We had some food in the suitcase; they didn't give us anything, and it was probably just as well because you couldn't go out anywhere. ["Go out" was my mother's euphemism for going to the toilet because she had to literally go outside at home.]

"We had these buckets to use, but it was torture to sit on it in front of everybody. In the daytime you got some light through the windows, but at night it was pitch black. The stench must have been terrible, but I don't remember it."

Now it was I who wished she would stop. I knew what was coming next, and I didn't want to hear it. I could see the platform in my mind, the confusion of the scared and tired people coming off the train, trying to accustom themselves to the glare of light after total darkness. I could see my mother getting her equilibrium, realizing that she'd been separated from her parents in the hubbub. I could see her terror. But I knew what I've always known, that I could never feel it.

She didn't stop. "Mengele said to me, 'You go that way.'"

She continued her narrative. "A lot of men seemed to be pointing in that direction. I ran to one of them and said, 'I want to find my mother.' One of the Jewish boys yanked me and said, 'You go that way. You'll find your mother tomorrow.'"

Now she paused. It struck me that she never talked about her father. "What about your father?" I asked her. "Whenever you talk about arriving at Auschwitz, you only mention your mother."

She pressed her lips together. "I loved my father very much," she said. Then she answered a question I hadn't asked. "There was no resentment."

I quickly broke in, torn between my desire to learn every detail and my wish not to hurt her. "No, I don't mean that. But you talk about your mother being old and having to take care of her, but your father was ten years older than she was. I just want to understand."

My mother sounded defensive. "It was such a mess. I can't think about it, what it was like."

"Please," I said, "don't be upset. I know you loved your father, but you never really talk about him. It's always your mother."

A change had come over my mother. She was now clearly intrigued by the omission of her father. Once again I watched her move outside her own memory, analyzing herself from afar. "You're right. Maybe it's because my father just took everything as it came, like I do. But actually, that's how my mother was, too."

She thought about it for a moment. "Really, there wasn't a discrimination. But my father used to sit around a lot, especially after the Hungarians came in. My mother was always running, even more than me. Neither of them was ever sick. Maybe it was a subconscious resentment that my father didn't make a living. If I needed anything, to buy anything, it was Mother I went to. She had to work so hard all the time, renting out that room, serving meals to strangers. Who knows?"

Her face was flushed. I thought it was enough. "Mommy," I said, "I'm sorry. I didn't mean to—"

"No, no," she said. "When I think of arriving there I think about my mother. Maybe it's because one time I looked up the day we arrived at Auschwitz, May 24. I marked that day for my mother's death."

I remembered that Bruno Bettelheim had once written that one reason many surviving children never really recovered from the loss of their parents was the absence of "tangible and physical" proof of their parents' death. Later I looked up his exact words: "According to Jewish custom, the gravestone is set only on the anniversary of the death or of the funeral, and it marks the end of the official period of mourning. The children of the Holocaust do not know the dates of their parents' death, hence they do not know when their period of mourning ought to have begun, nor when it should have ended." Setting this *Yahrzeit* date may have helped my mother accept her concentration camp experience in a way that my father had never seemed to.

I realized my mother had stopped talking only because she started again. "I tell you, for days, at least for a week, I did not believe my mother was dead."

I turned off the tape recorder. "Don't you want to stop now, Mommy?"

She seemed startled, shook her head no.

"We walked across the platform at Auschwitz, really at Birkenau. I remember the big gate and the sign 'Arbeit Macht Frei'—work will set you free—and that must have been reassurance that we were going to work.

"They took us in for showers and then they shaved us, for lice. I was standing next to someone who I didn't recognize at first. Then I saw who it was and I started calling, 'Nadia! Nadia!' She saw me and said, 'I'm here.' We looked at each other completely naked and completely shaved off and we started crying. My best friend, and I didn't recognize her!

"Right after we arrived they took away our suitcases. 'Put your clothing here, your pocketbook here.' They shaved your head. Everything had to go fast, fast. The women shaving us wore the striped dresses and the men had the striped pajamas. But we didn't get the striped dresses. When we went into the shower—maybe a thousand people, maybe five hundred, I don't know—they gave you soap and you had to do it very fast. I don't even know if I got the soap off. The water came and went. Then we got out and didn't have towels, no bras or underpants, just a dress.

"I remember that dress because I wore it for months. It was navy blue with little white flowers. It was shapeless, must have gone through the delousing from the last person who wore it.

"The only thing I held on to was my toothbrush. I went with it into the shower and I came out, with my toothbrush in my hand. I had my toothbrush all through Auschwitz. That's the only thing I saved. I went with it into the shower and I came out, with toothbrush. I just had it in my hand.

"The next morning they woke us and gave us coffee and bread, this dark heavy bread. It was the best bread I ever ate. By this time we hadn't eaten since we left the train and who knows when before. We ate the bread with black coffee, and then we were taken on foot to C Lager."

It was the best bread I ever ate.

As my mother said these words she lit up with a look of pleasure, as though she were describing her first dinner at Lutèce.

"In C Lager there were thirty-four stables, like they were built for horses. There were a thousand people. There were planks like bunk beds, three rows of them, and on each plank there were twelve people. They must have been there for a while because they seemed old. Ours was the best. At number ten next door the roof was leaking. I was in number eight, which became the children's block. The whole thing was called a lager, and each barn was a block."

Ours was the best.

It was awful to be in Auschwitz, to lose your mother and father on arrival, but not so bad. She might have been in the barn with the leaky roof. Was this optimism or a refusal to face reality or something else entirely?

I felt as though for years I had been staring at fragments, trying unsuccessfully to imagine this vessel that contained my mother's history. Now, for the first time, my mother was providing the sketch that allowed me to see what those bits and pieces fit into.

"They were going to leave some children. Altogether among the thousand people there were two mothers. One had two children, one was seven and her sister may have been ten. Another mother who had one child, six or seven. Otherwise they were all seventeen or eighteen. I was the oldest one at that time; I was twenty-one. I was with Baszi and Zeldi, who were sisters. Zeldi was carrying in the soup in big kettles. There were always potatoes on the bottom. The soup had some sandy stuff in it. Everyone stopped menstruating. I was the only one still menstruating because I never ate the soup. I washed off the potatoes to get off the grainy stuff.

"I never stopped my period, and it was a curse. We managed to make underpants out of—"

She looked at me. "Out of what?"

"I don't know," I said.

"I remember. You used rags. I remember we got a cover, like a comforter, and we would take the inside out and use it."

Then she smiled. "At the beginning we used to get something for dinner that was like baby oatmeal. They made it sweet. I gave everything away for it. I would give anything I had to get more of it. I would exchange my soup for a piece of bread and the bread for the oatmeal. They had this stinking cheese, and I loved it, too. Most of the girls couldn't stand it. It came in wooden boxes and it was runny. The girls who were dishing it out gave me the box, and I would scrape it out with a piece of bread. This was just at the beginning, and then they stopped bringing that."

They had this stinking cheese, and I loved it.

When I heard my mother's description of the food at Auschwitz, I understood why my closest friend never believes me when I compliment her on a meal. I understood why I was brought up to think that there were two designations for food: "delicious" and "less delicious."

———

▪ "It was quite a revelation, going around with Dorothea—a very good guide," said my mother. "All of a sudden I realized how horrendous it was. I always thought myself lucky because I wasn't beaten or even punished and I got enough to eat. I always felt I was just biding my time.

"You ask me what did I think about while I was there. In the lager one didn't think. One was thinking of the next meal, how eventually to save something, where to put it away so it isn't stolen from you, like a piece of bread or pieces of potato. But the biggest concern always was: How many more days?"

Her voice had changed into a singsong, not that different from the rhythmic chanting of Hebrew prayer. She seemed to have gone into a trance and taken me with her. It was only later, when I listened to her voice on the tape recorder, that I saw that she had composed a dirge to Auschwitz.

"*I remember* I always felt even while I was there that I was better off than my friends. When I saw the beds in the bunkers I remember how we used to sit there and I was telling everyone stories. The one they liked best was *Gone with the Wind*. I had read it so many times I knew it by heart. Every day I would tell them part of it.

"*I remember* being cold. We had to go outside at five in the morning and stand *Appell* [the roll call] until seven or eight, until they counted thirty thousand—everyone in Lager C. Twice a day, for four to six hours a day. I didn't have a scarf, so I cut the bottom of my dress and made a band to wrap around my ears.

"*I remember* taking potatoes I hid from the soup to my friend Manci's mother in another barracks, in the middle of the night. I felt so sorry for her. She was only forty-six or forty-seven but heavyset, and

I knew it must be so hard for her to climb up on those bunks. I guess it was dangerous to go there, but she was my friend's mother.

"*I remember* my friend Judy, a sweet girl with a beauty mark. A boy fell in love with her, and he would bring her things. Once he brought her a blanket, which she sewed into a little suit. She was the best-dressed girl in the camp. One day she had an infection on her *tushie*. Mengele came through for the inspection—we had to strip. When he saw the red mark on her, he sent her out to be killed. Poor thing! Her mother died of grief, and her sister went mad.

"*I remember* the day the news came that Hitler had been killed. The whole camp was excited, up in arms. Then came the news that not only was he not killed, he had all those people killed who wanted to kill him.

"*I remember* the girls were afraid they won't be able to bear children. They talked about it here and there. But the biggest concern always was 'How many more days?'

"*I don't remember* feeling despair. There must have been times. Ours was the annihilation lager. We weren't working and knew either we would be shipped somewhere else or, in time, you would not be able to function too much. You could get lice. Anybody who had anything on the body would be shipped out.

"*Wait. I do remember* there was a time when I had a doubt. I got a splinter on my leg from the bed that started gathering pus. I kept squeezing it, trying to get it to go down before Mengele came. He didn't want to take chances with anything that could be contagious. It opened up and left quite a gash. I was scared that he shouldn't come and look. That was maybe the only time I wasn't sure I would come out. But I was so lucky."

———

▪ There was the routine. The *Appell,* waiting for meals, thinking about meals, avoiding the punishing hand of the young Jewish woman they called "Piroshka." The nickname was both descriptive and ironic. *Piros,* pronounced "pirosh," means "red" in Hungarian, and Piroshka had short, fiery hair. But the *ka,* the note of endearment, was decidedly insincere, a bitter joke. They had to find amusement somewhere, and

Auschwitz provided little in the way of entertainment but gallows humor.

Piroshka's status was unclear. She wasn't a kapo, yet she came along every day for the *Appell*. It was thought that she provided special services to Graza, the German SS officer with the long blond hair. The young women in Szimi's bunk were fascinated with this idea, that Graza was a lesbian. This was a safe subject for speculation, better than, say, wondering about where they might be tomorrow or thinking about what had happened yesterday.

Their public relationship was more clear cut. Graza, who was beautiful, used the unattractive Piroshka for her dirty work. "She's so ugly the Messiah won't come because of her," the girls used to joke. It was a joke they told very quietly, because the redhead was skinny but very strong. The girls would whisper, "She's strong as an ox. She must get her strength from being so bad."

The *Appell* carried a powerful psychological force, impersonal—reducing humans to numbers—but profoundly personal as well. Twice a day all the inmates had to line up outside their barracks and remain there until everyone in their block, their lager, was counted. C Lager, Szimi's block, contained thirty barracks; each barrack held a thousand women. To understand the numbing importance of the *Appell,* you must understand that it took two or three hours to reach the count of thirty thousand each morning and another two or three hours each evening. The roll call began long before dawn, enriching the psychological complexity of the count with cold and disorientation.

When the numbers didn't add up, individuality was restored. No one could sit down until the missing person was found.

This rule was made very clear to Szimi one day when she knew the *Appell* had gone on much too long—past the usual allotment for early-morning sluggishness, or the beatings that periodically took place on the way to subdue a smart-ass or to teach someone to enunciate more clearly. The word came down the line: Someone was missing. The count in C Lager had reached 29,999 instead of 30,000. They would have to stand outside while the search went on for the culprit who dared disturb the ledger.

This disruption in routine tormented the women, who were too weak and hungry and demoralized to consider why the count might be off. The victory that one escape represented was the kind of philosophical judgment an observer might make after the fact. At that moment, if they could speak honestly or bother to think at all, they would have to admit they felt resentful toward the missing person, the inconsiderate one who was making them stand—all day, as it turned out. The morning *Appell* ran into the nighttime *Appell,* and then they were excused.

Their grumbling turned to sorrow a few days later. The word came back that the missing person was a seventeen-year-old girl. Her mother had hidden her in a dark corner because the girl was burning with fever, a kiss of death. When the daughter had been found, both she and her mother had been subtracted from the count. They had been replaced the next day to keep the numbers nice and even.

The *Appell* became the stage for many memorable dramas. An electric wire separated C Lager from the next camp, known as the Czech camp, where the kitchen was. The Jewish girls working in the kitchen would throw scraps over the fence to the inmates in C Lager. Szimi never scavenged there. Her friend Zeldi, who lived in her barracks, worked in the kitchen and made sure their soup had bits of potato in it. Instead of wasting away in Auschwitz, Szimi became bloated. Besides, they had been warned too many times about the voltage in the fences. Then, one day, the *Appell* was held up again. Later they learned that a girl had spotted some food lying near the fence. As she had bent over she had touched the fence and was gone, dead in a quick jolt.

The daily count put enormous pressure on the *Älteste* of each barracks—the person who might be thought of as the bunk counselor in this perverse camp. The *Ältesten* were Jews, collaborators by the harshest definition, sorry souls trying to save their necks by the most generous. They were responsible for making sure the numbers added up.

Szimi felt kindly toward her barracks' *Älteste,* Fela. She had been a medical student when she had been "taken." She never raised her voice or her hand. She quietly urged her "girls" in barracks eight to show up on time for the *Appell*—and they did.

Fela was one reason Szimi would describe number eight as the "lucky" barracks. Another reason was the roof, which didn't leak like the roof in barracks ten. The wet and drafty barracks ten was always coming up short in the *Appell,* as the inmates would sneak out during the night to another barracks where they might find a dry piece of plank to sleep on. Every morning Fela would find her barracks over-flowing while Yolan, her counterpart at barracks ten, would be frantic. The nighttime desertions meant she couldn't produce the goods, the bodies necessary to satisfy the count.

She struck a deal with Fela. She wouldn't report the deserters if Fela sent her overflow to stand in front of barracks ten for the *Appell.*

The deception was carried out openly. Graza, the SS woman, was aware of the early-morning scurrying to make sure that the subtotals as well as the totals were in order. She apparently didn't care where they slept, just where they stood.

Szimi became one of the "volunteers" sent to stand for the *Appell* at barracks ten. In these deadly hours of early morning, shuffling in the cold, she was both numb and alert to this, the only task of the day, an-nouncing her position among the thirty thousand in her block.

Yolan began to warn them, as she warned them every day, "I want you to stay here until the count is finished—"

Szimi mocked Yolan by finishing the sentence under her nose, just for the amusement of her friends, she thought: "—or you will be taken to the gates."

It was one of those bad Auschwitz jokes. "To the gates" was the eu-phemism for going to the crematorium.

Yolan could be excused for not appreciating the joke. She knew if the count was low the first at the "gate" would be her.

She stopped counting. "Who said that? Who said that?" she barked.

The commotion drew Piroshka and Graza, who had been a few steps behind.

As Yolan's gaze settled on her, Szimi couldn't believe this was hap-pening. She had thought she was safe, standing in the back. The women were lined up in rows of five. Usually only the front row had to keep completely quiet as the *Älteste,* the SS woman, and Piroshka made their rounds.

Yolan nodded toward Szimi and yelled, "It was that one!"

Szimi felt nothing except an urge to choke Yolan, who was shouting, "This one, she was opening her mouth when I said she should stay here!"

Szimi felt, rather than saw, Piroshka coming her way, a streak of red—that red hair on the skinny body. She heard the sound of skin being slapped—hard—and realized she felt nothing because Piroshka was beating up the girl standing next to her.

"No, no," Yolan said, "it wasn't her." With a nod at Szimi, she clarified who the culprit was.

Piroshka started toward Szimi.

What happened next was lucky by anyone's interpretation.

Graza stopped Piroshka. "Leave her," she said. "Leave her alone."

She looked at Szimi and said, "You promise to be here for every *Appell?*"

Szimi nodded. "I promise."

Though Graza had never talked to her before and would never talk to her again, Szimi didn't spend much time wondering about why the SS woman had spared her. If the former child genius couldn't comprehend the calculations she could make, how could she understand questions that had no answer? She understood something far more important to her well-being—that the one thing she couldn't afford to do was ask "Why?"

For years after the war my mother would stay in touch with Gertrude Winkel (right), the kind German woman who brought her food and clothing in work camp.

8

Heaven on Earth

■ We had moved into the higher elevation of the Tatra Mountains. The air was fresh as we passed through quaint little hill towns. My mother began humming along with the music that had just begun playing up front.

"It's a Jewish song," my mother said.

"You're kidding," I said. "They're playing Yiddish songs on the radio in Slovakia?"

Imagine that, I thought. This is like a movie. Just as I'm hearing these stories, these details, for the first time, somebody's provided a score. Too on target for my taste, but that's not the point. How can this music be playing here?

The same question had occurred to my mother. She leaned forward and began asking Leopold about the music in Hungarian, an exclamatory language that injects the illusion of excitement into the most mundane conversation.

When he had explained, she laughed and nodded.

"It's a tape," she explained, settling back into her seat.

"Zeldi used to sing all those songs in the camp," said my mother. "She had a very pleasant voice."

I listened to the music. I didn't know this particular melody, but its sweet, sad sentimentality was familiar.

My mother closed her eyes and translated for me.

"Where should I go?" she murmured. "All the doors are closed before me . . ."

She fell silent.

"Zeldi and Baszi and I, we were always together in camp," she said softly, her eyes still closed. "Nadia was somewhere else.

"We knew each other but weren't really friends at home. Our two fathers were friends. Their name was Schafar. They were sisters and had a temperament like Rozsi and me. Baszi was a worrier, even before, and Zeldi was happy-go-lucky. Baszi had that nature—a very good girl but carried the world's problems on her back. And what they went through! Zeldi got over it, but not Baszi.

"They had actually been taken in 1941 at the same time Flora was taken, to Kamenets-Podolski, because they were called foreigners by the Hungarians. They owned an inn up on a lake out of town. Their father was a very decent man. He never took a penny from those gendarmes at the inn, and they were protective of him until they came and took them away.

"They got released to come back to Huszt. The father made it across the border, where their uncle waited for them with papers proving they were Hungarian citizens. Then he—the father—died on the way home. The mother and children came to live in Huszt.

"We were all together in number eight, and Zeldi was the *Stubendienst*."

I interrupted. "What's a *Stubendienst*?"

My mother laughed. "Literally, now that I think of it, it means barracks cleaner."

"Zeldi was carrying the food in big kettles from the kitchen to us. They would bring the big kettles of soup, and in the bottom there were always potatoes. Zeldi would spoon it out and save the bottom for us.

"Then it was summertime and we took it easier. We weren't freezing. Then the fall came and we were cold again. At the end of September they began emptying the lager. The Russians were moving in very close. We heard every day that the Allies were showering Germany with bombs. We heard from the Jewish men. They had a radio or some other way to get the news, and they would come and clean the latrines and tell us what they heard.

"They started taking groups of two hundred women out from the lager. We didn't know if we were going really to work this time or if they were getting rid of us."

Her detachment became more and more marked as she went on. "The last week wasn't so good because the even-numbered barracks were evacuated. Whoever wasn't taken was pushed over to the uneven numbers. We decided we will stay together, Baszi, Zeldi, and I, so we went over to number eleven. Zeldi was still working in the kitchen, but in number eleven Zeldi wasn't carrying the food so the food wasn't there."

I was almost as transfixed by her dispassionate tone as by the details of this terrifying story. After months of waiting, having fallen into what seemed liked unending routine, she knew something dramatic was about to happen. After months of static, there was movement—and in Auschwitz movement more often than not meant death. Yet she recast the memory as something unpleasant, not disastrous.

The last week wasn't so good.

"As I said, the food wasn't there, so after a week we decided to try to get onto the next transport for the work camps. Baszi was afraid they wouldn't let her on, she was very skinny. I told her, 'You just go ahead. I will be in back of you and push you through.'

"So Baszi went through the crowd to where the train was and I went and then we were looking for Zeldi. Somebody said she went to the wire because their cousin was in the next lager. She worked in the kitchen, and Zeldi wanted to get some food from her. By that time it was falling apart. They weren't so strict.

"Then we saw that Zeldi was up front. She had gone ahead of us. But I had these high shoes on and I had to stop and tie them. Baszi was yelling, 'Come on, come on! We were looking for Zeldi, but she's already there. Let's go!'

"We started to go to catch up with her, but they cut off the transport just in front of us. Zeldi went and Baszi stayed. She was crying and crying.

"I said, 'Don't worry, we'll go.'

"Baszi said, 'Don't leave me!'

"I said, 'Don't worry, I'll never leave you. We'll go on the next transport.'

"Sure enough, next day, they were coming for transport and I was telling Baszi, 'Now we'll go through.'

"And we went through."

A new tone had come into my mother's voice. She was no longer recalling an incident, she was constructing a parable. She had within her that rabbinic impulse to find some lesson in the tales she tells. The lesson is always the same, and it's not necessarily a comforting one.

"And this is fate," she said with an oratorical flourish. "Very few on Zeldi's transport made it through, and even those who did went through hell. Their train was bombed, and that was only part of a very bad circumstance. Zeldi went to Nürnberg and wandered in many, many places and in very bad conditions. It was wintertime before she ended up, I think, in Bergen-Belsen. Baszi and I went to Zittau. And Zittau was heaven on earth."

———

▪ They must have looked like freaks—traveling in November without socks or coats, wearing the striped uniform of Auschwitz. Szimi had worn that print dress she got after that first shower for months. She had changed clothes once, after the transitory Hungarian Jewesses had been marched from Birkenau to Auschwitz for delousing. Her second dress was much like the first—a housedress taken from one of the carefully packed suitcases the prisoners had brought with them. It was only when she received her work assignment that she became an official member of the Auschwitz community. So she put on the stripes associated with Auschwitz as she left—on loan to Zittau, an engine factory in eastern Germany, five kilometers from the Czech border.

The German soldiers who waited for them there didn't seem to know what to make of the burr-headed women who stepped off the train. Six months had passed since Szimi's head had been shaved, but her hair was growing back slowly.

"Did you have lice, that they cut off your hair?" an old man asked her as she got off the train.

"We were at Auschwitz." She thought she needn't say more. Then she saw the response meant nothing to him.

"Where was Auschwitz?"

Szimi looked at him suspiciously. "You don't know what is Auschwitz?"

He shrugged. "I just came back from the Russian front."

She began to explain what Auschwitz was. But when she saw the incredulous look in his eye, she stopped.

———

▪ The terror was over. That was obvious almost right away. They would no longer cower like animals in stables built for humans. They were housed in a large building with central heating, in dormitory rooms where each girl had her own bed. They were humans again, living among human beings. The first week they shared the space with British prisoners of war, who handed out goodies from their Red Cross packages to these pathetic girls. Szimi, who had held on to her toothbrush from home throughout Auschwitz, had lost it on the way to Zittau. She began her stay there with a new toothbrush, courtesy of the Red Cross.

They would no longer have to go to the toilet on long latrines, using pieces of material torn from dresses and blankets for toilet paper. The toilets were behind a door.

They were greeted by the *Lagerführer,* a man of fifty-five or sixty who seemed elderly to Szimi, who had turned twenty-two in September. He told the young women that if they behaved he would protect them, and he kept his word. He arranged for them to bathe regularly, in warm water. On Sundays they were allowed to experience the satisfaction of real stew, with potatoes and barley and meat, not the regulation potato gruel.

These creature comforts may seem insignificant compared with the other major departure from Auschwitz in this new prison: There were no beatings. There was barbed wire around the perimeter of the compound, but no electric fences. This was a prison, not a death camp.

Yet Szimi would remember not so much the lifting of fear as the reintroduction of pleasure. Eating, sleeping, relieving and cleaning herself could now be thought of without dread. Her optimism no longer seemed delusional. She had seen the worst. Knowing this, it was easy to feel fearless again.

———

▪ Not even Szimi could keep the shine on this gilded first impression when the kindly *Lagerführer* was replaced by a more rigorous successor. On his first day he gave a speech that made one point clearly: Zittau was a work camp. Its function wasn't to restore the souls of young Jewish girls but to repair airplane engines. Like his predecessor he assured them that if they behaved, they would be treated fairly. However, his manner implied that they would do well not to find out what would happen if they did not.

There was always someone who couldn't tolerate ambiguity, who had to probe until the unspecified threat was spelled out. One day the inmates assigned to the kitchen were unloading sacks of potatoes. Someone slit one open, releasing an avalanche of potatoes. The women couldn't resist this unexpected dividend, so by the time the potatoes were put back the sack was half empty.

The *Lagerführer* called a special *Appell*.

"I told you I would be fair. From now on you will have a special Spanish goulash on Sundays."

Here was the recipe: one kettle of water flavored faintly with potato. That was Spanish goulash. Even Szimi had to admit it wasn't delicious.

———

▪ Each worker was assigned a Jewish girl to be his helper, to clean and carry and hold tools. The factory was working at top speed in this last phase of the war, operating twenty-four hours a day, with a twelve-hour day shift and a twelve-hour night shift.

For the week following Szimi's arrival the Germans used the morning and evening *Appelle* for a benign selection—to hand out jobs. During that first night's *Appell* the officer asked if anyone spoke German. In the past Szimi would have hesitated, not wanting to be identified as a Jew. That, clearly, was no longer an issue.

"I do," she called out.

Thus she got her work assignment—sitting in the office where the small tools were kept. When a worker got a tool, she put his number on the nail that held the tool. Her companions were two German women and the guard, an elderly man. He wore the black uniform of the SS, an indication that he belonged to the new guard, a Hitler man who had no use for the old standards of conduct for war. However, he quickly assured Szimi that he was really Wehrmacht, a member of the pre-Nazi German Army, men who saw war as a way to divide the world's bounty—not zealots trying to create a new social order that had no place for anyone not like them. The Wehrmacht belonged to a tradition that convinced itself that war was an honorable game so long as its rules were respected. Mass extermination of civilians, even Jews, wasn't part of the game.

Szimi saw no reason to quarrel with this nice man who helped pass the time with exciting horror stories from the Russian front, about men freezing to death while they waited to be shot.

One of the women kept to herself. The other was friendly, a soft-looking woman just a few years older than Szimi but already motherly.

"Why don't you have socks?" asked Gertrude Winkel.

It was quite an ordinary question to ask. It was November and already wintry cold in the Sudeten mountains. But a few months in Auschwitz had been sufficient to erase Szimi's memories of ordinariness. Socks were a long-forgotten luxury. By asking the question so innocently, Gertrude Winkel implied that she saw Szimi simply as a girl whose feet deserved to be kept warm.

She didn't ask the corollary question: Why don't you have underpants? However, the next day she brought underpants as well as stockings and a scarf and food.

Szimi would never forget that meal, a pot of sweet-and-sour red cabbage with meatballs. She was certain she had never eaten anything as good as that. Though she'd already eaten supper, she ate half the pot and saved the rest for Baszi.

Day after day Mrs. Winkel—she was married and had a young daughter—brought things for Szimi. Sometimes just bread and butter, sometimes a meal. One day Mrs. Winkel confided that it was possible that someone in her background might have been Jewish.

One night she followed Szimi to the toilet.

"The other woman has been watching," she whispered. "I've been transferred to another section of the factory. We'll have to meet here."

Szimi quickly came up with a scheme. "Don't worry," she said. "My sister is there. You can give it to her."

Her "sister" was Baszi. Szimi worried about her friend, who wasn't able to enjoy their improved circumstances. It wasn't the work, though Baszi had a more rigorous job, handling the tools for one of the German machinists. She didn't possess Szimi's special adaptability. Unlike her friend, she didn't view life as a movie, a suspended here and now. She didn't see the barbed wire surrounding Zittau as a frame for all existence, the way Szimi seemed to. She wasn't able to stop thinking about her sister, Zeldi, and her brother, Jossi. Had they survived?

Yet Baszi was Szimi's companion throughout, her coadventurer in what Szimi would describe as the excitement of Zittau, the romance of Zittau.

In Zittau, Szimi found there was room for flirtation. Not long after the Jewish women were installed in the dormitory, the British prisoners of war were moved out and replaced by Jewish men, young men brought in to work. A wall divided the men from the women, but the rooms were linked by heat pipes. She began talking with a Jewish boy from Luxembourg. One day she heard lovely singing floating out of the pipes. Her unseen lover had a friend with a strong baritone and was serenading her by proxy.

She had forgotten that boys thought she was charming. Yet she had her Jewish romance through the pipes and a more dangerous flirtation at the office—though she would deny there had been any sexual overtones to the long conversations she began having with the young Austrian worker who would stop to talk when he picked up his tools. Though he'd been brought up in the Hitlerjugend, the Nazi youth group, he seemed to have missed the lecture forbidding fraternizing with Jews.

They didn't talk politics. He told her about growing up in the Tyrolean mountains of Austria; she told him about Podkarpatská Rus. As time went on, she told him more, about Auschwitz, which he, too, claimed not to know about.

She must have felt very comfortable at Zittau, because she didn't feel compelled to hide her thoughts from him. When he told her, in late April 1945, that he would soon be called to defend Berlin against the Allies, she mocked him.

"To Berlin!" she said. "You aren't going to Berlin. We're hearing the war is over."

When he told her he had to do it, for "the Fatherland," she mocked him again: "You're Austrian. What Fatherland?"

———

▪ The sky lit up at night on May 7, 1945, as Russian rockets screamed over Zittau.

"My God," Szimi thought, "they're coming in."

Yet the prisoners weren't taken down to the bomb shelter. They went to sleep in their own beds.

The next morning Szimi awoke to a strange silence. She and the other seven women in her room sat quietly on the edge of their beds, waiting for an order from someone. When nothing happened, they began to roam around the compound with the other prisoners. The Germans were gone. They'd vanished in the middle of the night.

Like all successful people, these young survivors did what they had to do without thinking. They gravitated toward life by instinct, not introspection. They were the adaptable ones. Otherwise they would have been dead.

Not surprisingly, the kitchen was soon packed with former prisoners, scavenging whatever they could get their hands on. Szimi found herself holding a live chicken in her arms.

Baszi agreed to cook it if somebody else would kill it.

There were no volunteers. Szimi looked around and saw that the fear had returned. The exhilarating rush to the kitchen had been a momentary bravado. With freedom came squeamishness. Just a minute before, they'd been talking hungrily about chicken and rice. Now no one could face the chicken, which was angrily disputing their choice of menu. Maybe they couldn't bear to be identified as oppressors, even to a chicken.

Szimi heard herself saying, "I'll kill it."

As she clutched the chicken, she remembered watching the kosher butcher in Huszt do his job. It didn't seem so difficult to slit the throat of a chicken.

Someone handed her a knife, and she began. Blood spurted, but the chicken was far from dead. No matter how many times she hacked at its throat, the chicken wouldn't stop thrashing. Frantic, Szimi stabbed it again and again until finally it stopped moving.

She felt only fleeting disgust at the blood on her hands. Her mind had already darted ahead to the thought of chicken *paprikás* with rice, a thought she hadn't allowed herself for months—because she knew one thought led to another and she didn't want to be led back to her mother's kitchen. She had before her this poor mangled bird, and it wasn't a memory or a dream but the ingredients for a meal in the here and now.

Just then a boy she knew from Huszt came into the kitchen and told them they were just five kilometers from the Czech border. He and some friends were leaving and wanted to know if Szimi and Baszi wanted to join them. They were going home.

The girls consulted briefly, then decided not to wait for the chicken *paprikás,* just to go. Szimi would describe her elation like this: "We just left. We decided we wouldn't cook anything, just go. We left the chicken on the floor and never looked back."

━━

▪ Five of them set out together—Baszi, Szimi, the boy from Huszt, and two other young women from home. It was the kind of walk through the countryside Szimi used to take regularly, fourteen months before, when she had measured each step by the number of calories she'd burned off. In those days, which she now knew belonged to another life, her route had been unvaried; she would walk up the little mountain just outside of town, stop by the cemetery, visit the old ruins, come home again. Yet she had believed, then, in that safe little world, that she had unlimited freedom to do whatever she wanted.

On this unfamiliar road she felt strangely comforted by the return of that feeling of unlimited freedom. Luckily she had no mirror. She couldn't see herself in her striped concentration camp dress and her burr cut.

She was acutely aware of her lack of hair; her hand would occasionally sweep across her abbreviated hairline in an absentminded way, as though she were petting a dog. Yet she was conscious mainly of the sensation of pavement under her feet—and movement. She realized she was still looking at the world with concentration camp eyes, with the feeling that she was in a bubble floating by a place that had nothing to do with her. When she saw the dead bodies of German soldiers lying by the edge of the road, like litter tossed from the back of a moving car, she felt nothing, neither satisfaction nor horror. It was strange, when she thought of it; those were the first dead bodies she'd actually seen, except for the brief glimpse of the girl who'd been electrocuted by the fence at Auschwitz. Surrounded by death for months, she'd never seen a corpse, just smoke and fire.

That evening they arrived at the Czech border and stopped at a farmhouse. A German woman answered the door. This was the Sudetenland, the territory that had sparked the war.

It struck Szimi when she saw the expression on the woman's face. She was terrified of them, these scruffy ragamuffins.

"We come from the camp," one of them said. "We're going to sleep here."

Those were the words, more or less, that led their "hostess" to produce blankets and food. They lay on the floor in one room; she disappeared into the next. They were exhausted but couldn't sleep. One of them found a radio. That night, at midnight, while Szimi and her friends camped out on a German woman's floor on the border between the Czech Sudetenland and Germany, the news came: The war was over. Szimi had thought those words—*The war is over*—would produce a movie moment. An orchestra would play, she would break into dance. Instead she luxuriated in the mundane indulgence of drifting off to sleep with tomorrow on her mind. The next morning they would start for home.

The roadside had abundant pickings for scavengers. Shortly after they left the German woman's house, they collected a couple of abandoned bicycles. They made a plan. They would go to Prague, which they'd determined was the nearest big city, then make their way back to Huszt. They were living in the age of delayed communication—no faxes, not even phones that worked. "We were like free birds," Szimi would say, trying to explain what it was like to those who couldn't imagine a world without faxes or phones.

They kept walking, looking for more bicycles and not finding one. When they arrived at another farmhouse at the top of a hill, they asked the German man living there for a bicycle. He looked them over and didn't seem impressed.

"No," he said.

Szimi was indignant. Months of subservience had been erased from her memory by the previous night's experience. She had seen in the German woman's eyes that Szimi and her friends were the victors. They had a right, she felt, to take what they needed, but she wasn't able to do it. None of them had the wherewithal to defy this man's confident "No."

Then the thing happened that would further convince Szimi that the Gypsy woman—the "Jewish Gypsy"—in camp had been correct. It was the kind of moment that would encourage her, for the rest of her life, to have full faith in the most dubious twists of plot in movies and plays. As she and her friends reached the road, some Russian troops happened by and a lieutenant stepped out of the ranks and asked them where they were from.

In her careful schoolgirl Russian—all those months of studying *Anna Karenina* coming in handy now—Szimi said, or thought she said, "We are from Podkarpatská Rus, but we were in Auschwitz and we were here working in Zittau and we want to go home."

"Why were you there?" he asked.

"Because we're Jewish," Szimi answered.

She was surprised when she saw his response. It was clear from his expression, a mixture of fondness and fear, that she had made that connection, that conspiratorial link. She knew it before he said the words, even though she couldn't believe that this tall, lean man with the trim little mustache and the Russian officer's uniform was a Jew. She had assumed all Jews had gone to concentration camp.

"I'm Jewish, too," he told her, unnecessarily, "but no one knows it in the army because they wouldn't follow my orders."

Szimi pressed her advantage. "Maybe you can help us."

"What is your problem?"

"We need bicycles to go to Prague, but the man in the house up there won't give them to us," Szimi said.

The Russian took hold of her arm, and together they marched to the top of the hill. When the German man opened the door, the Russian spoke the phrase all Germans would quickly learn: *"Davai!"*—Give it to me!

Now Szimi had her bicycle, and she explained the rest of her problem to her *Landsman,* her fellow Jew: "Three of us know how to ride bicycles, and two of us don't."

The lieutenant spoke to his commander, who agreed to take with them the two girls who didn't ride bikes. One of the girls who hopped onto the Russian truck was Baszi.

The Russian showed Szimi and her friends the map. His finger landed on a town called Ústí nad Labem, Ústí over the Elbe River, the biggest city between them and Prague. "This is as far as you can go because in Prague there is an uprising against the Germans," he said. "The trains are not going yet. There's a railroad crossing and a pub right by it. We'll meet you there."

As Szimi and her friends set out, she saw the panic on Baszi's face. She felt compassion for her friend—she knew Baszi was a worrier—but she was annoyed with her as well. Hadn't she told her everything would turn out all right?

Of course Szimi wasn't acknowledging the obvious—that they had no idea how things would turn out. Baszi knew only that her parents were dead. She didn't know where her brother and her sister were, and Szimi knew even less. She had never heard where her father had gone that night on the train platform in Birkenau, and her brothers could be anywhere. She just knew she had somewhere to go and a way to get there, and that was all she was going to think about right now.

She waved to Baszi on the truck and yelled out, "We'll meet you at the pub in Ústí nad Labem!"

On the way to Ústí Szimi and her friends stopped at an abandoned house. It was there that Szimi changed her striped prison dress for a pair of slacks and a shirt. They hadn't exercised in months, yet they rode like trained athletes, running on the adrenaline of possibility and youth. Even after all they'd been through, or because of it, they felt invincible, as though they could outpedal the sorrow that would always shadow them.

In the pub at Ústí they found the familial welcome that would become habitual over the next few days and weeks, the bonding of relief. Their incarceration was no longer a badge of shame but a pass to free meals and rooms. "Stay here until your friends come," the pub owner invited them. Whatever they needed was theirs—that was the impression he gave them.

The three friends stopped by the railroad station next door, just as the Russian lieutenant had said, where they were told a milk train was leaving for Prague in two hours. They went back to the pub and told the owner that when their two "sisters" arrived with the Russian troops, please tell them they would all meet later in Prague. Szimi, apparently, had forgotten what she had told Baszi back in Auschwitz: "Don't worry, I'll never leave you."

———

■ The meeting should have been impossible. When Szimi and her two companions stepped off the train, they found themselves in the middle of a jubilant crowd that seemed spread across the entire city. Physically untouched by the war, the ancient spires and turrets of Prague—the "golden city"—looked like a fairyland. The electricity was out, so the trolleys weren't working; the streets were mobbed with pedestrians, milling around with the aimless giddiness of Mardi Gras drunks.

Szimi was giddy but never aimless. She dragged her friends through the mob in Wenceslas Square until they found the Alcron Hotel, which she knew was owned by a Mr. Krofta, the "Conrad Hilton of Czechoslovakia" and the husband of the woman she would always call "my famous cousin Olga." Krofta, who wasn't Jewish, had stayed behind while Olga left to wait the war out in America. He kept their little girl and was waiting for Olga's return, not knowing that she would leave him for a Swedish shipping magnate she would meet in America. Olga would become part of a minor international scandal by selling ships to China during the Cold War. Later she would settle in Switzerland and the family would lose track of her, knowing only that the Italian nobleman her daughter had married had died in a car crash.

But all that lay in the future on the day Szimi made her way to Mr. Krofta's apartment on Václavské Náměstí and announced herself to the housekeeper. As she waited for her cousin's husband, Szimi felt as though she was finally returning to the world again, as thoughts of Olga took her back to the gossipy comforts of Huszt, with its small scandals, its myriad family connections.

Szimi had known Olga first as Rozsi's piano teacher, then as an outcast. Olga wasn't a beauty, but she was tall, slim, and blond, and—it was said—she had an *effect* on men. She'd left Huszt for Prague after the young bank clerk who worshiped her committed suicide; he'd embezzled money to buy her things. Olga had given the gossips more to chew on when she appeared at his funeral not in white, the Jewish mourning color, but in black from head to toe, like a Gentile. In Prague, it was said, she had put her net out for Mr. Krofta—twenty years her senior—by sitting in the Alcron lobby every day until he noticed her.

The housekeeper returned with Mr. Krofta, a stout man in his early sixties, not handsome but nice looking, or maybe he just seemed so because of the sympathetic feeling Szimi saw in his eyes when she told him she was just back from Auschwitz. He sat her down at a huge, gleaming table in a formal dining room and ordered the housekeeper to bring tea and a babka, a cake. Though she had never experienced luxury like this except in the movies, she felt at home there. Her adaptability was upwardly mobile. She sat straight in her chair and remembered her manners, but forgetting to mention that she had left her friends waiting outside the door while she chatted and sipped tea.

"What are your plans?" asked Mr. Krofta (she never knew his first name).

She was direct: "I want to go to Huszt, but I don't have any money. Could you help me out?"

She was having trouble paying attention to his words as she concentrated on the sweet buttery crumbs of cake filling her mouth, her entire being, with little bursts of pleasure.

"Don't go back to Huszt," he said. "I'm afraid Huszt will stay Russian. What kind of schooling did you have?"

She told him she had finished high school in Russian.

He outlined a plan. "They need interpreters at the Alcron, where the Russian command is. You'll get a job there. I can't give you a room at the Alcron or at the Flora; the Czech government is there. But I have a *pension* a little out of the way. I'll give you a letter for the woman who is the caretaker, and I'll call her and let her know you're coming."

With that he called in his daughter, a girl of about twelve, introduced the cousins, and told Szimi how eagerly they were awaiting Olga's return—not knowing, of course, that Olga would never come back to him.

When he walked Szimi to the front door and opened it to let her out, he saw two young people sitting on the step. He turned to Szimi. "Are they with you?"

When she said yes he took the note for the landlady back and ordered two rooms, so the boy could have his own. He sent the rest of the babka along with them but no money. "You won't need it," he said, and he was right. Prague was on holiday. When the trolleys began running again, they were free. The Red Cross, the Jewish Relief Agency, and the Catholic Church had set up shelters, where "repatriates," as the refugees were politely called, could find free beds and food.

Szimi and her friends walked to the *pension,* less than two miles away, where the landlady gave them rooms and salami and bread. They decided they were too tired to go back to the center of town to find Baszi.

The next morning they stopped for free breakfast at the Catholic church stand. Szimi heard someone calling her name. It was Baszi, newly arrived on the morning train. Szimi didn't notice any resentment from the friend she'd left behind—but then, she wasn't looking for any.

Everyone was on the move, trying to find someone or else someone who knew something about someone. The atmosphere was charged with jubilation and fear. A roving photographer could capture a montage of grief or of happiness, depending on whether she snapped the picture when old friends fell into one another's arms or when they found out whom they would never see again. Szimi would always carry with her the happy photo album, the one in which everyone is smiling, everyone's best side is turned toward the camera. She wouldn't throw the other pictures away—she is incapable of waste—but they would remain hidden, neither discarded nor displayed, like a diary filled with secrets that she doesn't want to remember but doesn't want to forget.

Szimi and Baszi stopped for lunch at another free food stand, this one run by the Red Cross. Then they separated so Baszi could register with the police while Szimi went to the Alcron to see about the job Mr. Krofta had arranged. They agreed to meet back at the Red Cross stand at three that afternoon.

The Alcron was a madhouse as its new Russian tenants set up the peacetime command. Szimi stopped one soldier to ask about her job, then another. No one knew anything about it.

As she stood in the lobby, she felt distant from the frenzy around her, back in the bubble once again, watching a world that had nothing to do with her. She sensed rather than felt people shoving her as they rushed by. In this dreamlike state she said to herself, "I just came back from concentration camp. Why should I go back to work? There's food everywhere. This is really crazy."

She would never regret the decision except in one way. She never thanked Mr. Krofta for his kindness because she was too ashamed to face him after she rejected the job he found for her.

She drifted back to the *pension*.

Her friends asked her, "Where's Baszi?"

Szimi said, "Oh, she'll come later."

"Does Baszi know where to come?" one of the friends asked.

Szimi responded the way she always would to this kind of situation, with a brief moment of remorse followed by an expeditious fatalism. "You'll see, she'll sleep at the Red Cross and we'll meet her tomorrow."

——

■ Szimi had no doubt that she would keep her promise to Baszi—*I'll never leave you*. She had never been inclined toward literal interpretation and so wouldn't have considered leaving Baszi behind at the border a form of abandonment. (Her experience had assured her that she couldn't afford anything but the long view.)

The next morning, still wearing the shirt and slacks she'd taken from the German house two days before, she set out for the Red Cross station in the center of town, fully expecting to find Baszi there. As she walked down Wenceslas Square she again felt the exhilaration of the day before, as though she were reliving, magnified, the Saturday-afternoon promenades in Huszt. The streets were packed with people roaming up and down with expectant eyes. She allowed herself to absorb only the excitement of anticipation, not the accompanying terror so many must have felt.

She turned off Wenceslas Square onto Jindřišska Street, to the old hotel that the Red Cross had converted into a shelter and cafeteria for the "repatriates." She walked into the dining hall ready to pull Baszi to her and tell her about the place they had found to live—before Baszi could ask her "Why did you leave me?" Szimi would make her see the question was irrelevant before she could utter it.

She stood on her toes and stretched her neck as she surveyed the room, a short person's habit that made her seem younger than she was, twenty-two years old. Her cheeks, still round after Auschwitz, completed the impression of a precocious little girl.

After a few minutes she found the young woman who seemed to be running things and told her who she was.

"Oh, yes," she said. "Your friend was looking for you. She said to tell you she'll be back at noon."

It was just 10 A.M. Szimi was about to go out for a walk when she spotted a familiar face, darkly imposing, made even more striking by bushy black eyebrows. It was Dr. Salamon, the young doctor who had moved to Huszt a few years before and had been the most eligible bachelor in town until he married Anna Lazarovičs. Most of the Jewish girls in Huszt had had a crush on the good-looking doctor with the thick wavy hair, including Szimi, though she admitted this only to her friend Olga Mermelstein. He had, after all, been quite old, thirty years old, when he arrived in Huszt in 1939.

She saw that he was thin but still handsome, especially so in his partisan uniform (this was, after all, a girl who could speak fondly of Mengele, so fine in his uniform). And she saw that he was smiling at her and kept smiling as he walked toward her and hugged her. She was startled by the show of affection. He had always seemed so remote to her in Huszt, rather glamorous, always formal, even when he rode to see patients on his bicycle—before he had bought the car that indicated he had made it into the Huszt elite. He was also very tall—and seemed especially so to Szimi, who was five foot two.

He pulled her over to the table where he was having breakfast with a doctor from Budapest. They had the conversation that all the repatriates were having in Prague that May: Where were you? How did you survive? What do you know about the others?

The two doctors told her they had been in Dachau together. Three weeks before the war was over, the Germans had begun emptying the camp. During this march, to where they didn't know, Sanyi—Dr. Salamon—and his friend had slipped off into the forest, where they had soon joined a group of partisans.

Szimi told them her story, too. Anyone watching the conversation from another table would have seen simply an animated group of friends who hadn't seen one another for a while. The horror was squeezed out in the telling; the last year had become an adventure story. They even laughed sarcastically at the great Czech uprising on the last day of the war. Some Germans had been hanged in the Old Town Square, and the electricity had been cut. This show of bravado had turned out to be a pain in the neck, they agreed, because now there were no trolleys.

The doctor from Budapest left; he was catching a train home.

When Sanyi and Szimi were alone, his mood changed. The light went out of his eyes.

"Did you see Anna and Evika—little Eva—in the transport?" he asked her.

"No," she said. "We were on different transports."

"Tell me what you know," he said.

She told him what she knew about his wife and daughter, a child not yet three when the Germans had come to Huszt a year before.

"I used to see Anna quite a lot after they made the ghetto," she said. "Do you know about the ghetto?"

He asked her to tell him.

So she told him how the Jews of Huszt had been packed into a few streets and how she had stayed with Dr. Lakatos with her friend Nadia. Anna had been working as Dr. Lakatos's nurse, perhaps because her husband was a doctor, perhaps because her father was a prominent citizen.

She didn't tell him that she hadn't paid much attention to Anna, the pretty daughter of a wealthy man, because she hadn't even gone to *Gymnasium*. Though Anna was three years older than Szimi, Szimi had thought of her as "a simple girl" because she wasn't educated. In truth, she hadn't been much aware of her at all. Her marriage and her child had made her part of another generation. Szimi had different ambitions.

"It was said at Auschwitz that she had Evika in her arms and wouldn't let her go. She would have gone immediately," Szimi told him.

He didn't respond.

Szimi, who grieved so little for herself, felt very sad for him. Once again, as they sat silently, it occurred to her how lucky she was. Yes, her parents had died (though she still hadn't heard what, exactly, had happened to her father). But she felt sure she would soon be reunited with Hilu and Gyula. Even now, facing Sanyi Salamon's sorrowful face, she didn't worry about her brothers at all. They were young and strong and from the same stock as she. She glanced at the door and felt surprised they weren't there, just because she was thinking of them. She believed more strongly than ever that she was possessed of some magical power. She had moved beyond the trivial manipulation of numbers. She had it in her to influence the fate of human souls. This power, as she imagined it, wasn't entirely to her liking because she had no control over it. Sometimes when she broke a glass good fortune fell on the person she was thinking about; sometimes it didn't.

She realized Sanyi was leading her out the door, to take a walk while they waited for noon and for Baszi to come. They were caught up in the movement of the street, and that was the sensation she would always associate with him—of motion, of going somewhere. Since he no longer talked about Anna and Evika, she assumed that he was treating his loss the way she was treating hers, as something that had happened to somebody else a long time ago.

My father, Alexander Salamon

9

Daddy

■ After we returned home from Europe I began listening to the tapes. When I got to the story of how my mother left Baszi behind, I picked up the phone.

"How could you do that?" I asked her. "How could you leave her there? Wasn't there another train later on?"

There was an edge to my voice, as though I were Baszi's defense counsel. I knew Baszi, after all. She and her family had lived in Cleveland—the opposite end of Ohio from Seaman, where our family lived, but close enough for us to visit each other sometimes for Thanksgiving. Her children had spent a couple of summers in the country with us. She had died relatively young of pancreatic cancer. I remember her as a gentle soul who always remained the girl who couldn't ride a bike, who never learned to run faster than the demons chasing her the way my mother did.

As always when I ask these questions, my mother responded calmly, with neither shame nor defiance, but rather with bemusement.

"Looking at it today, it was really crazy," she said. "We got on the train and went to Prague. I just figured that in Prague we will meet."

I asked, "Had you ever been to Prague?"

"No," she said.

"Had you talked about where you might join up if you separated? It's a big city."

"No." She sighed. "How we will meet wasn't discussed."

The conversation ended.

A day or two later she called me.

"You see," she said, as though no time had elapsed since we last talked about what she could see I was positioning as her abandonment of Baszi, "everything always works out."

She sounded elated. I prepared myself for the rationale that was sure to follow and for the inevitability of my own willing complicity in it. I long ago lost whatever immunity I might once have had to my mother's persuasion.

"Tell me," I said.

"Here's what I realized about that time in Prague. We went back down the next morning and I asked the Red Cross worker if she'd seen my sister—I don't know why I called Baszi my sister, from camp, I guess—who I had been there with before.

"The woman said, 'Yeah, yeah, she left word she'll be back here at noon.'

"So," my mother continued, "when I looked around I saw this tall man from Huszt with a broad face and black hair in a partisan uniform and he was coming toward me. He was so handsome. We talked and talked and never parted from that day. So you see, if I had met Baszi when I was supposed to, I might not have met your daddy, and where would you be now?"

———

■ *Where would you be now?*

The instant she said it I was stunned by a rare flash of absolute clarity. It was at that moment, infected by my mother's heady analysis of fate's logic, that I finally understood what I had been looking for—first in Ohio, then in Europe. It was my father.

He'd left behind a legacy that might not seem like much but that was daunting in our little world. I'm not talking about the visible monuments—the plaque on the wall at the Adams County Hospital, the landing strip that qualifies as the county's airport, called "Salamon Airport" because my father donated the land for it (though I admit I take some pleasure in knowing our family name is on the maps pilots use, a pinpoint of immortality). I'm talking about the mythology that grew up around him—the sainted doctor—because he worked very hard not to let anyone see the truth.

And what was the truth? Not that he was evil or even less saintly than he seemed, but that he was mortal and had suffered.

It was my father who was responsible for the way I still think of Seaman, the town where I grew up. More than twenty years after I left, I couldn't stop thinking about summers there, how hot they were. Maybe they were really no hotter than summers were in other places where summers were hot. Maybe everything merely seemed more distilled in that little Ohio town—to me—and therefore more intense.

This question has periodically preoccupied me over the years, usually when I get together with my mother and my sister. The three of us have spent much time considering our perceptions of that place. Were the stars really so much more abundant, the crickets more animated, the snow deeper and whiter, the autumn leaves more vivid? We thought so but didn't trust our memories, knowing that our recollections were magnified by what had happened to us there and by what we wanted to believe was happening. It was our father who had taken us there, made it part of our blood, and then died—there, in Seaman, in the only home I knew as a child.

My father died two days after my eighteenth birthday. I loved him all the time, worshiped him most of the time, feared him some of the time—but I didn't know him. Until recently I figured that lack of knowledge was no more than the natural gap in a child's perception of a parent, which can be eventually filled in as everyone grows older, for those lucky enough to find the freedom with age to examine together events that were once too painful to discuss. Parents remain stuck in time when they die before their children know which questions to ask. Like actors in old movies, they never change. The best their children can hope for, as they accumulate experience, is a hypothetical under-standing.

The mysteries of my father have been particularly hard to unravel because he actively submerged so much of his own history. The difference between him and my mother struck me when I spent some time in my daughter's kindergarten one day. My mother is the child happily scribbling away without stopping. When she makes a mistake or wants to take her work in a new direction, this child simply scratches out the discarded idea and moves on. She proudly holds up this messy drawing, content to let anyone see what's been crossed out.

I could see my father in that other child, laboriously working on his "perfect" drawing. It is neat and clean and pleasing to the eye, and shows no sign of effort. For that you have to look under the desk, where many scribbled pages have been carefully hidden.

The things our father didn't tell us weren't insignificant to him or to us. He never told my sister and me that in an earlier life he had had a daughter (our half sister) and a wife (her mother) and that they had both been killed in the war. He didn't tell us when he was dying, either.

I kept diaries throughout my childhood. I looked in them recently, hoping to find in them clues about my father. Instead I found a meticulous accounting of my activities, as though I were trying to reassure some future reader that I wasn't wasting a second and that everything was wonderful all the time. Occasionally I make oblique reference to my father being in a "bad mood." But more typical was this note, on January 2, 1971: "D and I talked awhile. Was nice. I love him."

I rummaged through drawers stuffed with papers, some of them no more than scraps on which I'd jotted some thought I'd had, often while in transit—on a subway, or waiting for a plane to take off. On one of them, undated, I had written the following:

The 18 years at home compress into little picture capsules. There's Daddy, white shirt, dark pants, standing at the front door with the lacy curtains. He kisses us good-bye. We're on the way to school. I remember the slip slap of the hedges, trying to keep my dress dry.

Where's Poochie? At the end of the hedge. She was always there to walk us to school but where did she wait, exactly?

Some guys are hanging out in front of Hannah's Grocery Store across the street. Sugar crullers, six for a quarter.

Until I was in sixth grade and she was a senior Suzy and I walked out together. Did we hold hands? We did. We crossed Main Street and waved at Daddy. He was smiling at us. Why do I remember him feeling sad?

I feel an ache now. What is the feeling? Did I feel it then? I don't remember. I remember the feel of the road, a little crunchy, poorly paved.

There's Daddy staring at us through the lacy curtain. What did he feel watching us—me and Suzy and Poochie—make the turn and disappear?

Was he thinking about the office, all those patients waiting? Or the farm? Or was he thinking of her, of Eva, our dead half-sister? Did he think of her every time we stepped onto Main Street and a car sped by? Did he want to keep us locked in the house?

We lived in rural Ohio but traveled around the world, always including local synagogues among the tourist attractions. Our destinations tended to be places where our parents could look up friends and relatives from the Carpathian region, and they seemed ubiquitous even after Hitler.

Daddy was formal—he wore a coat and tie every day—but he was cool. When he saw Elvis on TV for the first time, on *The Ed Sullivan Show*, he told our mother he had just seen greatness itself. He bought us our first Beatles albums as well as a two-record set that explained the Old Testament in songs that were structured and paced like a Broadway musical (*"Dan Dan Dan-i-el, Come out of Is-ra-el . . ."*). When he saw we liked comic books, he found a deluxe comic book version of the Bible. We said our prayers every night before going to bed, a variation on a Christian prayer: "Now I lay me down to sleep, I pray the Lord my soul to keep. Guard me through the starry night and wake me safe with sunshine bright."

Over time he became more rigorous about our religious training.

On Saturday mornings, before making his hospital rounds, he would sit us down in the living room and we would all read the weekly Torah portion in English. He became extremely solemn as he composed explications on the Biblical passages. His task wasn't made easier by our tendency to giggle when it was our turn to read. We just didn't understand the source of the intensity with which he would read certain sections—this, for example, from Samuel: "Moreover I will appoint a place for my people Israel, and will plant them, that they may dwell in a place of their own, and move no more; neither shall the children of wickedness afflict them anymore, as beforehand . . ."

He would take off his reading glasses and look at us nervously, as though he were making a speech and we were an audience of strangers. He would say things like "We should be proud of our heritage and support Israel," but then he would say, "We are Americans first and Jews second." We would listen politely to what we called his "Sunday" sermons and pretend we didn't notice how teary-eyed he got.

He began driving us to Cincinnati on Sundays—a two-hour trip in those days, before the highway was built—for Hebrew lessons with a young Israeli rabbinical student. Our reward for this hardship would be a trip to the local Coney Island Park or the movies or both.

In turn, we rewarded him and our mother with obedience and adoration. At an early age we learned to pronounce everything our mother cooked as "delicious"—even when she insisted on serving us huge, heavy rolls of cabbage stuffed with rice and ground meat in the dead heat of summer. We accepted our bifurcated lives—singing "Deep and Wide" at summer Bible camp with our friends, dancing the hora with our relatives at weddings in New York.

We didn't, however, understand the current of tension that often seemed to be in the air or where our enchanting, sentimental father went when he slipped away from us into a silence we didn't know how to interpret. We knew these disappearances were, somehow, connected to our being Jewish and to the Holocaust (never mentioned by our father), but we couldn't identify his emotion or its exact cause. Was it rage or despair or simply disappointment at something we had or had not done?

I couldn't repeat with my father what I had done with my mother. There could be no road trips for us. So I set out alone to see what I could find. This leg of my journey took me back to Ohio, to the suburbs of New York, to Boca Raton, and to São Paulo (by phone). Over and over I asked whoever might be able to tell me: Who was this man?

My father would always remain a little aloof. Here he is with other doctors in Prague; he's the one looking away from the camera.

10

Set for Life

■ Sanyi Salamon was a man about whom there would always be much speculation. He had an arresting face, darkly sensitive like a matinee idol's. His large head and square shoulders accentuated the sensation that he was slightly larger than life, even when he was quite thin. He tended to remain silent until he was spoken to, a habit that many people, feeling judged, found intimidating. Yet when he did speak, his voice was soft and often hesitant. This made him very appealing, like the gentle lion in a children's story whose fierceness masks great insecurity.

It was easy to see why Szimi Rapaport would choose to see him as the fulfillment of the "Jewish Gypsy's" prediction back in Auschwitz. From that first meeting at the Red Cross she felt that he would be the one with whom she would have that long and happy life. If nothing else, he carried himself like a man of destiny.

That carriage wasn't accidental. From the moment he was born, on February 7, 1909, he was treated like a prince, the youngest—by far—

of seven children. In some households where money was tight he might have been seen as an unlucky accident. But the Salamons always spoke of him as the gifted one, the miracle child of "elderly" parents (his mother was thirty-six and his father was forty when he was born).

He came from a family that liked to give itself tribal characteristics. It was common for members of the Salamon family to generalize about Salamons. "Salamons like a good joke," they would say (meaning, Salamons love to tell terrible jokes and laugh uproariously at them). "Salamons are Gypsies," they would say (meaning that Salamons love schmaltzy music and to dance the csárdás until they drop). "Salamons are good at love, bad at business," they would say (meaning exactly what they said).

The Salamons were farmers in Homok, a village in the Carpathian Mountains. Marcus Salamon, the patriarch, Sanyi's father, was a tall thin man with a mischievous face and a big appetite. He was what they would call "a real Salamon"; "he would have given away his underpants," was how his relatives put it. Eventually he had nothing to give, having lost most of his property for reasons that might have had to do with the general economy or, just as likely, with his lack of interest in financial detail. There were rumors that he sold his land to pay his oldest son Louis's gambling debts.

No one could say for sure why he was forced to move his family to Kis Begany, a slightly bigger town than Homok, and to become a renter, not an owner. Even so, he remained a gentleman farmer, managing properties for other people. He never seemed beaten or even saddened by his reduced circumstances. His grandchildren remembered him riding from farm to farm on a horse-drawn wagon looking as though something amusing was going to happen. The grandchildren often spent the night, and most of them would end up in bed with their grandfather, who told them stories and didn't mind them crawling all over him like a litter of pups. (Their grandmother was the realistic one. She often seemed worried.)

Sanyi spoke little of his life there, but certain things were known. He spent a lot of time outdoors with his nieces and nephews, who weren't much younger than he was but young enough to worship him. On hot summer nights he slept with them outside, on a haystack underneath a

My grandfather (the smiling man with the beard) and grandmother (to the right of him) surrounded by their children and grandchildren. My father's the skinny guy with the mustache and suspenders.

pear tree where there was always a breeze. On those nights he had a way of peering at the stars with such intensity he seemed to be finding secrets in them that no one else could see. He took the children into the forest to pick berries and giant mushrooms and taught them to hide in blackened tree trunks during fierce summer storms, assuring them that lightning doesn't strike the same place twice.

He was earthy as well as ethereal. He liked to play cards and he liked girls, especially one special "friend," a non-Jewish girl who, his young cousins suspected, was teaching him "things." It was assumed in those days that a Jewish boy would learn about sex from Gentiles, then marry a nice Jewish girl.

A mythology grew around Sanyi. How, for example, he was the only Salamon child to finish *Gymnasium*, how in grammar school he had to walk from Kis Begany to Nagy Begany to catch a train for school in Beregszaz. When it was pointed out that this was a distance of only a mile or two, the adoring niece or nephew would scornfully remind the doubter that the roads weren't paved. When it was raining, the mud was up to your neck and the snow was even worse. But didn't Marcus often drive his youngest child to the station in the wagon or ask the hired man to do it? Yes, sometimes, but even then poor little Sanyi had to get up at 4 A.M. to be on time.

Sanyi himself never repeated these stories. Even as a boy he wanted no pity, no special treatment, and he always seemed surprised when it came to him.

There were only two Jewish families in Kis Begany and not many more in Nagy Begany, though there was a synagogue. When the Salamons were asked to describe what it was like for Jews in Nagy Begany, they would tell a joke:

"There was always a problem getting ten Jews together for a *minyan* on the Sabbath, and without a *minyan* you can't pray. Every Friday evening someone was sent to find a Jewish beggar to be the tenth man.

"One Friday they sent the rabbi's wife to find someone. She searched around until she found a beggar.

" 'Would you like to be the tenth man?' she asked him.

" 'Lady,' he said, 'I would like to be the first.' "

The Salamons would giggle at a joke like this until they cried—actual tears. *Salamons like a good joke.*

No one could remember who had given Sanyi the idea to go to medical school. Maybe healing the sick was what Sanyi was thinking about when he drifted off into silence on walks in the woods. Or, perhaps—most likely—he learned by negative example. Maybe he simply didn't want to follow in his brothers' footsteps. His oldest brother, Louis, fifteen years older than Sanyi—the *shlemazel,* the one with bad luck, he was called—was married with two children and one on the way when he left for America, promising he would send for his family when he had enough money. "Left" was the kind way of putting it. Louis had run away. He had run away because he was ashamed.

He'd lost a lot of money playing cards, and his father-in-law had bailed him out. The next time Louis ran up a big gambling debt, he couldn't bear to ask for money again. Instead he signed his father-in-law's name to a check, fully intending, he told himself, to pay the money back. He concocted the kind of plan that makes sense only to the panic-stricken. He would go to America, where money floated in the air like leaves from trees. He would bring his family to join him or he would come home, but either way his father-in-law would be paid. A nice theory, but no one was setting the table for Louis's coming-home party.

Jani, the second-oldest brother—Jani of the smiling eyes, they called him—was facing conscription into the Czech Army when he decided to leave. His best friend, who played the violin beautifully, had left for South America to find his fortune. He wrote to Jani, "It's wonderful here. Come join me." Though Jani was then living with an aunt and uncle who loved him, he couldn't resist the Gypsy's call and he was off. He caught a ship in Hamburg and met his friend in Buenos Aires. All was well until Jani's money ran out. He woke up one morning and his friend was gone and so were all his things. Jani had done a little boxing at home, so for the next few years he trekked from town to town, earning money in the ring. He made his way across Brazil, then Chile, picking up odd jobs wherever he went. Eventually he settled in Peru, as far from Podkarpatská Rus as the moon.

The third brother, Béla—the bull, because he was so powerfully built—stayed at home, where he proved to be as successful at farming as his father, which is to say not very. He worked for his well-to-do brother-in-law, who grew grain for the manufacture of alcohol.

Sanyi, however, had been designated the intellectual, the delicate one, almost from birth. Maybe his brothers had nothing to do with his decision after all. They hadn't set out on their wayward paths when Sanyi announced (or so it was remembered), when he was seven years old, "You'll see. I am going to be a doctor." It's believed a teacher had told his mother that he was very smart and should be encouraged. Certainly he was encouraged. When it was time for Sanyi to go to *Gymnasium*, a luxury in those days, he stayed with an aunt and uncle so he wouldn't have to lose energy traveling every day. Though none of his school records were kept, the family agreed that he was a brilliant student, especially in Latin. Whether he was or wasn't, he sped through school, finishing a year ahead of his class.

He was seventeen when he matriculated at Charles University Medical School in Prague, in the fall of 1926. He immediately began to smoke, to get the smell of dead bodies out of his nose. He began washing his hands frequently.

His sisters sent him weekly packages of cakes, smoked meats, and goose liver encased in fat so it wouldn't spoil, not thinking how unappetizing that particular delicacy might seem to someone whose head never cleared of the scent of chloroform. His brother Louis, in exile in America, couldn't afford to bring his wife and children over, but he always spared four dollars a month for his little brother, enough to pay for lunches at the school cafeteria. Even Jani in Peru helped subsidize Sanyi's medical education, sending what he could whenever he could.

Sanyi would mention these gifts repeatedly and with gratitude. That gratitude must have been layered with guilt because he would later tell his own children not to owe anybody anything.

He came home on holidays full of stories and surprises as well as chocolates. One summer a young cousin mentioned that he had heard the opera *Carmen*. The next day Sanyi appeared with the sheet music and a violin and played the entire score. Another day he showed up with an oboe and played that beautifully as well. Once again there was proof: *Salamons are Gypsies.*

He entertained the cousins with his adventures in the big city. One night he told them how he had been snookered by some cardsharps on the train to Prague. They would play a hand and Sanyi would think he had won. But one of the guys would yell out *kronula!*—and take the money.

"What's *kronula?*" Sanyi asked.

"You don't know what *kronula* is?" they said sarcastically, figuring, correctly, how to silence the country rube.

"Finally," Sanyi told his cousins, raising his impressive eyebrows for dramatic effect. "I figured it out. So the next time I yelled *kronula* first and took the money and those guys couldn't say a thing!"

He startled his sister Fanci—just as he intended—when he sent her a photograph taken of him during an anatomy course. She took one look and put it on a table, facedown.

"Sanyi and his jokes," she said, laughing and holding her stomach.

She refused to let her children see the picture, but they stole a look anyway and howled with delighted disgust. Sanyi, dressed in surgical scrubs, grinned at the camera, holding his hand spread wide in the air, a piece of intestine dangling from his finger.

Fanci's children couldn't wait for his visit that summer, to see what kind of mischief he would bring. Yet they were disappointed when he arrived, to see how serious he seemed.

"Sit down, Fanci," he said sternly, right after he walked inside. He nodded at her husband. "You, too, Jozsi."

Then he turned to Erzsika, their five-year-old daughter whom he had dubbed "Potza" when he had heard her whining after a spanking, "You hurt my *potza!*" she had wailed, rubbing her *potza,* her bottom.

"Potza, in the middle," he said.

She ran over to her parents, and they all sat waiting obediently. Then Sanyi revealed what the mystery was about. He pulled out a camera and took their picture!

Little Erzsika was enchanted. Who else had an uncle like this? A gorgeous man, she heard everyone say, but what interested her and her brothers was his mystery and his mischief. He wasn't like the other grown-ups. She would keep the picture he took of her and her parents for the rest of her life, and she would live a long time.

In the summer of 1931 Sanyi brought home the best gift of all, his ornate medical diploma rolled up in a strong cardboard tube. His family proudly noted that not only had he successfully completed medical school, he had done so in record time: only twenty-two years old and a doctor. He served as a medical officer in the Czech Army, then began a surgical residency at the hospital in Beregszaz. In his six years there he became, his colleagues later testified, a skillful diagnostician and cutter. He did it all—appendectomies, colostomies, hysterectomies, hernias, amputations. He delivered babies. Someone taught him how to relieve the ache of bursitis with injections into the joints. He soon acquired minor local fame for this specialty; he was believed to have a magic touch. The family's awe of him grew as he established himself in this mysterious world of blood and healing.

Sanyi remained a faithful son. He visited his parents in Begany almost every weekend, rebelling only by refusing his mother's pleas to give up his motorcycle. That's how he indulged his hot streak, tearing across country roads on his red Java.

He briefly worked at another hospital after Beregszaz; then he decided to strike out on his own. He chose an unlikely spot, a mountain village populated mainly by Ruthenian peasants. This decision to live the rustic life may not have seemed the obvious choice for an upwardly mobile country boy in his late twenties. No one knew what, exactly, had propelled him to the hills. Sanyi had always been an unpredictable romantic.

The experiment was not successful. The young doctor, who had acquired a certain sophistication in Prague, wasn't prepared for his patients, who were dirty and uneducated and who paid him with chickens and eggs and milk. He wasn't encouraged by the young nephew he brought along, Erzsika's brother Pityu, a fastidious young man who got upset when his fingernails weren't manicured. Rather quickly Sanyi decided that tending to the poor wasn't for him. He couldn't take the spitting and the stench. The two came home a week after they'd left.

After this brief fling with idealism he made his way toward security. He settled in Huszt, where he was immediately welcomed by the Jewish gentry. Though the town had eight doctors, none of them was as young or as handsome as Dr. Salamon, the reason many patients gave for trying him out.

With apparent ease he accustomed himself to the town's bourgeois customs. He could be seen joining the Saturday-afternoon promenade and playing cards at the Koruna Hotel with the other bachelors. He must have been aware that people were keeping tabs on him, wondering which of the town's girls would become the new doctor's wife.

He liked it there. He found that people laughed at his jokes. Women liked him best, but he was also adored by those children who were able to see past the intimidating façade (not all of them could). When a Jewish kid needed a medical excuse to skip school for the Jewish holidays, Sanyi would make it a game.

The twelve-year-olds found it hilarious when he would look at them and wink. "What did we put down last year? We don't want anyone to catch on to us, do we?"

He was an incorrigible tease. When a woman came to his office and said, "My arm hurts when I raise it," he would inevitably give a *shtick* reply: "So don't raise it." Then he would be so attentive the patient would not only forgive him but repeat the joke as though it was the funniest thing she'd ever heard.

He remained close to his family, making the hour drive from Huszt to Begany almost every week. He'd traded his motorcycle for a little white Tatra. His mother rested easier, though he still drove like a wild man.

One weekend he was in a particular hurry because his mother, who had never been sick, had come down with pneumonia and was quite ill. He pushed the Tatra until it rebelled. A tire blew in a small village. Sanyi had just changed it when an enormous woman came panting toward him, screaming in Yiddish: "Doctor, God should keep you well, my daughter is giving birth and she needs help. It's been going on a long time."

He could never say no to a patient, even one he didn't know. He followed the woman to her house and found that her daughter was indeed suffering. It was said of Sanyi that he could coax a baby out of anyone, and eventually he did it this time, too, but it took some doing. He waited to make sure the mother and the baby were stable and turned to leave. When he reached the door he found the way blocked by the new baby's humongous grandmother, who grabbed his arm.

Had she known him well, she would have realized he was angry because he spoke to her curtly. "What's the problem?" he asked.

Again in Yiddish, she asked him, "Doctor, tell me please, why do I burp so loud?"

He looked at her coldly. "Because you are a big pig."

Later, the family doubted whether he had used that rude language. Even in anger Sanyi was usually polite. But those who had heard him swore those were the words he had used when he told his mother the story shortly after he arrived at her bedside. She was weak and burning with fever.

"Listen, *Mamuke* [he would always call her "Mommy"] to what happened to me," he told her in his lightest voice.

When he got to the punch line, Sally Salamon laughed as heartily as if she had been born a Salamon, not married one. It was taken as yet another sign of Sanyi's special powers that the next day her fever broke.

———

▪ In the 1930s in those small European cities people hadn't yet lost the ability to tell a good story. There were competing diversions; movies and radio had become more and more available, displacing local celebrities with distant ones. Still, gossips were in abundance, collecting information and rumor and dispensing it with the flair for innuendo that would later become the province of the professional journalist. Inevitably people in Huszt began to notice that Sanyi Salamon seemed to be spending more time with Anna Lazarovičs than with other young women. Huszt may have been cosmopolitan in some ways—the clothing people wore to promenade wouldn't have looked out of place in Prague or Berlin—but it was very provincial in others. The social strata were fixed and obvious, and within that structure a match between a doctor with a promising career and the daughter of a prominent Jewish businessman satisfied everyone (except perhaps the girls who would have liked to take Anna's place).

Anna, a tall, striking woman with flame red hair, was the middle daughter of Samuel Lazarovičs, one of the handful of well-to-do Jews in Huszt whose money came from lumber. He had become partners with Nathan Rapaport when he bought some timberland from a Rapaport relative. Mr. Lazarovičs was one of the local gentry who had been entertained on occasion by Nathan's daughter Szimi, the little math genius. She was often in his neighborhood playing with his niece Olga Mermelstein.

Even without the business connection of their fathers, Szimi would have become aware of the fact that Anna Lazarovičs was spending a lot of time with Dr. Salamon. There were no secrets in Huszt. When she heard the news the thought passed through Szimi's mind that Anna was a bit simple for the obviously intelligent doctor (to whom Szimi had actually spoken only one or two words but who, she confessed to her friend Olga, she liked a lot).

But his relationship with Anna wasn't a bruising disappointment. Szimi's infatuation was an experimental emotion, a way of indulging a fantasy life that had no more expectation attached to it than the crush she had on Clark Gable. Besides, by the time Sanyi and Anna were officially engaged she wasn't spending much time in that part of town anyway. Her friendship with Anna's cousin Olga had weakened after Olga was shipped off to boarding school in Vienna. Olga, possessed of "promising eyes," had upset her parents by flirting too much, studying too little, and then making matters worse by openly expressing her devotion to her handsome Hungarian tutor. Olga was gone only a year—she came back to Huszt after the Nazi *Anschluss*—but that year made a difference. She returned from Vienna wearing makeup and more obsessed with boys than ever. Szimi was developing into an intellectual snob, interested mainly in friends like Nadia, whose interests (study, travel) she considered more appropriate.

Sanyi's affair with Anna was lightly touched with scandal, enough juiciness to titillate the local gossips but not enough to offend anyone. This was the "scandal": Before Anna, Sanyi had been going with her cousin, whose family owned a fancy mineral water factory in Polany. They were serious enough for him to take her to Begany to meet his family and for her to introduce him to hers. She especially wanted him to meet her favorite cousin, Anna.

One day she finally arranged this meeting near the creek on the outskirts of Huszt where all the young people went swimming. There were many versions of exactly what happened, but the Salamon family remembered it like this: Anna melted when she saw her cousin's boyfriend and told her mother so. Mrs. Lazarovičs had what the Salamons referred to as "Polish intelligence." By that they meant she was shrewd, even devious. Suddenly she developed terrible headaches and began sending Anna to Dr. Salamon for medicine. Sometimes the headaches were so severe she asked Anna to bring the doctor home for a house call. Yet miraculously, by the time they got there, she had fallen into a deep sleep from which she couldn't be awakened until Anna had a chance to serve the doctor some tea and cake.

"We loved Anna," the Salamons would say, "even though she took away her favorite cousin's almost fiancé."

She was tall and slender and modest—nothing like her older sister Lilly, who modeled herself after the popular Hungarian actress Katalin

Karady, keeping her hair suspended in a huge whirling mass and plastering herself with thick makeup. Anna listened to Sanyi, who told her he liked to see her face as it was. It didn't hurt Anna's popularity with the Salamons that her father was one of the most prosperous men in Huszt, that she had flown to Romania in an airplane, and that she had all her clothes made at the best shops in Budapest. It was said that she had fifty pairs of shoes in her closet. They noticed that after he met Anna, Sanyi began wearing suits with the distinctive cut of expensive tailoring. There were no longer holes in the bottoms of his shoes.

Privately the Salamons admitted they were a little concerned about Anna's mother. When she came with her daughter to meet Sally Salamon, she said something they didn't like. "We are going to make for Sanyi five-centimeter slacks," a strange expression they interpreted as meaning that Sanyi could wear the pants in the family but they would be constricting. Anna would call the shots.

Sanyi slipped easily into those five-centimeter pants. He seemed content to accept his place in Huszt society as part of a promising young couple, respectful of tradition but thoroughly modern. Their wedding picture might have been taken in Prague or Paris or New York. The bride wore a flowing white silk dress, plain except for an exquisite spray of cloth flower petals clinging to the neckline. The groom matched her simple elegance in a dark suit, a crisp white shirt, and a white handkerchief in his pocket. Everyone agreed: They were stunning.

After the wedding they moved into Anna's grandmother's house, a few doors away from Anna's parents. Not long after that Anna went on a shopping trip to Budapest and returned with eight new suits for Sanyi, as well as appropriate shirts and shoes and socks. She had grown up accustomed to luxury and seemed happy to introduce it to her husband. A maid brought them breakfast in bed; they slept on red satin sheets.

Seven months later, on September 28, 1941, the Salamons understood why the wedding had been put together so hastily. Anna gave birth to a daughter they named Eva. Though it was duly noted that the baby was remarkably healthy for a premature delivery, the gossip was good natured. What could you expect, the ladies would say, from a handsome guy like that? The Hungarian Jews were obsessed with physical beauty, ascribing great powers of intelligence and character to those who possessed it.

Olga Mermelstein, Anna's cousin, found this exemplary couple a little boring. After she returned from boarding school in Vienna, she often visited Anna to play with the baby. Sanyi, her new cousin-in-law, seemed satisfied with so little. He and Anna rarely socialized. He moved his medical office next to his home. When he wasn't working, he was completely absorbed in the most mundane actions of his little daughter. As soon as Eva was big enough, he put her into the basket on his bicycle and took her with him on nearby house calls. To the disappointment of the girls still interested in a casual flirtation, Dr. Salamon was a happy homebody.

His practice prospered. He provided general medical care and con-

**My father and his first
bride, Anna Salamon**

tinued his surgical career as well, having maintained his relationship with the hospital in Beregszaz where he had done his training. The clientele for his bursitis shots grew, though it was suspected that some of the women who became regular visitors to the office simply wanted to spend a few minutes laughing at the doctor's bad jokes. By all accounts, he felt himself to be set for life.

There was only one flaw in this placid scenario, and it was a fatal one. The life Sanyi Salamon had chosen for himself was out of step with the times. If it was security he was looking for—and that certainly seems to have been his desire—he had picked the wrong time and the wrong place. He had set down roots in acid soil. Sanyi would learn, most cruelly, what all doting fathers learn: He had absolutely no power to protect his child from fate.

Yet the realization of this awful fact would still come as a shock, even though the European war was well under way when Eva was born. Despite everything they were hearing about what was happening to the Jews elsewhere in Europe, these events seemed remote from Huszt.

When the Hungarians reoccupied the Carpathian region, the war became less remote. The rights the Czechs had attached to Jews and other minorities were stripped off like old wallpaper. Still, the situation didn't seem terrifying. Every family had a pogrom story brought out for family gatherings along with the good china and silverware. Bad times had come and gone.

There was a general lack of appreciation for the progress in terror. The tales from beyond were dismissed as *bubemeinses,* old wives' tales. In this atmosphere it is possible that Sanyi was able to convince himself that everything might be fine. His young family was thriving despite the upheavals around them. When local Jewish men were being drafted into service in "work camps" Sanyi went, too, but only for a couple of weeks. After that he was released, though not for the reason he thought he would be—that he had been an officer in the Czech Army. But he was a doctor and he was too old, over thirty. The work camps seemed even less ominous because of his nephew, who started showing up in his home in Huszt on official "leaves" from one of them. They played cards, laughed at each other's bad jokes, and allowed themselves to subscribe to the theory of self-delusion that had become popular among the Carpathian Jews. They made themselves believe that a fluke of geography would save them. In the end, being neither here nor there—not quite Czech, not quite Ukrainian, not quite Hungarian— would be an advantage.

It wasn't an insane theory. The restrictions on the Jews in Huszt under the Hungarians remained manageable for a long time. Yes, Anna's father had to turn the supervision of his sawmills over to the Hungarians, but he was still able to bring in money with "unofficial" business. The police took radios from some Jewish homes and sealed others so they could receive only the official broadcast from Budapest (though everyone easily figured how to tune in to the BBC). People took comfort in rumors that Regent Horthy's wife had Jewish blood. Surely that offered some protection, if it was true.

By early 1944 miracles were starting to seem plausible. The news was good. Through Hungarian-language broadcasts on the BBC they heard the Hungarians had taken a terrible beating on the Russian front and the Russian army was closing in on the Carpathians. Encouraged by the Russian advance, the local partisans had become more aggressive. Everyone knew there was a great deal of guerrilla warfare going on in the mountains nearby. The weaker the Nazis and their allies, the more audacious the partisans.

Throughout the war Sanyi had never seemed inclined toward heroism. He kept to himself, occupied with his wife, his child, and his patients. He seemed willing to keep up the pretense that life was normal. Yet he would be remembered in Huszt as a war hero, despite his best efforts to sit out the war with his family.

The details of what happened that night are murky, but the story was remembered like this:

One evening, in early spring 1944, a stranger came to the Salamon house.

"We have a patient for you, a man with a broken leg," the man said. "Can you come?"

The man's method and manner made it obvious who "we" were. "We" were partisans. He also didn't have to explain the hidden meaning in that deceptively straightforward request for medical attention. He was asking Sanyi to commit treason against the Hungarian government.

It's said that Sanyi didn't hesitate, and that would be consistent with his later actions. He would always say "Never volunteer," and he never did. But he was known to be incapable of refusing medical attention to anyone who needed it.

He went into the woods with the partisan and found his patient. He was a Czech, described as the "technical commander" of the unit, most likely the radio expert. In any case he was a parachutist who had dropped into a tree. His leg was broken. Sanyi had been recommended as a good bone man by other doctors who had helped the partisans.

The setting of the leg went smoothly and Sanyi went home. The story might have ended there, but Sanyi, apparently, had been designated a friendly doctor. Over the next few months he was called on repeatedly to make surreptitious house calls in the hills.

The arrival of the foreign parachutists and the ensuing months of successful skirmishes led the partisans to premature celebration, a victory ball before they emerged from battle. Or perhaps they got drunk and noisy that night in March because they could no longer fight without getting drunk first.

The Carpathian partisans paid dearly for their cockiness. They were picked up by the Hungarian anti-espionage forces, vicious men who seemed to get a kick out of brutality just for the sport. They must have forgotten to listen to the BBC because they didn't seem to realize the end of the war was near—or maybe they were more pitiless because they knew their party was almost over. Their motives are irrelevant. The fact was, they wanted to hurt these partisans and they wanted to hurt everyone associated with them, including the doctors believed to be treating their wounds.

It was inevitable that someone would break under torture. The Hungarian special forces were notoriously cruel, and there was stiff competition for that special notoriety. This was, after all, the war that brought cruelty into the modern age—mechanized it and bureaucratized it. By the last year of the war the viciousness seemed to rise in proportion to desperation. As the Hungarians were torturing the Huszt partisans—kidney punches were a specialty—the Germans had begun to evacuate Huszt's Jewish civilians.

If logic hadn't become a lost art by then, it would have been an astonishing decision. The German Army was desperate for ammunition, clothing, and food. There weren't trains to spare, not a cattle car. But the need to sweep up every stray Jew in Europe had a particular urgency because it now appeared that the Final Solution was the only part of the Nazi plan that was working well. So while German soldiers went hungry, their commanders were paying top dollar for freight cars to ship out the Hungarian Jews.

It came at different times for everyone touched by the war, the moment when you looked up and realized you were staring at an eclipse of the sun. If you were lucky enough not to be blinded by horror or killed, your way of looking at the world would still be irrevocably altered. The most pleasurable light would forever be dimmed by fear.

For Sanyi it happened like this: Someone couldn't take the beating. That poor soul's confession was Sanyi's eclipse, the darkness that transformed him from an unassuming family doctor into a war criminal accused of high treason. One day, he was pedaling around Huszt with Eva in his bike basket; the next day, he was a prisoner in the jail at Szigetvár, where guards specialized in torture that left no marks. His travel through the criminal justice system was remarkably expeditious: top priority for traitors.

Within days he was transferred to Kassa for a trial, which ended as expected: He was sentenced to death by hanging and shipped to Budapest. Anna and her father had hired a lawyer to appeal the sentence, but the days of appeal were gone. Whatever influence in official circles the Lazarovičs family had once taken for granted no longer existed.

The word spread quickly through all of Huszt. Sanyi's sister, already herded into a ghetto in Beregszaz, heard that her brother had been tortured and then hanged by the Hungarians. She begged everyone not to tell her parents, also in the ghetto, what had happened to their darling Sanyi, and it is believed they never knew.

Hope seemed gone for him. Two other doctors from Huszt who'd helped the partisans had already been killed, one by firing squad, one by hanging. But Sanyi's death sentence was momentarily commuted by the fast approach of the Russian army and the concomitant push by the Germans to ship out the Carpathian Jews. Sanyi posed a dilemma: Kill him as a traitor, or kill him as a Jew? His captors were spared the conundrum. As the Germans marched into Huszt and ordered the establishment of the ghetto, all the political prisoners held in Kassa were transferred to Dachau. Sanyi left for Dachau thinking his wife and child were safe. Anna entered the ghetto believing her husband was about to be killed. Their worst fear—that they would never see each other again—was correct, though they both believed it was Sanyi who was doomed.

He never spoke about his months in Dachau, except to say he wasn't treated so badly because he was a doctor and was of some use to the Germans, who operated infirmaries inside the camps.

He would refer only to the final days, the part with a happy ending. He had learned his lesson in Huszt, he would say, not to trust fate—a lesson underscored by the year he spent in Dachau and Buchenwald. When the Germans began shipping out the concentration camp prisoners, he was prepared to risk everything to get away.

The Germans seemed determined not to leave the Jews behind to be liberated, yet security had grown lax. The High Command may have been intent on killing the Jews, but the men carrying out the orders were tired and hungry. Sanyi found it relatively easy—or so he implied—to jump off the train carrying him out of Dachau and to run into the woods with friends.

He spoke to his brother Louis's eldest son, another Pityu, of the terror he had felt hearing the dogs coming after him—the horrible weakness and finally the despair. Pityu, an ardent Sanyi admirer, couldn't believe what his uncle told him next: that he had sat down in the woods and told his friends to leave, that he was too weak to make it and he would drag them down. There was only one interpretation for this desperation, Pityu felt certain, and it wasn't the obvious one—that Sanyi was, after all, mortal. No, he must have known that Anna and Eva were gone. Otherwise he would not have asked to be left behind.

He wasn't left behind, however. His friends wouldn't allow him the easy way out, of dying and forgetting. They dragged him to the Czech border, where they eventually joined a partisan regiment. Sanyi never discussed what exactly he had done with the partisans, though it was believed he had acted as a medical officer.

He never confided in Szimi what had taken place in the woods. She knew only one thing about Sanyi and the partisans: They had given him the uniform he was wearing when she met him at the Red Cross station in Prague on May 10, and she had never seen anyone wear a uniform so well.

My half sister, Eva Salamon

11

The Accounting

■ It was a long walk to the boarding house room Mr. Krofta had arranged for Szimi—all the way across the Moldau River to the other side of Prague. Yet after a long afternoon of walking and talking and eating, Sanyi took her all the way home. She wasn't surprised, nor was she surprised when he told her to meet him again the next morning at the Red Cross station. She wasn't surprised by her intense physical desire for him, by the urge she felt to have him next to her. By the end of that afternoon the only thing that would have surprised her would have been separation from him. She didn't have a doubt about it: They would be together always.

Later she would say, a little impatiently, "It wasn't a time you can talk about, it was a time to live." It was impossible to explain the strange combination of exhilaration and deprivation she felt as it began to sink in. The life she had known no longer existed.

She had meant to grow up and leave Huszt to find her fortune. It just hadn't happened as she had planned. In her dreams there would always be a home to return to, a mother to write encouraging letters and to welcome her back if things didn't work out. Instead she felt like a shipwreck survivor, adrift in a city where thousands of people were, like her, trying to find a toehold somewhere. She sensed that she was part of a vast re-creation, that she was experiencing a new version of the Biblical story of Genesis, starting with Day One.

The next morning, as planned, she met Sanyi at the Red Cross station. He introduced her to Dr. Gross, a former classmate, who had already managed to establish himself with the Ministry of Social Work. Social work was the biggest industry in town. Every day more and more people made their way to Prague, mainly from Poland, Hungary, and Ukraine. They were heading somewhere else, to Palestine and America, but in the meantime they needed housing and clothing.

When Dr. Gross heard about Szimi's *Gymnasium* education and her grasp of languages, he urged her to get a job at the ministry. With the job would come an apartment.

Sanyi told her he had already found a good position for himself, as the staff doctor at the Boruvkovo Sanatorium, the hospital for members of the Czech government as well as foreign diplomats. His immediate superior, the man who had hired him, would be Oskar Klinger, personal physician to the Czech president, Edvard Beneš. Sanyi would have a room at the hospital, though he'd been assured that he could move into an apartment or a even a house as soon as he decided what he wanted to do. He had a double status as partisan and surgeon.

Szimi liked being part of this purposeful discussion. Only two days had passed since Szimi had backed away from Mr. Krofta's job offer, but it had been a substantial two days. She already felt herself to be established in Prague, ready to settle in. For the first time in more than a year, planning didn't feel dangerous or futile. Open-ended freedom no longer seemed so enticing. What she wanted now was to please Sanyi Salamon, and he seemed to think that it was a good idea for her to follow Dr. Gross's advice.

That afternoon Szimi went to see about the job at the Ministry of Social Work. She was immediately hired to supervise the distribution of clothing collected by Catholic charities. During her tour of her new workplace she regarded the piles of winter pajamas, dresses, coats, and slacks with the wonder she had once thought reserved for the Pyramids. Some of the clothes were new, some were secondhand, but the sheer volume gave her goose bumps. She felt the way she had in the storeroom at Zittau after the Germans left, giddy with the prospect of plenitude. The clothes on the top floors had been donated by Americans, she was told. Downstairs, however, the clothing was bounty taken from German homes after the war. The looting had come full circle.

The philosophical implications of where the clothes had come from didn't interest Szimi in the slightest—not then. While her new employer explained her duties as they walked through the rooms of clothes, Szimi was calculating what she needed. Her head filled with new wardrobes for herself and everyone she knew. Yes, this would be a fine job.

Not long after Szimi started working, Sanyi came to her.

"I'm going to Huszt and to Beregszaz to see what I can find," he told her. "Would you like to come?"

Over time he would stop being startled by the way Szimi's face could change. She usually seemed to be smiling, or about to, like a beloved child whose experiences had led her to face the world with agreeable expectations. Yet he would discover those rare occasions when her face would reflect her actual experience. Her features twisted into a mask of hatred as her lips pressed together, trying, it seemed, to contain unspeakable rage.

"There's nothing for me there," she said tersely. "I'll never forget them watching us as we walked up the street, like we were animals."

She said no more.

Her definitiveness would have seemed more natural coming from someone else. But Szimi didn't indulge in bitterness. Bitterness contradicted her vision of herself as the lucky one. Yet it was bubbling there at a slow simmer, now hot enough to scorch her natural impulse to collect what was hers.

She hadn't forgotten how she and her mother had packed up all their valuables, the candlesticks, the good bedclothes, Gyula's nice suits, the few pieces of silver—how little there had been, now she thought of it. They'd jammed it into a hole in an opening in the wall between the outhouse and the stable where they kept the buffalo. *Drink a glass of buffalo milk every day, and you'll never be sick.*

Her dowry. A ritual that now seemed far more remote to her than China had, when she and Nadia had been making their plans. How worried they had been about those possessions. That made her sick. How could she bring back those candlesticks? Every Friday night she would be reminded of those final days.

Maybe Hilu had gone home and would find the stuff, though he had no way of knowing where they'd hidden it. Did it matter? Money was a curse. She remembered how much trouble they'd taken to sew money into her mother's corset, and then how they'd torn the corset apart in terror on the train. She was angry at herself every time she thought about it—if she would allow herself to think about it—her insistence that her mother help her remove the money when the soldiers shouted at them. That breathless disemboweling of whalebone in the pitch black of the cattle car, the frenzied tossing out the window of bills, the hope that somebody needy would retrieve the money so it wouldn't go to waste. Terrorizing her mother needlessly, thinking that obeying orders would save her life.

What foolish optimists they had been from the beginning, she thought. Worrying about money and things as if they were going on a trip to a spa and leaving the house untended. They had been in a frenzy that last week before the ghetto, trying to look at their house the way a burglar might. She remembered clumsily rolling up the dollar bills they'd bought on the black market and stuffing them into the grate behind the chimney, trying to keep her sooty fingers from soiling her clothes.

That money was gone. She'd learned that from a Huszt man who had come to Prague with news a few days before. He told her that cousins of her father who had sat out the war in the woods had gone to Huszt as soon as the war was over. They'd settled in the Rapaport home—which had been abandoned by its Hungarian occupiers—and had begun doing business in denatured alcohol, a dangerous and illegal business. They had been careless as well as lawbreakers. One night when one of the cousins had been pouring alcohol from a jug into a bottle by candlelight, the moonshine had exploded. She had gone up in flames in the Rapaport pantry. Szimi assumed the money had gone with her.

She told Sanyi none of this. To him she said only, "If you see Hilu, tell him I'm here."

He promised he would and he left.

She wasn't worried that Sanyi would be lonely on his trip, because he had found a companion—Olga Mermelstein, Anna's cousin. It didn't occur to Szimi to be jealous of her friend Olga, known for her electrifying effect on men, even though Szimi believed the Mermelsteins would have liked to keep Sanyi in their family. Everyone knew that more than one Lazarovičs cousin had expressed interest in soothing their widowed cousin-in-law's grief.

Yet Szimi reacted to love no differently than to life. Once her plans were in place, she became certain of an inevitability that would make everything work out. This may or may not have been a psychological trick, but she thoroughly believed in it. Otherwise she wouldn't be so shocked when everything didn't work out. It helped that she gave a generous interpretation to the idea of things working out: much easier to find the happy ending when you are willing to reconstruct the story to fit it. Because she assumed she would spend eternity with Sanyi Salamon, she had no doubt that he shared the assumption. She arrived at this conclusion as swiftly and surely as she had used to multiply numbers—without bothering to understand the computational process.

She might have felt differently had she known that Olga Mermelstein was certain that Sanyi was in love with her. Or maybe not. No one took Olga's presumptions all that seriously. She was so accustomed to having men pursue her that she assumed all of them wanted to. So even when she swore that Sanyi had asked her to marry him on their trip to Huszt, no one who heard the story believed it. Why would she have said no? they wondered. Olga had a reply: "I couldn't marry him though he was a good-looking man. I thought of him as a cousin."

No one doubted that Olga believed her story. It was just that she had a special way of interpreting things. On the other hand, who knows what might have been said on a trip like that, a dangerous trip through territory that had already been annexed by the Russians? They traveled by train, by car, by foot to a city that was no longer theirs. Only three or four Jewish families remained. The Mermelsteins' stately home had become headquarters for the Russian command.

Together Sanyi and Olga faced the indisputable evidence that there was nothing to return to, that what they had been was history and what they were to become was unknown. Perhaps Olga understood Sanyi's lament for his lost wife and child as a plea to help him begin again.

Her story could be true and not true at the same time. Everything everyone said about Sanyi Salamon was always subject to interpretation. People tended to look into his eyes and see the reflection of their own desires and insecurities—though it was entirely possible that he was simply daydreaming when he stared off into space. It is also possible that Olga's memory was correct and that in a flash of passion he did ask her to marry him—even though this interpretation would remain unacceptable to the keepers of Sanyi's flame, who couldn't believe he would consider a flighty girl like Olga for a minute.

On that final trip to his past he made two stops—his boyhood home near Beregszaz and his married home in Huszt. Though Olga cynically thought he was scavenging for jewels left by his wife, it appears from his bounty that his search was more discerning than that. Sanyi wasn't like Szimi, ready to eradicate the past.

Little remained. He was able to fit the remaining evidence of his first thirty-six years on earth into a small satchel. He returned from Huszt with the following: his birth certificate and that of his daughter, Eva; the birth certificates of his brother Louis's two sons; his mother's wedding ring (hidden in the yard behind his parents' house); two photographs of little Eva and another photograph, of Anna and himself on their wedding day. He brought back a piece of marble embossed with pictures of his wife and daughter, and he brought back his medical diploma, which he found on a pile of rubbish behind his in-laws' house in Huszt, where Anna and Eva had moved after he was arrested. As Olga had suspected, he also collected Anna's diamond rings, though she was wrong about his plans for them. He saved them until he found a place for them, with Anna's sister, Lilly.

He seemed a haunted man as he went around town, trying to find out what had happened to friends and family. He spent an afternoon, for example, debriefing Pityu Klein, a seventeen-year-old boy whose father was another doctor in Huszt. After hiding in Vienna during the war, the Kleins had returned home. The boy had no information for Sanyi but went along to the Lazarovičses'. Pityu watched the doctor slowly patrol the house, scrutinizing wall spaces and corners that might have been agreed-upon hiding places. From the ceiling rafters he retrieved a piece of metal that, after a lengthy examination, he tossed onto the floor.

Pityu picked it up when Sanyi moved on. The boy was confused. Why had Dr. Salamon thrown away the medal of honor the partisans had given his wife after he'd been arrested?

Sanyi had only one question for Pityu Klein—the same question he asked everyone. It was the question he'd asked Szimi when they had first met back in Prague: "Do you know what happened to Anna and Eva?"

Perhaps he kept asking because no one was able to give him a satisfactory answer. No one could tell him directly, "Yes, I saw her taken on such and such a day." What he got was supposition. She must have been on the third transport because no one had seen her on the first or the second. She must have been sent to death immediately because she had a child in her arms.

How difficult it must have been for him, that ambiguous answer: *She must have been.* The repetition of the question indicates a persistent unwillingness to accept what seemed obvious to everyone else. Eventually, however, he had to settle for ambiguity. Eventually he must have realized the answer wasn't going to change no matter how many times he asked the question. After that trip he fell silent on the subject of Anna and Eva.

———

▪ I first found out about them when I was nine or ten or eleven. It was summer and our house had become, as it did almost every year, a summer camp for my New York cousins. We usually spent our days outside, at home or on the farm. During one of the summers of President Johnson's Great Society we all enrolled in the government-sponsored physical fitness program. Unaccustomed to this mingling of my separate lives, I was relieved to see that my Seaman friends and New York cousins played together effortlessly.

But one day, maybe it was raining, we—the cousins—were lounging in the spare room that was attached to my father's office. I loved that room, piled with papers and books, furnished only with an old desk and a pull-out couch upholstered with scratchy green fabric. I would spend hours there, absently rubbing my bare legs on the couch's rough material, relieving the itch of mosquito bites, while I read the piles of books I'd drag home from the bookmobile that visited town once every six weeks. That back room also had access to the attic and its treasures. It was in the attic I found the only diary my mother ever kept. It was blank except for one entry, which I remember vividly: "Today Julie said, 'I hate you Mommy.' Why does she say things like that?"

That day we cousins were discussing what had happened to our family during World War II with a touch of the horrified excitement of children exchanging ghost stories at Halloween. Someone said Erzsika, my father's niece, had lost a baby during the war. So did Uncle Béla, said someone else, adding, for dramatic effect, "and his hair went from red to white overnight." I went for tragic irony, telling the story of how my Uncle Gyula had survived the camps but had died when the Allies upset his stomach with fatty food. I got the response I wanted, a series of exclamations from my worldly cousins: "Gross!" "Idiots!"

It was perversely pleasurable, adding up the casualties—or it was until my cousin Marsha made an additional entry. "And there was Uncle Sanyi's wife and baby . . ."

"That's not true," I snapped at Marsha, feeling utterly betrayed. Why would she, of all people, make up such a hideous lie? Marsha, the older daughter of my father's niece Aliska, was my idol. Slightly older than I, she was adorable in every way. No one, in my view, was prettier than Marsha, or sweeter, or more fun, and she had the astonishing ability to stay skinny even though she could easily eat three or four sugar crullers at a sitting.

I could see from the shock on her face, more than from anything she said, that she was telling the truth and that she assumed it was something I already knew.

I ran from the room to find my sister, Suzy.

"Did you know about this?" I asked her.

She confessed that she had and had planned to tell me someday, when the time seemed right. Later she told me that she had found out from an old newspaper clipping in the attic when she was eleven or twelve. She had taken the newspaper to our mother.

"What's this about?" she had asked. "They made a mistake."

"No," said our mother. "They didn't make a mistake. Daddy was married before, and he had a daughter."

"What was her name?" Suzy asked.

When she heard the little girl's name was Eva, her middle name, Suzy was shocked.

"Is that who I'm named for?"

Szimi looked at her dispassionately. "I guess so."

This matter-of-factness would become familiar to Suzy. Later, when she asked her mother how babies are made, Szimi kept flipping through the mail while she answered.

"Oh, you know, a man sticks his pee-pee in a woman's pee-pee and they have a baby."

Neither of us mentioned the revelations of that day to each other for a very long time. But until my father died both my sister and I were haunted by this unnamed presence. Suzy would find Daddy sitting in the living room, hunched over a hassock where he spread out his newspapers and magazines. Whenever he stopped reading and stared out the window, she was sure she knew what was distracting him.

"He's thinking about them," she thought. "He'd rather be with them. He's thinking about his daughter."

Many years later, after my sister had become a doctor and was married with two children and living in Boston, I noticed she had on display in her study an old photograph of a wide-eyed little girl.

"Who's that?" I asked her. "Mommy?"

She told me the child was our half sister, Eva. I nodded but didn't ask her where she'd gotten the picture or what had triggered the decision to frame it and put it out. My reticence came not from a lack of curiosity but from something else, some mixture of terrible sadness for that lost child—and competitiveness. For so many years I, too, had wondered how big a place she occupied in my father's heart (perhaps, how much of *my* place), and now here she was again, staring at me from my sister's desk.

———

▪ I had always thought of Huszt as my mother's city, not my father's, and now I understood why we knew so little about the time he had spent there. But during my travels with my mother and Arthur, the story I brought away from Huszt was my father's more than my mother's.

We arrived there hot and cranky after being held up at the Ukrainian border for four hours. My mother was determined not to spend the night in Ukraine—and not to spend any money there. She exchanged a total of three U.S. dollars to cover our day's expenses (a sum that turned out to be more than enough; our restaurant meal for four came to two dollars and change).

The countryside was beautiful, especially after Slovakia, which was littered with the architectural detritus of the Communist era. It seemed that no stretch of landscape could be looked at without the ruinous spectacle of an ugly box building. Western Ukraine was unspoiled by anyone's idea of progress; the broad, rolling hills looked much as they must have when my parents were young. Field workers still labored with their hands, helped mainly by horses and carts; only an occasional small tractor appeared to remind us that time had, indeed, passed.

As we approached Huszt, my mother began scanning the scenery for landmarks and could identify none. I could see she was unnerved, and her spirits weren't helped when a policeman stopped us for speeding just as we were about to enter town. She leaned forward from the back seat and explained that she was an American returning home. The policeman, a young man with pink cheeks, seemed to forget why he had stopped us in the first place and offered detailed directions to the center of Huszt. Once inside this small city, we saw a reemergence of the grandly drab architecture we'd been subjected to in Slovakia.

"What's wrong?" I asked my mother, who was visibly upset.

"I don't know where we are," she said. "Nothing looks familiar."

We began looking for someone who could tell us where the synagogue was. No one seemed to know what we were talking about. Finally, in what seemed like the center of town, we found a group of young men who seemed to know what we were looking for. We followed where they pointed and found ourselves in an older part of the city near an open-air market. There we found the synagogue where my mother's family had prayed and an old peasant woman who told us she was Jewish. The door was locked. The old woman agreed to take us to the synagogue caretaker, climbed into our car, and promptly lost her way. Our search party widened as a friendly high school teacher picked up the trail for us on his bicycle and two pretty little blond girls helped us to the man's house. I photographed them all and collected a pageful of addresses written in Cyrillic lettering.

Over the next few hours my mother found fragments of her Huszt, which had been swallowed up by the new Huszt after the war. Her family's house had been torn down and replaced by a shoe factory. The movie theater she had visited so regularly had been razed; its owner had committed suicide after the war. Even when she found the alley that had once contained the heart of Jewish Huszt—the *mikvah,* the butcher, the bakeries—she felt no real recognition. Everything was different.

This sense of alienation continued until we stumbled onto her high school, an airy building that had been brand new when she was a student there in the late 1930s (and was much newer than my high school in Seaman). My mother's return home really began at that moment. From the school she readily found the street that used to lead her home. It was a narrow cobblestone street lined with flat-looking one-story stucco buildings with tile roofs. My mother told us these were very nice homes, though it was hard to tell because they opened onto interior courtyards invisible from the street.

As we walked up the street, the synagogue caretaker, who had come along with us, mentioned that one of the town's few remaining Jews, Mrs. Klein, lived in one of the houses. At that moment an old lady's head emerged from the window. With her bright white hair pulled into a delicate bun and her old-fashioned black clothing, she might have been a character in a children's fairy tale. She was at least ninety, with an intelligent face that still had gracious lines, though her chin was stubbled.

Back home in Huszt, my mother finds friends she hasn't seen for fifty years, Mrs. Klein and her son, Pityu.

"Mrs. Klein?" my mother asked her in Hungarian.

It took the old woman only an instant.

"Szimi?" she said, as though five years, not fifty, had passed since they'd last seen each other. A minute later another face appeared in the window, a man with big dark eyes, chipmunk cheeks, and graying hair. It was Pityu, Mrs. Klein's son, a lawyer who was a year or two younger than my mother.

Minutes later we were inside their home, the same place Mrs. Klein had lived with her husband, Dr. Klein, who had died in the 1960s. Now she and her son, Pityu, lived there with his wife, a Russian woman who remained in the kitchen while we were there—except for a brief appearance to serve us coffee.

Their apartment was immediately familiar to me; I'd sat in a variation of that apartment dozens of time as a child, listening to my parents speak Hungarian to friends and relatives in Israel, Europe, New York, and South America. The high-ceilinged living room was crowded with books and cut glass and other "fine" things—all of which had had to be replaced after the war because her things had been stolen while she was exiled in Vienna, Mrs. Klein explained. We were served coffee in delicate demitasse cups, and a precious box of chocolate was unearthed from a cupboard. I sat on the couch doing what I've always done in similar situations, smiling demurely while trying to fill in the blanks between the few Hungarian words I understood. *"Szép lány,"* Mrs. Klein said periodically, smiling at me, "Nice girl." I didn't know it, but Pityu Klein was recounting the day my father had come back to Huszt after the war and taken Pityu with him to find what he could.

———

■ A year after we returned and I was deep into the writing of this account, my mother presented me with a package, a manila envelope on which someone had scrawled IMPORTANT.

"What's this?" I asked.

"I thought it might help you," she said. "Daddy kept this in a cardboard box in the drug room." (Our house was divided from my father's office by a small room containing the medications he dispensed to his patients.)

"What's in it?" I asked.

"I'm not sure," she said. "His papers and things."

We were having this discussion in the large messy room in Old Saybrook that my mother uses as a catchall: The washing machine and dryer are there, an ironing board, bookshelves and books, a spare refrigerator, bottles of soda, cans of tennis balls, piles of clothing bought on sale (the markdown tags still dangling from the sleeves), old photographs, a couch, fold-up chairs, and a table. In the middle of this clutter I began pulling out the contents of the envelope. There were papers—many yellowing documents written in Czech, Hungarian, and Russian. But what took my breath away were the "things." Leaning on a pile of dirty sheets, I found myself face to face with a sober little girl in a pretty playsuit.

"That's Eva," my mother said, telling me what I already knew.

I didn't have to ask about the next photograph. My father's wedding picture, and the bride wasn't my mother.

Some time later I asked my mother, "Didn't you ever look in that envelope? Weren't you curious?"

She looked at me as if I were speaking a foreign language. "That was Daddy's," she said. "Why would I look?"

———

■ The envelope yielded valuable documentation: letters, medical school records, tiny scribbled notes my father had written to himself, birth certificates, passports. But I needed more information about my father. Tibor Mermelstein, brother of my mother's childhood friend Olga, visited me in my home with a friend of his from Huszt. I found myself mimicking my mother as I prepared for the interview—buying rye bread and whitefish, slicing peppers and tomatoes—laying out the kind of food I thought would make them feel at home, even though both of them had lived in the United States most of their lives by then. I called Olga in São Paulo, finding on the other end of the phone a shrewd, tough Hungarian who remembered my father's trip back to Huszt very vividly. From other relatives and family friends I culled bits and pieces, finding myself easily transported back, even during an interview with my father's nephew Miki on the terrace of his condo overlooking a tropical golf course at Boca Raton.

From them I could only conclude that my father, on returning to Huszt, had been sickened by the brutal pruning of his family tree. What were the Salamon sins? Exuberant reproduction? Too many bad jokes? It would have been better for him to rage at this fate, but he didn't know how. The anger stayed inside him like a dangerous chemical whose corrosive effects were erratic and largely unknown.

He had other business. He wouldn't return to Prague until he had accounted for as many relatives as he could. It was a dismal accounting. His wife and child—gone. His three sisters and their husbands—all gone. His parents—gone. Nephews, nieces—too many of them gone. His brother Béla—missing somewhere in Russia; he had been one of the Jews who had been forced to march ahead of the Germans to detonate land mines, then was accused of being an enemy collaborator by the Russians.

There was some happiness. He found his nephew Miki, who had already managed to make some money by playing the market in fluctuating exchange rates at the border. He heard of others who were thought to be alive; a few plus signs on the ledger.

He met Szimi's brother Hilu and urged him to come to Prague to see his sister.

"I will come eventually," said Hilu, "but I'm waiting for my brother, Gyula, to show up. We'll come together."

A new life begins. My parents get married, August 20, 1946.

12

Born Again

For a woman smitten with love, Szimi was complacent about Sanyi's ten-day absence. Her new job absorbed her; she discovered she thrived on a sense of purpose after so many years in flux.

She liked sorting the clothes into piles, recording what there was, setting aside a few nice things to take home every day. But that was only part of her job. She never adapted to the other component of her new life as a social worker. Three times a week she traveled by trolley to the suburbs where the Jewish Relief Agency had set up camps for refugees en route to Palestine and America. She was to find out what they needed and then arrange to have the food and clothing delivered.

After a week she made her first trip to one of the camps. By then, dressed in new clothes, she was the tidy young bureaucrat, confident and self-important. The earth had shifted, and she had landed on her feet. The new world was here, and she was part of it. The days of Auschwitz, her days of nothingness, were gone.

She was shocked by what she saw at the camp and more shocked by what she felt. The ragged travelers, most of them from Poland, Hungary, and Ukraine, seemed dirty to her—"loathsome" was the word that came to mind, she was ashamed to admit. She wanted to go back to the city, to isolate herself from these people.

Leave me alone! she wanted to scream.

Instead, she showed her identification to the fat Czech guard who met her at the entrance.

"I want to ask you something," he asked her. His breathing was heavy. She felt a chill. Did he think she belonged inside, with them? Even before his question sank in, she could hear that his tone was neutral. "What are they doing over there?"

She looked. Some religious men were swaying back and forth, chanting in Hebrew. "They're *davin*ing," she said coolly. "Praying."

He nodded, his curiosity satisfied. No big deal—to him. She felt humiliated. Was he associating her with them, those *shtetl* Jews from Poland?

Her own thoughts disgusted her. She knew if these poor people were Christians she might still condescend to them, but she would pity them, too. Her reaction was part of her heritage as a bourgeois Jew in liberal Czechoslovakia. The Jews there felt equal, yet they also felt the equality was an illusion. Christians were one degree superior by birth, so it was imperative for Jews to be two degrees better, at least. Jews who failed to do so were sluggards, a drag on the prosperity of the whole race. The "modern" Jews looked at the "backward" Jews as *dreck,* garbage, remnants of an unpleasant past, blocks to the future.

As Szimi surveyed the transient Jews wearing rags, her revulsion was far more profound than the old snobbism. Ragamuffin men wailed their prayers, and the women—they seemed so weary—shuffled around in sackcloth dresses. Watching them, she realized how she must have looked to the Nazis, a lower form of humanity—Jewish scum. Little stood between her and these refugees, only a bath and a set of new clothes.

Yet no matter how often she returned—and she went to the camps three times a week—she couldn't bring herself to talk to any of them, to find out where they had come from or where they were going. She did her job efficiently and impersonally, collected the information and left. She was always happy to get back to the office, to the pretense that she was just another young career gal starting out on her own in the big city.

By all appearances, that's exactly what she was. As Dr. Gross had promised, Szimi's new job came with an apartment. Within a few days she moved into 4 Štrossmajer Street, an attractive Art Nouveau building that had been completed just before the war. She moved into an airy one-bedroom apartment, with a maid's room, on the second floor.

Soon, Štrossmajer 4 became a magnet for everyone she knew from Huszt. First her old friend Olga Mermelstein showed up. Within days Olga's two brothers, Otto and Tibor, and their father arrived. Szimi was especially glad to see the man she called "Uncle Shamu," an "elderly" man of fifty-two. She felt a special kinship with Mr. Mermelstein, remembering the wonderful high school graduation trip to Budapest she'd taken with him and Olga and her brother Gyula. Once, when Gyula had been sick, Mr. Mermelstein had dispatched his chauffeur to take Gyula to the hospital. Szimi suspected he had hoped Olga might find Gyula attractive, but it had never happened.

Friends of friends found their way to Štrossmajer 4 carrying empty suitcases that Szimi would fill with clothing and sheets she brought home from work. In this haphazard way they re-created the Huszt bourgeoisie. Everyone who came to Štrossmajer 4 left well dressed.

The war seemed far away, though it was hard to close the books with so many people unaccounted for. In the expectation that Hilu and Gyula would soon arrive, Szimi set aside suits she thought they would like. They would be so proud of her, she was sure, having everything ready for them. She asked everyone who came from Huszt if they knew anything about her brothers. No one had seen them. Szimi didn't mind: "No news is good news," she would say.

Maybe it was just as well that she wasn't home when a man came to Štrossmajer 4 looking for her. He left behind a small blue photo album and a message with one of the Mermelstein boys.

He was from Huszt, a friend of her brother Gyula's. He came with news that validated Szimi's theory: *No news is good news.*

"Gyula should have been here with me now," the man had said. He'd been taken to Mauthausen not long after Huszt had been cleared of Jews. He hadn't shriveled to bones. He hadn't become a *Mussulman,* one of the walking dead. Just the opposite: When the Americans had liberated the camp—just a few weeks before—his appetite had been intact. He had gone with enthusiasm at the fatty pork stew the ignorant, well-meaning soldiers had served the inmates. After the meal he and his friend had got hold of a map so they could plan their journey home. As Gyula studied the route, he had keeled over. A heart attack, the friend assumed, or maybe food poisoning. The liberators accidentally killed many survivors by feeding them food they couldn't digest. Gyula was thirty-four years old.

The man from Huszt said there had been too many bodies to hope for a proper burial. He had done what he could, had prayed for Gyula as his body was dumped into a mass grave with all the other Mauthausen corpses. The friend had searched Gyula's pockets before he was taken away, and there he had found the photo album.

When Szimi heard the story that evening, she didn't seem to react. She may have been in shock. She had been so certain that Gyula was alive. Without comment she took the album to her room and shut the door. She went through it page by page, studying the pictures. There were Hilu and Rozsi and their mother. Mostly there were pictures of her, wearing her gray dress with the lace collar. They were the photos she'd had taken by the professional photographer on her graduation trip to Budapest. Coquettish in this one. Serious in that one. She smiled at how good she had looked in those pictures, never better.

Then she began to cry, big heaving sobs, with a giving in to grief she hadn't allowed herself until then. It was the happiness in the pictures that did it. She had kept adjusting to new circumstances, never looking back. Now "back" was in front of her face, in this wallet-sized portfolio of pictures.

How was this possible? She had been certain that Gyula would return. This album directly contradicted her unwavering faith in one principle: *Everything will turn out all right.*

She interpreted her devastation as anger. Yet her anger wasn't directed at the evil Nazis or the unthinking Americans. She was furious at fate for failing to reward her for her faith in the silver lining.

It hadn't been easy, not even for someone with her special vision. Yet she had persevered. When her mother had died, she had managed to twist logic and say, "She was actually quite lucky. It would have been too awful for her to endure Auschwitz." Her poor father hadn't been quite so lucky. He hadn't been killed right away, she'd learned recently, but had worked in a mine for six weeks before he'd collapsed. Yet, she thought, he couldn't have stood it to live without Mother. He was too old to be alone. As for the rest, she simply hadn't thought about them.

But Gyula's death stumped her. Not even Szimi could find a rationale for his death. Gyula was closest to her, the kind brother who had protected her from her jealous sisters and always encouraged her to fulfill her promise (which, he implied, was extraordinary). Gyula, she had been sure, was like her, touched by magic. How could he be dead? Until now she had refused to accept disillusionment. For the first time in her life she believed what the tired old women in Huszt used to say: "Life is like a baby's shirt, short and shitty."

Gyula's death confirmed what she secretly knew but had been unwilling to accept. The Szimi Rapaport smiling at the photographer in Budapest no longer existed. The past was sealed.

When had she last cried? At first she couldn't remember, it must have been so long ago. Then she recalled it wasn't long ago at all, a little more than a year. Those tears had been shed for Gyula as well, when she had thought her effort to get him out of jail had failed. She bitterly remembered how triumphant she'd felt when those tears had convinced the *tábornok* to let Gyula go. She remembered packing a suitcase for Gyula as the ghetto in Huszt was forming, and his message: "I can do more good here than there." She'd slipped the album in with his clothes at the last minute, afraid that she wouldn't be able to save her precious pictures in the ghetto and certain that Gyula would protect them for her. There was no consolation in knowing that she had been right.

———

▪ After Sanyi returned from Huszt, he and Szimi began seeing each other every day. His schedule at the Boruvkovo Sanitorium was hardly strenuous—a few checkups, an occasional surgery, plenty of free time. The war was not a subject of conversation. After that first meeting at

The courtship. Boating on the Moldau River.

the Red Cross station they referred to it obliquely, as a marker for other experience rather than experience itself.

It was as if they'd made a pact. They were now something else, not fragments of historic fallout, not "Holocaust survivors," but a happy couple in love starting a new life together. They spent lazy afternoons boating on the Moldau River and walked all over the city, which Sanyi had come to know quite well during his years at medical school. Their travels expanded when Szimi enrolled in the medical school at Charles University and acquired a student pass. She rarely went to classes and never took an exam, but she kept up her registration so she could ride buses and trolleys free anywhere in Prague.

They told each other stories from their past, deleting the most painful parts. Some of the gaps were understandable, others were not. Easy to see why Sanyi chose not to discuss his lost wife and child with his new lover. Not so easy to understand why he never mentioned to Szimi that he had once loved to play the violin.

Szimi never probed Sanyi's secrets. She was intimidated by him— not by his profession and his age but by his sensitivity. She understood that despite his imposing size and demeanor he was delicate in a way she was not. He was a poet, she was a pragmatist.

Yet she also felt they were the same in some fundamental way, absurdists who chose to see life as a silly joke, not a bitter one. She constantly found proof for this proposition, even in the way she interpreted Sanyi's choice of anecdotal material. She could see in his telling of Salamon family lore that he shared her weakness for amusing parables about human foibles as well as sentimental movies with improbably happy endings. She loved, for example, a story he told about his brother Louis, who had been sent to live with an aunt for a while to help ease the family's financial burden (Salamon children were always being shipped off to one relative or another). The first night he was there his aunt had served carrots for dinner. Louis detested carrots but hadn't wanted to be rude. His parents would have killed him if he had been sent home. So he had eaten the carrots right away, figuring the rest of the meal would drown out the taste.

"Ah, you like carrots?" his aunt had said.

"They were delicious," Louis had muttered.

She laughed with Sanyi as he told her how the aunt had refilled Louis's plate over and over. Not wanting to hurt anyone's feelings, Louis had had no choice but to clean his plate every time. The only thing he had eaten that night was carrots.

In the romantic version of the Prague years, the only version that ever went on record, Szimi and Sanyi found they were a perfect match. He confessed to her that he had noticed her in Huszt. Actually, he told her, he had noticed her backside. She had been dressed for skiing, bundled up like a snowman, and he remembered thinking as she marched up the town's main street, "How could such a little girl have such a big *tuchas?*"

He shared her ability to carry fond memories from persecution. One day he asked her if she could cook a *delicious* dish he'd been served by the Hungarians when he was in jail: sauteed potatoes, onions, and egg noodles. The best thing I ever ate, he told her. How then could she resist telling him about the wonderful stinky cheese she'd eaten in Auschwitz that no one else seemed to appreciate! They would spend years together exclaiming over the tastiness of the most mediocre food. They complained only if the soup wasn't hot and the portions weren't large.

They began sleeping together almost immediately. Their sex life was very much like the rest of their relationship—passionate yet strangely remote. They were shy with each other, never looking at each other naked, never talking about what happened between them when the lights went out. Szimi would remain elliptical about that part of their life except to say, "In the darkness it was a different story." When pressed, she would giggle and offer an oblique explanation.

"I remember many years later a friend of mine called me up and told me about this amazing article she'd read in the *Reader's Digest* about foreplay. Did I know about it?

"When she explained, I said, 'Of course I know about it.' Then I felt sorry for her because for the first time I realized not everyone knew what Sanyi did."

That was that.

Szimi felt no need to confide in anyone about the pleasurable hours she spent with Sanyi in his room at the Boruvkovo Sanitorium. It may have been a new world, but she still felt constricted by the rules of propriety that operated in Huszt. She didn't want the Mermelsteins or her other friends to know she was sleeping with someone she hadn't yet married. The "yet" was always present in her thoughts, even though the subject had never come up.

How could marriage not be inevitable? One by one Salamon relatives began showing up at Štrossmajer 4, directed by Sanyi, who never stayed there himself. She had plenty of room; in September she had acquired a second apartment in the building. How that came about also became part of the sunny version of how-it-was-after-the-war.

Szimi had been living at Štrossmajer 4 with the Mermelsteins. She was the only one working, so she made an agreement with her roommates. She would bring home food and clothing; they had to keep the apartment clean. One day she urged the Mermelstein boys to be especially vigilant with their chores. She was bringing home a friend from work.

That evening when she arrived home, she found seventeen-year-old

Tibor chasing thirteen-year-old Otto with a wet mop. The living room floor was flooded with dirty water.

She exploded. *"Asta kutya faia neked mindaynate!"* This Hungarian phrase roughly translates as "Doggonnit," but Szimi gave it the force of a sailor's epithet.

The next day she spoke to her boss at the Ministry of Social Work and got another apartment, on the top floor of Štrossmajer 4. The word got out quickly. Her friend Baszi moved in immediately with her sister, Zeldi, and brother, Jossi. Her brother Hilu finally comprehended that Gyula wasn't coming home, and he moved to Prague. Then came the Salamons, one after the other, dispatched by Sanyi, who had nowhere else to put them. Though they were all the same age, more or less, young people in their twenties and thirties, Szimi was clearly the leader—not just the income producer but the organizer and the arbiter of disputes.

She became the master of the fast answer. No sweating the details for her. She filled the vacuum the others found themselves wandering through. At a time of uncertainty she provided a North Star. This is it, she would say with absolute certainty, and everyone would assume that "it" must be so.

Just when it seemed that every corner of the apartment was full, another relative or friend, more flotsam, would float in. None of the new arrivals was more poignant than Baba, Sanyi's fourteen-year-old niece, deposited at Štrossmajer 4 one day by a relative whose response to finding the young girl at *her* door had been "My God, what do I do with you?"

This relative had tracked down Sanyi at the Boruvkovo Sanitorium, and he had given her the usual instruction. "Take her to Štrossmajer 4."

They stood at the door, a grown woman and a tall girl.

"What do you want?" asked a friend of Baszi, another "temporary" guest.

"We're looking for Miki Hermel," said the woman. "Sanyi Salamon sent us."

Without saying a word Baszi's friend slammed the door in their faces. A minute later the door opened.

"Baba!" Miki yelled, and hugged his cousin and brought her inside.

Before he could introduce her to the roomful of strangers, the relative who had brought her was in the elevator, gone.

The chaos didn't seem to affect the young girl much. She had learned to numb herself to far worse. Everyone was dead: her mother, her father, her brother. She should be dead, too, but they had thought she was older than thirteen when she had arrived at Auschwitz because she was so tall. For a year she'd worked in the building next to a crematorium, sorting the contents of confiscated suitcases into piles. Her ability to make herself numb had come in handy when she had forced herself to swallow the food she found hidden in the suitcases while smelling the death from next door.

In midwinter she had been taken from Auschwitz to Buchenwald in an open railroad car, exposed to cold and terror as bombs exploded around them en route. From there she had been herded to Dachau, then herded onward again, this time on foot, through the snow. Her feet and fingers had turned brown with cold. She had forgotten all that when they arrived at Bergen-Belsen. There she had seen mountains of corpses, felt swarms of lice. She had retreated further into numbness. When the English had arrived to liberate the camp, she had got diarrhea from eating rice and pork. Then she had erupted in boils.

Baba could endure this noisy bunch while she waited for Uncle Sanyi, her mother's favorite brother.

First she would meet her uncle's girlfriend, who was at work when she arrived at Štrossmajer 4. Not much of a meeting. When Szimi walked in the door that evening and was introduced to her latest houseguest, she didn't say a word. She just stared at this young girl— a child, really—with her clearly Salamon characteristics: wide face, high cheekbones, thick unruly hair. A pretty girl but a mess, a gangly teenager dressed in a *shmatta*, an old rag, her feet lost in man-sized sandals.

Baba wanted to become invisible. She thought she knew what the stare meant. Everyone seemed to have the same reaction to her since she had returned from camp: "What the hell is this?"

Szimi had merely been caught off guard. She hadn't had much experience with young girls. She had always been the youngest in the family, and Rozsi's daughter had been just a baby when they had left for Palestine. The little Mermelstein boy had lived with her, of course, but his father and sister and brother had taken care of him. Baba stymied her. She didn't know what to tell her.

She would, of course, come to a decision about what Baba needed. When she came home from work the next day, she handed Baba a navy blue skirt, an all-cotton white blouse, and a red sleeveless pullover sweater. "There," she said. "Now you'll be fine." For Szimi, that was that.

Baba couldn't argue the point. Compared to where she'd been, she was fine. But she wasn't finding a new life for herself the way the others were. There wasn't a corner for her in that apartment. All day long people were playing cards, making jokes she didn't understand. Some nights so many people slept there she felt as though she were back in camp, crowded into a bunker with strangers. Some of the people who came by were downright unpleasant, like the family from Huszt who stayed long enough to infest the place with bugs.

Everyone was nice to her. Baszi taught her to cook; at night the "boys" would tease her and offer her glasses of the awful beer they brought in big pitchers from the pub up the street. Sometimes she spent the afternoon at the Mermelstein apartment downstairs, where she and thirteen-year-old Otto taught each other how to kiss.

Szimi, who wasn't home all day, insisted that Baba was "fine," but Sanyi began investigating schools for his niece, a nice boarding school, perhaps, where she could be with children her own age, where someone would know what to do with her. The only thing he could find was a school run by nuns. He couldn't do it. Baba had already suffered because she was a Jew. He wouldn't risk having her suffer anymore, not even girlish taunts. So she remained at Štrossmajer 4.

They would all eat together—eight, ten, twelve people. Baszi did most of the cooking and got better at it as time went on. These survivors had moved on. They didn't bow their heads in thanks at having plenty to eat. They gleefully mocked Baszi's amateur *knedle*—the Czech dumplings supposed to be big and fluffy, so delicate they could be cut with a thread. Hers were rock hard. They complained about the lack of good meat in Prague that summer and fall.

They knew their luck had changed for sure when Béla, Sanyi's brother, showed up. If Béla, for whom nothing came easily, had made it through—that's what they called survival—then they could risk being optimistic. Surely it was safe now to look ahead.

No one could tell by looking at them that all of them had "made it through." Photographs show well-dressed, good-looking young adults only slightly serious, like people who hadn't been photographed much, just like most people in those days. They would remember the Prague period as a lark, peppered with the manageable risks and thrills of a happy adventure. Reconstructing themselves *was* a lark after the horror show they'd experienced.

The population at Štrossmajer 4 kept rising and falling, regulated mainly by Szimi's tolerance for her whimsical houseguests. She kicked Baszi's brother, Jossi, out after the police stopped by one time too many to investigate the Carpathian black marketeers he brought into the house. Szimi wasn't above a little black-market trading of the cigarettes her American relatives sent her. But anyone stupid enough to attract the attention of the police didn't belong in her house.

Her own brother Hilu was arrested on the street one day, for un-

The group at Štrossmajer 4. *Standing, from left:* Hilu, Kic Sanyi, Pityu, Miki; *seated:* Béla, Szimi, Baba, Erzsi, Sanyi. They were invincible, or so they felt.

specified charges. As he was carried off to jail he screamed, "I'm a survivor, you bastards. You can't do this to me after I've been in concentration camp." Szimi bailed him out, and they both promptly forgot about it. None of them took anything that happened in Prague seriously in those days. They were invincible, or so they felt.

———

■ When the group at Štrossmajer 4 surmised that something "was cooking" between Szimi and Sanyi, as they slyly put it, their relationship became suspect. Why, it was wondered, did they use the formal *maga* when they spoke, not *te*? In Hungarian, grammar reflects emotional commitment: Intimates never say "you," *maga*, they say "thou," *te*.

There were two trains of thought. One saw the linguistic peculiarity as a sign of deeper problems: There must be a wall between lovers who called each other *maga*.

Others, however, took this refusal to use the familiar form as a sign of hauteur. Before the war, at least, socially prominent people distinguished themselves from the masses by addressing each other formally, even in private. Maybe Sanyi and Szimi thought they were better than everybody else.

Szimi knew people talked about it. Yet she couldn't imagine using *te* with Sanyi. She used the familiar *te* with everyone she knew. It was too casual, too ordinary.

Instead they called one another *zolotik*, a Ukrainian-Czech mixture that means "little golden one." Sanyi used it first, almost immediately. Then one day Szimi tried it out on him and saw that he liked it.

She was always careful to make sure that he liked what she did, because he had a way of retreating inside himself that terrified her. When he was upset, he vanished. His body might still be there, but his face would become a stone-cold mask, as if he knew the only way he could control himself was to reveal nothing.

One evening in the fall of 1945 Baszi and the man she was dating were going dancing at a nightclub. When Miki heard about it, he asked Szimi if she'd like to go; Sanyi was on call at the sanitorium that night. Sure, she said, love to dance. Miki was older than she was, but he was Sanyi's nephew, almost hers.

They had so much fun they almost missed the last trolley home. Szimi ran out of the nightclub ahead of them and saw the trolley coming. She was yelling at them to hurry when she saw the headlights of a car. She woke up the next morning in the hospital with a concussion. Sanyi was there. *"Zolotik,"* he said when she came to. But she could sense his fury, which she interpreted as concern for her. Later, Miki told her he had been terrified to call his uncle because he was well aware of another Salamon characteristic: They were wildly jealous. That would become the way Szimi's accident was remembered: as the time Sanyi got angry. No one could pinpoint words, not even a raised voice, but it was always agreed that Sanyi didn't like Szimi to go anywhere without him. Szimi would come to learn this about Sanyi the way she found out almost everything, obliquely, through hints and signs and portents.

Of course, another explanation for Sanyi's response is possible. He hadn't been able to give Szimi the good time she'd wanted. She went to the movies three, four times a week because she couldn't resist. He always refused to go, telling her he couldn't do it yet, not until he was out of mourning, a length of time he had determined internally, by a formula that ran not, according to tradition, from the moment of death—he didn't know that—but from the moment he had *acknowledged* the death. The deaths.

Because they never discussed it, Szimi wouldn't know what, exactly, the nature of the anger was that he felt when he found her in the hospital after her night of dancing. Was it jealousy, as everyone agreed, or fear of yet another loss? Who knows? The age of introspection hadn't yet arrived.

On one subject Szimi became uncharacteristically direct.

"When are we going to get married?" she asked Sanyi repeatedly in the spring of 1946.

"How can we get married?" he responded. "There's no place for us to live. Your apartment is loaded with people, and we can't live at the sanitorium."

"Why don't you get an apartment?" Szimi asked. "I don't understand."

"Yes, you do," he said curtly.

Actually, she didn't. What was he thinking? At Štrossmajer 4 there wasn't a free centimeter of space, and she knew very well that Sanyi could have had an apartment through his connections at the sanitorium. He could have more than an apartment if he was willing to exploit his war record the way everyone else was doing. He was a bona fide war hero, with papers to prove it. He had already been offered his choice of homes, the finest villas.

He always said no.

"Tell me again," Szimi would order him, bewildered by his refusal to take what was offered him. "Why shouldn't you have it?"

Over and over he repeated his answer: "I want to be free to leave this place. If I get too comfortable, I may not want to go."

The answer didn't quite satisfy Szimi. She didn't question Sanyi's fears. She understood he was receiving privileged information about the political situation from a good source, Dr. Klinger, the president's physician. Sanyi himself tended the diplomats and government officials who used the hospital. She knew he heard things. Everyone understood that the Russians, happily ensconced at the Alcron Hotel, were most likely not temporary visitors. Mr. Krofta himself had told Szimi on her first day in Prague not to return to Huszt because the Russians would be there.

She understood Sanyi's unwillingness to settle in, but she didn't understand why he couldn't accept something temporarily. She had become so accustomed to living in the moment that it wouldn't occur to her to equate comfort with permanence. She had survived, but her sentimentality had not. She didn't long for a home the way Sanyi did, so she didn't fear losing one.

His demands were minimal but nonnegotiable. Yet she wasn't angry at him, because he seemed so eager to please her. He brought her flowers often and, after he declared himself out of mourning, he took her wherever she wanted to go.

One evening he told her enthusiastically about the convention a group of American doctors was holding at a beautiful resort in the Tatra Mountains. He was invited and she could come along.

When he told her the news, Szimi's response shocked them both. She slapped him in the face, just like the insulted ingenue in a movie.

"How could you make me so angry?" she asked him.

"Why are you angry?" he asked her, laughing.

"What do you think, taking me along like some kind of prostitute, *zolotik?*" She put a mocking edge on their nickname. "If you want me to go to the Tatras, it's time to get married."

"Okay," he said. "We'll get married."

It was as simple as that, or so she would remember, because they agreed it would be that simple. In Huszt, the entire community would have been invited to a wedding to establish the latest link in a chain of history. Sanyi had had that wedding. The chain was broken, the link was gone. What purpose would be served by a big wedding with so many significant chairs left unfilled?

The arrangements were made. Most important among them, Sanyi finally used his connections to get an apartment—for his relatives, so they could leave Szimi's place. Szimi's friends, Baszi and Zeldi, agreed to move in with the Salamon relatives.

They would marry in the *Alt-Neu* (old-new) synagogue in the old Jewish quarter, with the group from Štrossmajer 4 in attendance—everyone but the Mermelsteins. Szimi insulted them by not mentioning the wedding until after it was over. Olga's father, especially, couldn't understand why she had snubbed him after all his kindness to her.

He didn't know she was angry at Olga. Not because she thought Sanyi had proposed marriage to Olga. All she knew was what Sanyi had told her—that Olga had been trying to steer him toward Anna's sister.

The wedding would go down in family history as a bit of slapstick comedy—starting with the slap-induced proposal. Sanyi had performed surgery the morning of the ceremony. When his nephew Miki came to pick him up at the hospital on August 20, 1946, he was still wearing his surgical scrubs. While Miki waited, Sanyi quickly pulled off his pants and started to put his jacket on over the same white shirt he'd been wearing.

"Is that how you're going to your wedding?" Miki scolded him.

Sanyi obediently changed shirts and they raced across town to the synagogue. Just as the ceremony was about to begin, Sanyi reached into his shirt pocket to give the ring to Miki, his best man. There was no ring. Then he remembered: He'd put it in the pocket of the shirt he'd been wearing early in the morning to make sure he didn't forget it. The two of them hailed a taxi and retrieved the ring.

Later, when Szimi had grown comfortable with the feeling of Sanyi's mother's ring on her finger, she would laugh at her cockamamie wedding. That was Sanyi. Absentminded about everything but medicine. Head in the clouds.

They spent their honeymoon at the medical convention in Spišská Nová Ves, a resort town in the Tatras—warm days, cool nights, purifying air. They hiked; they rowed on the clear waters of the giant lake there.

Yet later, when Szimi closed her eyes and revisited the scene of her honeymoon, she had only the briefest sensation of brisk wind and sun. Instead she remembered one of the medical meetings she had sat through with Sanyi, a slide presentation of a new technology in childbirth. The American doctor explained how a spinal anesthetic would allow a mother to watch the delivery of her baby without feeling pain. Szimi couldn't take her eyes off the slides, graphic photographs of an actual birth. It was a little frightening, trying to make the connection between this clinical view of procreation and the sweet, mysterious things that went on between her and Sanyi in the night. She felt as though she were seeing the human body for the first time.

An extraordinary moment, proving again that Szimi Rapaport was a marvelous specimen of self-preservation. She had willed herself into a state of grace, into believing that she was just another naïve girl capable of being slightly shocked and titillated by the warm vulgarity of adult life. She was innocent again, unable to remember stripping for Mengele, the mass showers.

Uncle Louis (lower right) reunited with his children, in America after the war. He hadn't seen them for more than twenty years. Szimi is standing, with her arms around Rozsi.

13

America

■ Sanyi continued to search for what remained of his family. Through the Red Cross, he found another niece, Aliska, as they called Aliz, Louis's youngest child and only daughter. She hadn't yet been born when her father had left for America, an eternity before. Poor Aliska, Szimi would say, she was not lucky, and Szimi didn't know the half of it.

Aliska and her brothers had grown up waiting. Though they lived with their mother's father, who was wealthy, their mother never wanted to buy anything for them or for herself because they would be leaving soon. "We don't need that," she'd say. "We're going to the United States."

For years the family collaborated on this narrative, the story of how Louis would be sending them affidavits soon. They would live in America for a few years and then come home to visit, wearing clothes like they saw in the movies. The children heard that Louis had rectified the terrible thing he had done to their grandfather and knew he sometimes sent them money, all of which enhanced the story's plausibility. The affidavits would soon be on their way.

After ten years, or maybe it was fifteen, Malvin, their mother, discouraged them from continuing what she had come to believe was fiction. The story line had become too painful for her. She mentioned their father less and less frequently, leaving it to Louis's relatives to maintain his memory for his children, which they did, during the summers they spent on Grandfather Salamon's farm.

Yet she didn't separate from the Salamons. She was a guest at Sanyi and Anna's wedding and encouraged her children to love their father's family. When Sanyi brought her a copy of *Anna Karenina* from Prague, she treated the book like a holy object.

Over the years the children began to accept this phantom father as a storybook character who had nothing to do with them. They felt curious about him, but not resentful—not until 1942, when the Hungarians, trying ever more inventively to figure out ways to weed out the Jews, began to examine the citizenship of residents of Podkarpatská Rus more rigorously. In a deadly game of political musical chairs, the Hungarians ordered the Carpathian people to produce proof that they belonged in the place where their families might have lived for generations. Those who hadn't collected the right papers as governments had come and gone lost their seats. They were shipped off to "the border," the place where stateless people could be shot because they fell under no government's protection. That was the theory, and that was the practice.

Louis began to loom large in the family's consciousness, in a way he never had, the day the gendarmes took Malvin Salamon and two of her three children to Budapest. There, in a detention center, they found Louis's ghost hovering, up to no good.

"You are no longer citizens," an official explained. "When the head of a household leaves the country for more than ten years, he and his family automatically lose citizenship. Your husband is an American citizen. Go to the United States."

It was a double curse from Louis: Not only had he been unable to fulfill his obligation to his family, but he had made them aliens in their own country. They didn't know then that it was a triple curse: Louis had never become a U.S. citizen and never would.

Once again Louis was saved by his father-in-law, in these last days of grace when money still counted—even if it was Jewish money. Malvin's father sold some property to bribe the appropriate officials. His daughter and grandchildren were released. Back at home they became legal residents again but were aware their status was tenuous. They had to register at the mayor's office every week.

It was a brief respite. A year later, in the spring of 1944, not even Malvin's father could save them. They were uprooted with everyone else—the boys sent to work camp, the rest to Auschwitz. Malvin's father was killed immediately.

Whatever bitterness Malvin may have felt for Louis was transformed into tenderness for her children. She nurtured their sensitivity, tuning them into beauty and suffering to perhaps an unhealthy degree. Malvin was closest to Aliska, the child born after Louis left for America. It was Aliska who accompanied Malvin to Auschwitz, where they stayed for six months. They sorted the clothes and belongings confiscated from new arrivals—not knowing that Baba, their cousin and niece, was doing the same thing in another building.

In October, as the Germans began dispersing the Auschwitz prisoners, they were transferred to Bergen-Belsen, taken at night to maximize the terror. Before they were marched onto the trains they lined up for yet another *Appell*. Aliska and her mother stood close together to make sure they wouldn't be separated, only to find the cutoff point for the first cattle car came right between them.

It's useless to try to imagine what went through their minds that night as they rode to an unknown destination, unable to find air to breathe in the densely packed wagon, yet entirely alone. Aliska, who had learned at Auschwitz to move beyond despair to the grace of obliviousness, now found herself fully conscious of her surroundings. Without the protection of her mother's comforting presence, she saw her grim fate clearly.

The train pulled into Bergen-Belsen right next to a crematorium. The newcomers heard their welcome committee screaming in the dark.

Aliska hung back while the others were marched ahead to the barracks, hoping she would find her mother.

Nothing. Finally she followed the crowd. Two hours later, still listlessly stumbling in the night, she literally bumped into her mother. For a moment they had one of those life-affirming experiences survivors would grasp at, a small spark of light to contradict the overwhelming blackness. They cried and vowed never to be separated again, caught up for an instant in sweet denial of their inability to keep that vow.

They stayed in Bergen-Belsen for six weeks. Then it was time to move again. There were rumors that the Germans were panicking, on the run and taking their slave labor—evidence of their crimes—along with them. But the rumors, even if they were true, brought no elation as the women traveled from one work camp to another, always by night and always in stinking, crowded wagons. In one town they cleaned bomb debris off the streets, in another—always thinner, always weaker—they shoveled snow. A month before the end, in yet another town, they were sent six hundred meters underground to work in a salt mine. They thought their systems were inured to shock by then, but the pressured salty air introduced new pain.

Malvin's body rebelled. For days she suffered from diarrhea until she couldn't face work. On her second day in the barracks the block commander sent her to the infirmary.

When Aliska went to visit that night, she was told no visitors were allowed, but when she said who she was coming to visit, the nurse didn't hesitate.

"Go in," she said.

When Aliska saw her mother, she understood the urgency she thought she'd heard in the nurse's voice. In a day's time her mother had shriveled, or maybe in her weakness she had lost her power to make her daughter see her as she had been before.

Aliska left, promising to bring a comb the next day. There was no next day, however, not for her mother. Then Aliska was on the road again, now by herself. Two days here, two days there, never knowing where she was and not caring. The doors would open and they would be hustled out, to do some job or simply to wait to be loaded into the wagons again.

It was May when the doors opened to a new greeting. No *"Raus!"*—Out! Instead, "Hitler is dead!" Clean wagons with red crosses painted on the side arrived and carried them to clean straw beds, blankets, and tables laden with food—though the Red Cross workers instructed them not to eat too much. Aliska obeyed but stuffed some potatoes down the front of her dress, not believing there would be more later.

Having accustomed herself to misery, she didn't adapt easily to comfort. Traveling by boat from Denmark to Sweden, whose King Gustav had opened the doors to refugees, she dutifully voiced her appreciation of small luxuries—eating dinner with proper place settings on tables covered with cloth, tasting grapefruit for the first time. She expressed her thanks for the new dress and underwear she was given on arrival and for the high heels that she could barely walk on.

During the six weeks she spent in "quarantine" on a farm just outside of Landskrona, she was physically revived by food and sleep. But internal life had vanished for her. She welcomed sleep even though it was torture, filled with dreams of her dead mother. Yet those tormented reunions were better than nothing, which was what she had when she was awake. During her few waking hours she paced the yard, wobbling on the new shoes she'd been given, the only shoes she had.

One of the Danish refugees who spoke German and Swedish told her someone wanted to meet her. A local woman, a woman in her forties, about the same age as Aliska's mother, had been stopping by the camp every day on her way home from work at a nearby sugar factory. The refugees had become a tourist attraction, the most interesting thing to pass through this small town since the circus. Her name was Liza Hagman, and she had no children. She had become captivated by the skinny, pretty girl she always saw, silently patrolling the yard on high heels.

They met through a translator and found a meeting of needs that quickly developed into affection. Liza brought gifts—first sandwiches and cookies, then sandals. Unable to speak the same language, they built the most powerful kind of intimacy, based on loving assumptions and implications.

On Mother's Day Liza took Aliska to her home, to meet her husband, Oswald, and his ten brothers and sisters and their families. It was a modest, comfortable house. Liza and Oswald were not wealthy; he worked in a shipyard, she worked in the sugar factory. Yet when Aliska walked into the living room she was overwhelmed. Not by the abundance of food, though the spread of cookies and cakes and delicacies she didn't recognize was almost beyond her comprehension, but by the presence of all those Hagmans, who struck her as incomparably warm and loving. She wasn't overcome because she had never experienced anything like that, but for the opposite reason, because she had. She ate nothing.

After that, Liza and Oswald began to visit Aliska every day. At the end of six weeks, when the Red Cross was about to move Aliska to another town, the Hagmans urged her to stay with them. They would adopt her.

Aliska, however, wanted to find her brothers. She left for a town called Raftele. Despite letters and calls from the Hagmans, she continued to wait for news from her family—an act of faith since she didn't have her father's address in America and didn't know where the rest were or if they were still alive. Finally a telegram arrived from her Uncle Sanyi in Prague, who had located her through the Red Cross.

"Don't go home," he wrote to her. "[Your brothers] Sanyi and Pityu are in Prague and will be going to America as soon as they can, and will send for you."

Aliska didn't hesitate. She called Liza and Oswald. She would stay with them while she waited—if they still wanted her.

They wanted her very badly. For two years she lived with them. She learned Swedish and went to work in a clothing factory, where she earned more money than she could spend. Her mother was dead, her father still hadn't claimed her. She had no difficulty calling Liza and Oswald, as they wished, "Mama" and "Papa."

———

▪ After their marriage, Szimi began to share Sanyi's urgent desire to leave, only because she realized he wouldn't be happy until they did. They weren't quite alone at Štrossmajer 4; Baba and Hilu had stayed with them in the apartment. Sanyi didn't like to eat there. Most nights

Szimi continued to meet him for dinner at the Boruvkovo Sanitorium; he would come to the apartment only to sleep.

She wrote to her sister Rozsi: "Sanyi can't wait to get out of here. He has a great job and earns about 40,000 crowns a month. He could earn a lot more but the problem is he's not money hungry. Neither am I, nor stingy. I just want a good, comfortable life."

Though she applied for visas to both America and Palestine, as Sanyi wanted, she would have been happy to stay in Prague. She was oblivious to the precariousness of the political situation, too caught up in the magic of this city that had been physically untouched by the war, its architecture of many ages still intact. With its Renaissance castles and Gothic cathedrals, Prague was to her a fairy-tale land, the perfect setting for someone with her appreciation of superstition and folklore.

Her demands for happiness were small. "I'm always happy again and again about my apartment, when I come home and it's nice and warm," she wrote her sister. "And I can write that I got everything on my own, which I am proud of."

She had everything she needed and more. Meat was scarce, but vegetables had been coming into the marketplace in abundance that summer. Szimi always played all the angles, including figuring out who to charm. Not long after she had become a regular at the Boruvkovo Sanitorium dining room, for example, the housekeeper there began sending her home with delicacies like good cheese and salami.

There was cultural nourishment as well. On the day Sanyi decided his mourning period was over, they began to go out every night—to the movies, the opera, the theater. They found something else they had in common—a willingness to weep at fiction without the inhibition they felt about weeping at life. "We are very good together, we love each other, and I think that's the most important thing," Szimi wrote her sister.

Sanyi began to prepare for their departure, collecting his academic records from the *Gymnasium* in Beregszaz and from Charles University, which provided him with a list of every course he had taken and when he had completed it. He tracked down the man who had been chairman of the hospital in Beregszaz where he had done his residency and received confirmation of his six years of training and the "highest recommendation" that he be recognized as a surgical specialist.

He also collected a glowing recommendation from Dr. Klinger, who said that he had not only proved himself an "excellent doctor," especially in surgery and gynecology, but that he was also "professional and humane." While at the Boruvkovo Sanitorium, Dr. Klinger wrote, Dr. Salamon had delivered eight hundred babies, including "serious cases that demanded surgery. . . . To the patients he showed compassion, to his co-workers he behaved as a real colleague, and to his subordinates he was always correct and tactful."

Among the many official documents he put into his file, he included a notarized letter from the Russian Embassy, confirming that he had been an active partisan from the spring of 1944.

Then they waited.

Szimi and Sanyi agreed their preference was Palestine. "I hope the Jews will still achieve something," Szimi wrote to Rozsi. "When all is said and done, there's been enough submissiveness and resignation. For once we have to have a country." In that same letter she urged her sister not to sound so downhearted. "You have to enjoy the day because you can never know what tomorrow brings. If we have survived all that happened, there's no reason in the world to be sad."

Taking her own platitude to heart—*you can never know what tomorrow brings*—Szimi had taken steps toward America as well as Palestine. Almost a year before, she'd gotten her Uncle Matyi Weiss's address from Rozsi and written a letter of introduction.

Now he was called Marty Weiss. The youngest of her mother's eight brothers and sisters, he had left for America in 1924 and had not been heard from since. He was generally believed to have been successful, mainly because sometime in the 1930s his wife, Anna, a tall busty woman with a face like Marlene Dietrich's, had visited her family in Satu-Mare wearing very fine clothes and holding her chin in the air. In fact, Marty had been foundering. After he arrived in New York he worked as a truck driver, bricklayer, and construction worker and hadn't made money at any of it. But he always expected to do well. As soon as he could he bought a car, drove to Florida, and vowed to return there when he could afford a swimming pool and his own palm trees. He confessed to making this vow years later, sitting under a coconut tree by the swimming pool he owned, overlooking Biscayne Bay in Miami Beach.

When he returned from Florida the first time, he got construction work on the Empire State Building, which was just going up. He would point at the building with the pride of authorship, always thinking big. That job brought him enough money to send for Anna. When his brother Herman, a Talmudic scholar working as a chef in the Catskills, laid eyes on her, he asked Marty, "Why did you do this? She won't work. She'll just boss you around and take your money."

Herman wasn't completely correct. Anna did work. She and Marty were hired as a "couple." He was the chauffeur, she was the cook. The problem was, she didn't know how to cook. Her mother had had high aspirations for her. She hadn't taught her girls to cook, she had sent them to a Catholic girls' school that trained young women in business.

Finally Anna said, "This stinks." That's how she talked, like a gangster's moll with a Hungarian accent. So Marty went to school to learn how to fix radios. They began to pick up old radios at junkyards and repaired them for resale, then moved into refrigerators and other appliances.

You see, Szimi would say, the silver lining. Hitler may have destroyed the family, but at least he was good for Marty Weiss. When the war came, no one manufactured new appliances anymore. Marty's fix-it skills were in great demand, and so were his used goods. There was surplus cash: Marty invested in real estate, Anna in Treasury bonds. In 1940 Marty Weiss was forty years old and nearly a pauper. Five years later he was well on the way to becoming a millionaire, already in semi-retirement, spending as much time playing chess and smoking cigars with his friend Willie Schwartz as he spent at Jamaica Refrigeration, his new appliance company.

He and Anna had no children. For the longest time they couldn't afford it. There were slip-ups; she would talk of "getting scraped." Then it was too late or they'd gotten too obsessed with other things—him playing chess, her minding the business, keeping track of the pennies, even after they were no longer hard earned. Marty returned to Florida, as he had said he would. He and Anna bought their mansion on the bay in Miami Beach, with its walled-in garden with coconut palms and orange trees and a swimming pool. Anna began dressing in the outlandish spangles that were then fashionable among the newly well-to-do, insisting on "the finest things" but always buying on sale. She never learned to cook. They hired Hungarian women to make Marty's favorite foods, and on the cook's night off they ate at the Polly Davis Cafeteria, plain food at very reasonable prices.

Though Anna usually handled the correspondence, Marty answered his niece's letter himself. He sent a check for a hundred dollars, instructions on how to apply for a visa, and assurances: Don't worry, we'll take care of the affidavit, we'll vouch for your economic well-being. From that moment on, Szimi regarded Marty Weiss in the way that few people did, as a generous man.

Every so often Aunt Anna sent a package of cigarettes and chocolate. Those were the cigarettes Szimi traded on the black market; Hilu took the chocolate, hiding it for private, greedy consumption. They followed Marty's instructions and applied for visas to America as well as Palestine. Sanyi had his affidavit from his brother Louis, who, ironically, had never become an American citizen.

By the time Szimi and Sanyi married, she had been waiting for clearance from both countries for more than a year. By then, despite Sanyi's earlier insistence on Palestine, she and Sanyi were agreed that they would go to the country that sent them the first visa. Szimi pointed out that there were similar advantages and disadvantages. Both of them had family in Palestine and America, neither of them spoke either Hebrew or English. Let fate decide.

So when their visas cleared for America, two months after they married, they chalked it up to destiny. Luckily, destiny had some earthly connections. Their boat tickets came not from God or fate or any of the providential beings Szimi thought were at her command. It was Uncle Marty (whose fortunes had turned just in time to save them, Szimi would insist) who arranged for Sanyi, Szimi, and Hilu, to sail in January from Sweden.

———

■ The corny movies Szimi had seen about the immigrant experience had led her—falsely—to expect her own crossing to America to be a series of joyous epiphanies. She wasn't prepared for the actual experience—a vulgar comedy featuring her brother Hilu gorging on rich food until he made himself sick.

She didn't know what to make of this brother. He had little of Gyula's charm or kindness. Sometimes she thought he might be *really meshugge,* and then she would erase the thought. "Poor Hilu," she would say, "he can't help it that he is how he is."

Prague had been woozy with love after the war. The survivors, especially, had seemed intent on pairing up, as though eager to start replacing the dead.

But Hilu remained alone. Few women met his high standards, and the ones that did couldn't be bothered with a crank.

Baszi came to him with a proposition. She had a friend, a young woman named Mary, who needed papers to get out. It was unclear whether money was exchanged or not, but Hilu agreed. There were ugly rumors—that he took the marriage more seriously than Mary did and wanted her to behave, as they coyly put it, "like a wife." Whatever did or didn't happen between them, her relatives in America sent her a ticket six weeks before Hilu's did and she left, carrying the rings Sanyi had brought back from Huszt in a tube of toothpaste. Hilu saw her only once after that, when, months later, he went to see her in Philadelphia to pick up the rings and to deliver her divorce papers. Szimi was certain he had cursed her. She died six months later, twenty-three years old, from a blood clot that formed after an appendectomy.

But all this was before him when he set out with Szimi and Sanyi on their second honeymoon. They spent five days in Paris, then took the train for Göteborg, Sweden, where they would board their ship, the *Drottningholm.*

When Sanyi wrote to Aliska that he and Szimi would be leaving for America from Sweden, she arranged to travel to Göteborg to meet them. Her adopted "grandfather" was curious and decided to come with her to meet her relatives.

He was a man of modest means, but he chose a fine restaurant for them to pass their few hours together. When Szimi, Sanyi, and Hilu reached the restaurant he had chosen they realized how meager their Prague bounty had been. It wasn't the fine silver and china that impressed them but the quantities of food. Before they sat down to give their order, Aliska's "grandfather" showed them the *smörgåsbord* of appetizers, proud as if he'd prepared it himself. They stopped eating long enough only to tell the waiter what they wanted. No meat shortage here. They ordered duck and chicken, mouths watering, but by the time the food came they were so stuffed with herring and gravlax and bread they could barely take a bite. Szimi didn't know which hurt more—leaving slabs of duck on her plate or watching Sanyi insist on picking up the bill.

They left with aching bellies and lumps in their throats, surfeited by emotion and food, carrying messages from Aliska to the father she'd never seen. "Tell him I can't wait to see him," she said. Not a word of reproach.

After she left and they'd settled into a hotel, Hilu, Szimi, and Sanyi went walking to see the sights.

Hilu saw only chocolate. To him it seemed as though there were chocolate everywhere, as if everything he'd been denied for five years had been turned into chocolate and shipped to Göteborg. No more self-denial after scorning those without self-control. He'd been at Mauthausen, too, at the same time as his brother Gyula, and had never known it. But when the Americans had come with their fatty meat, Hilu hadn't touched it. Idiots, he had thought. My stomach's too weak for that. He had eaten only bread and rice and had been strong enough to drag a cousin stricken with dysentery to the medics for help. He later regretted this act of charity because he didn't think the cousin had showed appropriate appreciation.

No more abstinence for Hilu. He stopped in every store, swallowing hunks of chocolate as if it were bread and he had come direct from Mauthausen, not two years of eating well in Prague.

"Enough!" Szimi barked at him, always snappish with Hilu, who inspired snappishness. "We're going on the ship. You'll be sick."

Hilu threw her own words back at her. "You never know what tomorrow brings," he said. "Leave me alone."

The *Drottningholm* was a rebuilt liner, one of the first to carry private passengers after the war. It wasn't a huge ship—14,000 tons, a nice size, not luxurious but many steps up from steerage. The cabins were tiny but adequate—two bunk beds and a little bathroom, not an inch wasted. Sanyi and Szimi had one cabin, Hilu shared another with a stranger.

Szimi and Sanyi took stock for an instant before dropping their things and hurrying up on deck. They didn't want to miss any of it. They were fascinated by every detail—the sea smells, gulls squawking, the elaborate mechanics of the crew preparing for leave-taking.

Suddenly Szimi realized Hilu wasn't with them and the ship was about to leave. She grabbed Sanyi's arm in panic. "Where's Hilu?" She had the sensation that he was on shore and they were leaving him behind. Her fault, she thought, for not having patience with him.

Then Hilu was at her elbow, panting, pulling her arm.

"Come downstairs!" he said urgently.

Szimi's concern immediately converted to annoyance. "Why go downstairs? Where were you? Why don't you watch what's going on? When do you think you'll see something like this again?"

Hilu looked at her with pity. "You think this is something? Come downstairs. See what I've found. In the dining room they're giving away delicious cookies and cakes with tea."

Szimi said, "I'm not really hungry."

She saw his disappointment and felt guilty for brushing him off. That's what their relationship had become, a cycle of scorn and guilt, each resenting the other's stubbornness and not understanding how they could come from the same family, then feeling remorse because they were, after all, brother and sister.

"It's fine," said Sanyi, who was always kind to Hilu, who repaid him with unabashed worship. He might complain about Szimi, but never about Sanyi. Sanyi was his idol, tall, good looking, a doctor—and he had all that hair. At thirty Hilu was already going bald.

They went below to the dining room, but the tea service was over. Hilu grinned at Szimi a little crazily, feeling some strange triumph at showing his sister she should listen to him. If she had come right away, she and Sanyi could have the same rich buttery taste in their mouths that he did. Szimi could see an entry being made in Hilu's registry of insults.

Szimi and Sanyi were lying on their bunks when there was an insistent knock.

"This is terrible," said Hilu as Sanyi opened the door. "I went to see about dinner, and we can't make the first seating. We're in the second seating, and I saw the table we have. They put us with seven big Swedes. Huge! They'll eat up everything on the table!"

Sanyi calmed him down—Remember the *smörgåsbord*, plenty to eat for everyone—and told him they'd pick him up for dinner.

When they came by, he called out that he'd meet them later. Oh, did they eat well that night! No matter how much they ate, even the big Swedes, there was more. *Delicious!* Sanyi and Szimi pronounced it, over and over.

Szimi ate until she realized she felt dizzy. The ship was rolling wildly. She ran to their cabin and made it just in time to throw up everything she'd eaten. A relief. After that she was fine, even though the ship didn't stop rolling for the entire week of the voyage.

Hilu, however, didn't budge from his cabin. By the second day he begged them to get him some whiskey, the only thing that would settle his stomach, he was sure.

"It's a dollar a shot," Szimi replied unsympathetically. They didn't have a spare dollar.

The second day Szimi began talking to a Slovak woman on deck and told her about Hilu.

"Don't buy their liquor," the woman said. "I have a bottle you can have."

For five days Hilu stayed in his room, drinking whiskey and throwing up. He refused to leave. Sanyi urged him to go up on deck, the fresh air might revive him.

"Go away," Hilu said.

On the sixth day Hilu's cabinmate begged Sanyi and Szimi to do something. The stench was killing him.

Sanyi came to Hilu again, this time using the unyielding tone he'd discovered few people seemed willing to rebut.

"You have to get up," Sanyi told him.

Hilu nodded, no argument left in him. Sanyi gently guided him into the bathroom and washed him. He got him into clean clothes and onto the deck.

For a while he did seem revived. Then the tea cart came, and Hilu tried a cup. Minutes later he was by the side of the ship, head out to sea. He glared at his sister and brother-in-law and disappeared once more. He didn't emerge from his room again until they reached New York.

Weirdly, Hilu's misery added to Szimi's enjoyment of the trip. Not that she was happy to see him suffer (maybe just a little, to see him punished for his gluttony). But his sickness gave her a chance to see just how tender Sanyi could be, so kind to her difficult brother. More and more she felt he was something apart, her conviction fed by the observation that Sanyi was one of the only people on the ship who didn't get sick, not in the roughest seas.

They spent most of the week wrapped in coats and blankets on the deck chairs, unable to take in enough of the salty air—which they also pronounced delicious, no matter how cold it was. They were never short on conversation, each finding great fascination with the minute details of the moment: how the ship worked, what they had for dinner. Sometimes they talked about the future, eagerly anticipating the abundance they would find in America. Szimi felt comforted by Sanyi's enthusiasm. He would no longer feel compelled to hold himself back. He wouldn't mind being gripped by the tentacles of prosperity.

The closer they got to New York, the more certain she felt that she hadn't been unduly optimistic in the letter she had written to Rozsi: "I just want a good comfortable life, and he will certainly be able to offer me that at any time."

My sister, Suzanne Eva Salamon, with our mother

14

The False Spring

■ They arrived on January 27, 1947. Szimi was sweating. She was sweating because she was wearing two coats, thick woolen stockings, and a warm dress, layered, just the way she had been when she went to Auschwitz. Big difference, though: It had been May then, and the layers had been for expediency, to get around the one-suitcase rule, to pull a fast one on the Germans by turning herself into an extra suitcase. Now it was the dead of winter, and she simply didn't want to be cold.

Instead she was hot. For a minute she thought she was burning with excitement. Then she realized it was seventy-five degrees outside, a false spring. She took the warm weather as one might expect she would, as a sign of rebirth. She'd been wrong about Prague. This was her new life, she was sure of it.

As the ship made its way into New York Harbor, she and Sanyi—and Hilu, wobbly legged but stomach settled, finally—stood on deck with all the other passengers, solemnly staring at the Statue of Liberty. Finally she had her moment of overwhelming joy, a moment meant to be scored by Gypsy violinists. She had tears in her eyes and checked to see Sanyi's reaction. His eyes, like hers, were on the statue, and she was sure his eyes were wet, though she had to admit she was looking at him with blurry vision. Glancing over at Hilu, who seemed choked with emotion, she wondered wryly if his tears were for the statue or for the sight of land.

The solemn mood lifted as the ship moved up the Hudson River toward the dock. Manhattan's dense skyline seemed to sparkle, so sleek and modern after ancient Prague, another fairyland—exotic but utterly familiar from all the movies.

They cleared customs in two hours, then walked out onto the street, not knowing who was going to meet them. They waited only a minute before a tall man, smiling, came toward them, waving them toward a car.

It took only a minute to place him. This was Geza, Aunt Anna's brother-in-law. They had met him in Prague right after the war. He'd gone there to see about starting a business importing fine Czech cut glass. Even then it had been apparent that Marty's success ate at him, mainly because Anna and his wife, Olga, never let him forget for a minute that Marty had made it and he had not. His trip to Prague hadn't helped him. Szimi had taken him to the showroom for the best cutlery and china. Geza, who had been in the import business, told Szimi that the price of the cut glass was too much for him. By the time he paid the duty and the transportation, he would be losing money. Even if the business had seemed less dubious on paper, even a guaranteed gold mine, Geza wouldn't have done it. The government was in flux. Geza wasn't ready to risk making an investment in Czechoslovakia.

So here he was, playing gofer for his in-laws. He explained that Marty and Anna were in Florida, where they now lived for half the year. But they had left everything ready for them. There was a furnished apartment waiting for them, he told them, in one of Marty and Anna's buildings in a place called Queens.

As soon as they began driving Szimi began unbundling. Pulling off layer after layer of clothing, with the warm wind blowing in through the open windows, she felt an incredible lightness. It was going to take a much less active imagination to be the lucky one here; she could sense that already.

As they pulled up to 88–22 Parsons Boulevard—a large red-brick square, not sleekly designed like Štrossmajer 4—Geza apologized for the apartment before he showed it to them. "Small," he said, "but you're lucky to have it, apartments are scarce now, nothing was built during the war."

Beautiful, Szimi and Sanyi said of their functional studio with a pull-out couch to sleep on and none of the charm or grace of the apartments in Štrossmajer 4. They were sincere because this tiny box had an unparalleled luxury feature: It was theirs and theirs alone. Anna had rented a room for Hilu in a private home not far away. In Szimi's eyes the studio on Parsons Boulevard was their honeymoon suite, marking the real beginning of their marriage, the first time they would live together without company.

They weren't alone, exactly. Hilu joined them for dinner every night, and at least once a week the Salamons got together—more and more of them as visas came through and new relatives arrived.

Within a day of their arrival Szimi met Sanyi's oldest brother, Louis, in the Bronx—Louis, the generous *shlemazel,* the unlucky one. She understood immediately why Sanyi loved him so much. He had a sweet disposition and seemed so eager to please. His two sons had already joined him, and they were expecting Aliska soon.

He had settled in with a family called the Kugels, tiny people who adored their tall boarder. Szimi's first impression of Louis was of a tree surrounded by stumps. There seemed to be many little Kugels, nice short men whose nice short wives ignored them while they catered to Louis and to his relatives.

There wasn't a hint in this happy, noisy scene in the Bronx of where Louis had been since he had left so many years before to try to pay off his gambling debt. No one would ever know what his miscalculations had cost him or be able to calculate the compensating balance. If he had stayed in Czechoslovakia, would his wife be alive or would he be dead, too, giving his children no second chance?

Louis may never have articulated this question, but his deep eyes hinted that he had thought of it. He never complained about his lot—

he worked in the unforgiving heat of a laundry until he was old, and never made his fortune.

But he once confided in Szimi what it had been like for him, how hard he had tried to bring his family out. When he'd arrived in America in 1924 he had got a job with a relative who owned a laundry. He had worked hard and got enough money after a few years to open his own dry-cleaning store. It was boom time, the late twenties, and he opened another one and another one and then lost it all in the crash of 1929.

Every month, through the worst times, Louis had sent money home—for his family and for Sanyi, never losing his pride in his little brother. It was that other American story, and Szimi had seen that one in the movies, too—about the good man who doesn't get what he deserves, who never finds the pot of gold.

Louis was best at finding trouble. Even after the crash, back working in a laundry, he saved enough money to bring his family over. His cousin told him he knew a judge who would "expedite" things at Ellis Island. Louis needed two thousand dollars. The cousin might as well have asked Louis to pick a star out of the sky, Szimi would say, such a huge sum. Yet Louis would have found a way to heaven for his family, and he came up with the money for his cousin to give to the judge. Two days later he read it in the paper: The judge had been arrested, and so had his connection on Ellis Island. Eventually Louis convinced his cousin to send affidavits for the family, but by then it was too late. The troubles had started in Slovakia, and Malvin had already taken the children to Budapest and internment by the Hungarians.

That was Louis's story. His children had their own interpretation, though they hesitated to offer it. For years they had wanted to believe that their father was going to send for them, and for years that's what their mother had told them would happen. Then they heard words like "weakling" attached to their father, in hushed conversations they weren't supposed to hear.

After all that had happened, it was inevitable that the children would start to hate their father, much as it pained them. Even when they found it in their hearts to forgive Louis for what he had done to them— the absenteeism, the false promises—they found it hard to forget that he had left their mother to die. When the war was over, Pityu, the oldest, living at Štrossmajer 4, couldn't stop himself. He opened his heart to his father in a letter, an outpouring that could be distilled to this: "You don't know how you've sinned. Not against me or my brother and sister, but against our mother."

Louis didn't write back. Instead he sent tickets for his sons and assurance that Aliska's would come as soon as her visa cleared in Sweden. When "the boys," now in their early twenties, arrived, Louis told Pityu, "Everything you said in your letter was right. I expected that from you, but all I can tell you is this: Life was against me."

The boys went through the motions of forgiveness because they didn't know what else to do, though Pityu got angry all over again the first time they played cards together. It struck him immediately: His father was a terrible card player! When he had bet the future of his family at the card table, he hadn't had a chance of winning!

But Pityu didn't have it in him to hold a grudge. Whenever he was struck by a flash of hatred, he would feel immediate, horrible shame. He forgave his father because he had no choice. Louis may have been a weakling and a lost soul, but he was the father Pityu had been given.

Pityu couldn't carry through the pact he made with his brother Sanyi, the middle child. They had agreed that when they qualified for citizenship they would change their names and separate from the father who had betrayed them. But in the five years between arrival and citizenship Louis did all he could to atone for the past. The boys lived with him until they married, and he gave them what affection he could.

When it came time to carry out the pact, Pityu got cold feet. He went to his Uncle Sanyi, his adviser on such matters, and confessed the plan.

"Big" Sanyi didn't hesitate. "You can't change your name," he said. "If it's good enough for me, it's good enough for you."

In this way Sanyi resolved the powerful conflict within Pityu, who had been unable to choose between betrayals. He left it to his brother, to little Sanyi, as he was called, to openly defy their father (though little Sanyi never explicitly told Louis why he had changed his name to Salaway). In keeping with the family's constitutional aversion to admitting anger, Louis ignored the insult and continued to see all his children almost every week as long as he lived.

Aliska also made a pact only with herself—never to discuss any of it with anybody. It bothered her that Louis never once asked about her mother. It infuriated her when she found out later that her mother had once received an anonymous letter from America strongly implying that the kindness Louis was receiving from one of the Kugel women wasn't strictly maternal. Her suspicions about his relationship with the Kugel women were sharpened when he married one of them after her husband died. Had Aliska's father left his family to rot simply because he was having too good a time?

Since this was not an acceptable hypothesis, she stored it away. Her anger became part of a stew of bile in her stomach, the lid kept tight, never revealed by her gentle exterior. But periodically her body rebelled. She spent weeks and months unable to eat or sleep, calming herself with sedatives, certain her illness was the direct result of swallowing too much heartbreak.

Louis was in despair over his daughter's agony, but when he asked her what was wrong she wouldn't answer.

Was Louis irresponsible or a weakling or simply too human, an inexperienced navigator of his own life? It could be said he had been an idiot to leave, prideful and stupid. But there had been a precedent for his decision. His own father-in-law, whom he admired, had gone to America in the early 1900s and made enough money to return home and buy land, become prosperous. If Louis's timing had been better, or maybe his luck, he wouldn't have had to apologize to his children, in their twenties, for missing their childhood, for missing the death of their mother. On the other hand, maybe he wouldn't have been alive at all.

———

▪ Szimi found these first months in New York with Sanyi to be pleasantly vague, free of pressure because they understood Sanyi couldn't look for a serious position until they learned English. He would have to pass an English-language exam before he could apply for a medical license. They lived off their small savings—they'd sold a few *objets d'art* they'd bought before leaving Czechoslovakia—and Sanyi collected the

The war was good to my Great-uncle Marty and his wife, Anna; here they are in front of their beach home.

fee for a surgery he had done in Prague on a man whose father lived in New York.

The feeling that they were on an extended holiday continued through the summer. Anna and Marty returned from Florida and immediately opened their beach house on Long Beach, not far from Coney Island. They invited their immigrant relatives to join them there for the warm months. Szimi and Sanyi found themselves immune to Anna's sharp tongue. Marty made it clear that his niece was not subject to Anna's rule, and Sanyi didn't need clearance from Marty. Anna instantly proclaimed him her pet.

Anna would always refer to Sanyi as "gorgeous," but his special status with her came not from his looks but from his fingers. Not long after she returned from Florida she was complaining loudly about the pain in her neck, cursing anyone who tried to comfort her. Without a word Sanyi went behind her and put his hands around her throat. Anna began to shriek, first in outrage, then in pleasure. "A genius, that man," she would tell anyone who would listen, especially after Sanyi began supplementing the massages with shots of cortisone.

Keeping Anna happy in this modest way was a small price to pay for that summer in Long Beach. Anna and Marty kept a strict routine that offered their guests much freedom. Every morning Marty rose early, had breakfast, then played chess and a set or two of tennis with his friend Willie Schwartz, who owned half the house. By 11 A.M., the Weisses left for the city to make the rounds of their various real estate properties and appliance stores.

Szimi and Sanyi developed their own routine. The moment the older couple left, Szimi fried onions and garlic for that evening's dinner. (She hadn't planned any menu but was certain that onions and garlic would be necessary.) Then she and Sanyi headed for the beach, every afternoon, lying there for hours, welcoming the lulling oblivion of the sun.

Their only expense was the movies, and they were cheap. They went every night, putting the permanent imprint of Hollywood slang on English that would become grammatically impeccable. Szimi, who felt she had to justify this luxury, insisted that the movies were necessary to help Sanyi pass his language exam. In this case, Sanyi was the pragmatist. That summer he enrolled in an English course specifically designed for foreign doctors.

While preparing for his language exam, he scrawled notes for the response to an essay question: "Describe a person whom you know to be an ideal teacher."

The draft, written in the stilted prose of a new English speaker, may not have been especially profound or lyrical to the objective reader—but it seemed so to those who knew him. They could find in these lines a confirmation of Sanyi's tender nature, one of the few clues that came direct from the man himself.

> *I have a very good friend. We used to go often together. My friend loves nature very much. He very often goes walking in the forest where he collects vegetables and insects. He is very fond of people, especially children. He is a man of the teaching profession.*
>
> *My friend is tall and he is dark complexioned. He is thin, but strong. Long ago the teachers taught differently from today. The*

teacher was not a friend of the children. The children did not have confidence in the teacher. They were afraid of the teacher.

My friend belongs in the category of modern teachers. Today's teachers answer all the pupils' questions whenever possible. The teacher does not belittle the pupil or try to embarrass him. He tries to encourage. The teacher must know his subject and he must know how to make it palatable. He tries to vary the lesson, to get away from the old routine. The teacher must possess a good sense of humor.

My friend was that kind of teacher.

Yes, I say "was" because I do not know whether he is still alive. During the Second World War both he and I were taken to a German concentration camp. After the war I did not find him at home, and I have heard nothing about him. . . .

He passed his English exam. Then he quit the grueling emergency room job he'd just started that winter, and enrolled in a refresher course in medicine to prepare for his boards. It had been fifteen years since he had graduated from medical school. He'd heard the most experienced doctors flunked the New York State exam if they didn't take the cram course. Szimi began working for her Uncle Marty as a bookkeeper.

One day that spring Szimi prepared to go to work as usual: She drank a glass of chocolate milk for breakfast, dressed, and went to the bathroom to brush her teeth. Before she knew what was happening the sink was filled with chocolate milk.

When she told Sanyi that night, he broke out laughing.

"Maybe you're expecting," he said. She could see he was excited, so excited she swallowed her doubts—was this the best time, with him studying, not bringing in money?

That summer they could go to Long Beach only on the weekends. Szimi had her job at Jamaica Refrigeration, and in July Sanyi began his internship at Lebanon Hospital in the Bronx, just north of Yankee Stadium and a long way by subway from Queens. It was an exhausting schedule. He worked every day and every other night for the princely sum of twenty-five dollars a month for the first two months, then fifty dollars. They had no car and no phone; after a year of spending almost every minute together, they barely saw each other during the week. On weekends Sanyi had to study for his medical boards, which would be coming up that fall. The vacation was definitely over.

Yet Szimi felt happy. After so many years of being afraid to look to the next hour, much less the next day, it was a luxury to plan. She learned this from Sanyi, the pleasure of anticipation. While she had to struggle to commit herself to any particular course of action, he loved to imagine what might happen next.

It no longer seemed delusionary to have expectations, to think they could be part of the postwar boom. They saw themselves as travelers on Noah's Ark; they'd weathered the storm and now could start over. They were impatient with those who questioned their faith—skeptics who had no doubt that the flood would come again next time God got angry. Szimi's own cousin, who had lost her little boy at Auschwitz, had an abortion rather than risk losing another child. Sanyi had tried to change her mind with an impassioned speech on behalf of life.

That autumn Sanyi passed his exams, one after the other. He finished the last one in November and was still waiting for the results in December when his brother Jani came to visit from South America. They hadn't seen each other for thirty years.

On December 13, 1948, Szimi went into labor. Sanyi was on call that night, so Szimi had prepared a chicken *paprikás* for her brother Hilu and the sister of an aunt who dropped by for dinner occasionally. When Szimi mentioned she felt funny, the older woman suggested she might be ready to have the baby.

At 10 P.M. Szimi went downstairs to the building superintendent's office and asked if she could use the phone. Sanyi was strangely diffident. When she told him she thought she should come into the hospital, he seemed reluctant.

"So late at night?" he asked, as though the baby would wait until morning.

Finally he agreed she should come. She put some things into a suitcase and walked to the subway in the snow with her brother Hilu. It took them almost an hour and a half to get to the Bronx, where Sanyi met them in the waiting room. New York was a gentler city in those days; at midnight, having deposited Szimi with her husband, Hilu returned to Queens because he had to go to work the next morning. Sanyi walked him to the subway, then came back to Szimi, who was waiting in the room where he slept when he was on call.

When he returned he handed Szimi over to the nurses for "preparation"—it was standard practice to shave women's pubic hair and give them an enema to make the delivery more pleasant for the doctor. After that she was left alone to wait in a hallway. She waited and waited, wondering where he was, trying to shut out the sounds of the woman screaming at the top of her lungs: "Doctor, doctor, help me!"

For two hours she waited for Sanyi, furious at him for his indifference to her. Should she scream like that other woman?

Finally, at 3 A.M., Sanyi came by to see his wife, explaining that he had been in the delivery room until then. He was the doctor assigned to answer the screams of the woman who had been driving Szimi crazy.

She wasn't interested in anyone else's problems.

"The pains are almost constant," she snapped at him.

He brought out the anesthesiologist he'd been working with to have a look.

"Who's her doctor?" he asked Sanyi, his annoyance obvious to Szimi. "Why hasn't he been called?"

Sanyi called the obstetrician. When he arrived, panting, he, too, snapped at Sanyi: "Why did you wait so long? The baby's head is right there."

Szimi was angry. Sanyi had seemed embarrassed to claim any relationship with her, as though it were inappropriate for him, a lowly intern, to bring his wife there. Before the obstetrician arrived she had hissed at him, between pains, "You know, you don't have to bow to anybody. What's yours is yours, and that's what matters. What's yours should come first, and the rest will follow."

She was even angrier when she realized there wasn't time for an anesthetic. She just pushed the baby out, then fell asleep. As she drifted off she saw Sanyi's face and heard the baby screaming and thought about how beautiful the snow had been that night, covering the streets like a fluffy down quilt, as she and Hilu had walked toward the hospital.

The next morning when she woke up, she forgot the fury of the night before. The first thing she saw was Sanyi's smiling face and the second was a vase of long-stemmed red roses and a card: "Thank you for the beautiful gift." All day long he kept coming in and out, in between patients, looking happier than Szimi had ever seen him. He seemed transformed, lighter, like a former invalid who finally accepts the doctor's prognosis: *You'll be fine.*

———

■ That adorable baby girl would be the bridge between past and future. She would be told, when she was older, that she carried the names of her two grandmothers. This was true of her Hebrew name, "Sarah Braha," but not her English name, Suzanne Eva. She wouldn't be told that she carried a secret memorial to her father's first daughter, a secret because her existence was never mentioned. It seemed that Sanyi had submerged her life as well as her death into his deepest consciousness, as though her memory would stymie his efforts to refute the undeniable evidence that God could be merciless. He wasn't a religious man, but he believed in God the way Szimi believed in fate, as a way to rationalize his own desire to carry on without bitterness, to convince himself that there was a master plan whose happy end would justify the irrational sacrifice. He had an almost desperate need to believe in goodness, in the progress of the human spirit. Indeed, it could almost be guaranteed that, on the rare occasions he displayed anger, the cause could be traced to a betrayal of that belief.

So when Anna Weiss, Marty's wife, promised him a car if he passed his medical boards, he expected her to buy him a car. He waited for weeks, then months, then finally went with Szimi and bought an Oldsmobile. They put down $480 on $2,400, and Sanyi stopped talking to Anna. Szimi couldn't believe it. When Anna entered the room, Sanyi simply behaved as though she weren't there. Week after week this went on, as the Weisses joined the Salamon families for weekly card games. Sanyi continued to pretend that Anna's words didn't penetrate his ears.

Szimi was proud of him for calling Anna's bluff but also a little frightened. She had sensed from the beginning that there were reserves of passion to this man that she couldn't penetrate, as cold and deep as mountain lakes. She made a promise to herself that would profoundly influence their lives together: She would see to it that nothing would get near Sanyi's wounds.

Anna missed being the object of Sanyi's jokes. Even more, she desperately needed her cortisone shots. It didn't take her long to figure out why he was ignoring her. She was a shrewd woman and a masterful holder of grudges herself. When Sanyi went to make the next car payment, he found the entire bill had been covered. He called Anna and thanked her profusely. Neither of them referred to the weeks of silence.

———

▪ Six months after Suzy was born, Sanyi's niece Baba arrived, to occupy the living room of their new one-bedroom apartment. They had meant for her to follow them right away, but her visa had been held up—for more than two years. She came with a skill; she'd learned how to sew bras in Prague.

She'd lived for a while with her Uncle Béla, Sanyi's brother. When her American visa hadn't come through, month after month, she had applied to the agency taking care of Jewish refugees for passage to Canada or Australia. They sent her, with other homeless youngsters, to a home near Versailles, to wait for repatriation to Canada or Australia.

Not long after she arrived, a telegram arrived from her Uncle Sanyi in America instructing the agency to hold Baba until her American visa cleared. She spent most of her days wandering around Versailles with other girls, careful not to make close friends, because they kept leaving. After seven months everyone was gone but her. The Joint Committee put her into a hotel in Paris by herself. They began to warn her that they would stop supporting her if her visa didn't come through soon, so she began looking for a job. Her French was poor. She hadn't bothered to learn much because she had always assumed she was on the verge of departure. Finally it happened. She took a train to Cannes, boarded an Italian ocean liner, and spent ten days under the tutelage of an elderly Italian man who protected her from the younger men on board and taught her how to eat spaghetti.

In New York she found a re-creation of Štrossmajer 4 in Szimi and Sanyi's apartment on Parsons Boulevard. They would barely finish dinner and the apartment would fill up with friends and relatives. Everyone gathered at their house to watch the tiny television set Marty had given Szimi when the baby was born. Milton Berle. Howdy Doody. The Carpathian crowd appreciated the burlesque humor, the unapologetic silliness.

This time, however, Baba blended in. She occupied herself with the baby, who was clearly the center of this little universe. Sanyi couldn't spend enough time with Suzy. They had no money to spare, but they did have a movie camera as well as a still camera.

It took Baba a while to understand that her uncle's passion for his child was, like all of her uncle's passions, complicated by words he would never speak. The love he felt for Suzy was touched with fear that was far deeper than the normal primal reaction to unknown danger.

Baba thought she might have caught a glimpse of the terror he felt the night she encouraged him to go out for a meal and a movie with Szimi. She would watch the baby, just as she often did during the daytime.

When they left, they seemed as she'd remembered them in Prague, laughing, greeting the night as though the most marvelous surprise was waiting for them.

They came home less than fifteen minutes after they'd left.

Sanyi didn't explain anything, just gave Baba a kiss on the cheek and walked over to Suzy's playpen and stared at her.

"We walked a couple of blocks, and all of a sudden Sanyi just stopped," Szimi told Baba. "I don't know what got into him. He got a look on his face and said, 'Let's go back.' "

Baba was less surprised by Sanyi's abrupt change in plans than she was by Szimi's child-rearing philosophy, which more or less paralleled her laissez-faire attitude toward life ("Everything will work out").

Baba was shocked, for example, when she accompanied her aunt to the A&P supermarket. She watched Szimi park the baby carriage outside and start to march inside. When Baba hesitated, she motioned impatiently for her to come along.

"What are you waiting for?" she asked.

"You aren't leaving the baby, are you?" Baba asked.

Szimi looked at Baba and shrugged. "You can wait out here if you want to," she said, laughing at what a worrier poor Baba was.

———

▪ They began building a legend of the New York years, just as they had in Prague. For Szimi the beginning would always be marked by the moment *Gone With the Wind* came to play at Radio City Music Hall, in revival. She had been waiting for nine years to see the movie, ever since she'd heard about it in 1939, a few lives ago.

Szimi (no different, perhaps, from the millions of other young girls who read the book over and over) had come to identify with Scarlett O'Hara. She found this identification perfectly plausible. Hadn't she, like Scarlett, triumphed over the loss of everything? She was smarter than Scarlett, of course, never taking her Rhett Butler for granted.

She would never forget the way the book had helped her escape from Lager C, day after day, as she told the story, in installments, to her bunkmates. She sometimes wondered—only fleetingly—whether something was lacking in her, some spiritual depth, because she took solace not in God but in popular literature.

She made elaborate preparations for the movie. By then she was five months pregnant with Suzy and always hungry. The night before, she prepared a huge batch of garlic meatballs. The next day, she carried the meatballs on the subway into Manhattan with her. She resisted the temptation to dip into them, even though the smell had saturated her senses by the end of her first viewing of the movie. She wept all afternoon, for Scarlett, for herself, for what they both had lost.

Sanyi met her after class, as planned, in the lobby. They bought tickets for the evening show and went downstairs, to the grand lower lobby of Radio City. There, sitting on one of the plush velvet benches, they ate the meatballs and splurged on the theater's expensive ginger ale. Szimi cried just as hard the second time—maybe more because she felt the reverberations of Sanyi's emotional reaction as well as her own. That night it occurred to her that they were safe: Misery was no longer part of their lives, but the stuff of fiction.

The Seaman Depot, 1882–1966

15

The Sign

■ Periodically it occurred to Szimi that time was passing. Sanyi was about to complete his residency at Lebanon Hospital and should be looking for a permanent position. However, she didn't hesitate to agree when he came home with an enticing proposition—one that would delay their quest for that comfortable life but that would give them a wonderful summer with the baby. He'd answered a newspaper ad for a position as the camp physician at Lake Huntington, a summer resort in the Catskills. Baba could come with them; they got her a job as a chambermaid. When Szimi heard the salary Sanyi would be getting—$10,000 for the summer—her qualms were settled. Sanyi could look for work later.

At Lake Huntington Szimi played tennis every day, leaving Suzy with the counselors at the day camp. Sanyi's duties were minimal. There was plenty of time for swimming and boating in the afternoon. They experienced Borscht Belt excess and got paid for it—the huge meals in the dining room, the weekend shows with Jewish celebrities like Myron Cohen. Some nights Szimi thought it was possible to keep life on hold. Perhaps this was life, a state of flux.

Sanyi, however, was ready to settle down. He had always been ready to settle down. He was forty years old, and a decade had passed since he'd moved to Huszt and started his life there. He returned from Lake Huntington invigorated, fully equipped with his recommendations, his degrees, his certification. He might not have been the blithe optimist that Szimi was, but he felt ready for things to fall into place.

He answered an ad placed by a young dentist who had extra office space on lower Second Avenue. They agreed on a rental price, and the dentist fixed Sanyi's teeth and Szimi's for the cost of his materials. Perhaps they should have noticed that he seemed to have a lot of time on his hands, but he was so nice, and he was so confident that if Sanyi put out a shingle, patients would come.

The word spread through the expatriate community of Jews from Huszt, and patients did come, out of loyalty and nostalgia. For these same reasons Sanyi refused to charge anyone from Huszt. He expanded the policy to any Jewish refugee from the Carpathian region, thus completing the guarantee that he would make no money. Even if he had charged them, they were an unreliable clientele. Most of them lived in Queens and the Bronx and weren't really interested in traveling long distances to see the doctor, or possibly they were embarrassed by Sanyi's largesse.

Every day Sanyi traveled to Second Avenue from Queens to sit in the office whose rent he could barely manage, staring at the equipment he'd spent his Lake Huntington savings on, waiting for patients who didn't come. He never spoke of how he felt during those long empty hours, afraid to take a walk for fear a patient might arrive.

He never spoke to Szimi of failure, or of his fears. He proceeded as though everything were going according to plan. He applied and was accepted into the Medical Society of Queens County, which automatically qualified him for membership in the state society. Yet the certification may have only exaggerated his sense of failure, eliminating all excuses. Sometime in the spring he started going into the office later, coming home earlier, spending more and more time in the park with the baby. Szimi went back to work for Marty.

Sanyi learned of a doctor who had an office near the old Wanamaker's department store on Twelfth Street. The man did nothing but workmen's compensation cases. It was an impersonal practice that carried with it none of the affection Sanyi had known in Huszt and none of the prestige of the Boruvkovo. But the doctor offered him $500 a month, which was about $500 more than Sanyi was making. He worked there for a few months, then asked the doctor if he had a future or if he would remain a salaried employee. When the doctor didn't answer the question, Sanyi took refuge, once again, in Lake Huntington.

It became a cycle; winter failure, summer solace in the Catskills. After the second summer at Lake Huntington Sanyi was hired by another workmen's compensation doctor doing business in the garment center.

"Don't worry," the doctor told him, "I know everyone in the garment center, no night calls, eight hours a day, you'll work a couple of weeks for me, then I'll introduce you around."

Sanyi found that the eight hours a day usually stretched to sixteen hours and sometimes twenty. The weeks went by, and there were no introductions.

"What's your rush?" was the doctor's response to Sanyi's inquiry.

A few more weeks passed, and Sanyi asked again.

"Why are you after me?" the doctor snapped.

Sanyi didn't say a thing. He packed his things and left.

Next came the call from a friend, a Hungarian surgeon, who told him about a doctor on the Upper West Side named Hauser who'd had a heart attack and needed someone to keep the office going. It was agreed they would split the proceeds fifty-fifty and that Dr. Hauser would come in only once or twice a week until he felt better. Sanyi was surprised to find how many patients Dr. Hauser told him to treat free of charge. Then it turned out one was the butcher who provided

Dr. Hauser's meat, another the grocer who swapped food for medical care.

The man was a *ganef*, a thief, but Sanyi had come to expect that in New York. He had come to accept his position as greenhorn, to endure the humiliation, because even with Dr. Hauser's "generosity" to his food suppliers, Sanyi was finally earning a good living. He was making between $800 and $1,000 a month, and Hauser had promised him a full partnership, "in due time."

On a day in February he agreed to "work something out," and in March he said "Yes, yes, yes" when Sanyi approached him again. In April he said, "Absolutely," and then he gave Sanyi a list of all the equipment in the office with the estimated value.

"When you pay me half the value of the equipment, we'll become partners," said Dr. Hauser.

Sanyi knew that Hauser had begun his practice fifteen or twenty years before, and most of the equipment looked as though it hadn't been new then. Yet he was being charged the price of brand-new stuff.

"Fine," said Sanyi politely, and he never went back again.

When he got home that evening, he told Szimi, "Guess what. We're going back to Lake Huntington."

That spring each of them came to the same decision: They could no longer pretend that New York's promise extended to them. This began crystallizing for Sanyi when Hauser handed him that list. He felt as though he were the country rube facing card sharks again, trying to figure out the rules of *kronula*.

For Szimi the catalyst was television. When she started working at the appliance store—which had expanded from radios and washing machines to televisions—she used her employee privilege of buying wholesale to exchange the tiny one Uncle Marty had given them for a twelve-inch model.

It was 1951, and she felt a constant terror gnawing at her. The television made it impossible to ignore the Cold War. Even the slapstick comedies didn't give her relief. She knew about escaping into fantasy while the world collapsed around her.

One Sunday afternoon they watched one of the alarmist news documentaries that were helping to feed the nation's paranoia. Using detailed maps and authoritative voices, the documentary explained how New York City would be doomed by an enemy attack—which roads would be closed, the enormous logjam that would ensue.

When the film was over, Szimi turned to Sanyi, who hadn't yet told her he wanted to leave the city. "Let's get out of here," she said. "I don't ever want to be enclosed again."

They returned from Lake Huntington at the end of the summer of 1951 with a united purpose. Sanyi, now forty-two years old, had decided emphatically that the anonymity and sense of failure he'd found in the city weren't for him. He had always been exempt from that Salamon characteristic—good in love, bad in business.

My parents and Suzy spent summers at Lake Huntington, New York.

Szimi never felt it was the lack of money that bothered him. When they had first come over, many patients he'd treated in Dachau had contacted him, asking him to write on their behalf to the German government, which was offering reparations to everyone who could prove they'd been interned in concentration camp. He had always complied. When Szimi asked him why he didn't apply for reparations himself, he looked at her so sorrowfully she wished she hadn't raised the question.

"How can they pay me for what they took?"

No, money wasn't it. She knew he needed something else—affirmation of his uniqueness, an appreciation of his gifts.

She, on the other hand, was simply impatient to get on with it, to feel they were making headway toward that comfortable life. For the first time since they'd come to America she lost confidence in Sanyi's ability to provide for them, unable to understand why a fantastic doctor like him couldn't get started. It was sometime in this period that the balance of power between them shifted. Until then, she had been the inexperienced one, the adoring younger wife. Now she became more willing to offer her opinion, slowly building to the day when Sanyi would say, with what always seemed like affection: "I am the head of the family, and Szimi is the neck." Meaning, he might rule the roost so long as he turned the way Szimi wanted him to.

The family put it another way: "If it weren't for Szimi, Sanyi wouldn't have a dime." He, like his father, would "give away his underpants" so long as he was adored.

Szimi's decision to become actively involved in the job search had a specific beginning—the day Sanyi returned from his interview at the Bureau of Indian Affairs. He gave his report to Szimi with excitement. They were looking for doctors on Indian reservations. They could move out west, to Arizona. Wouldn't it be wonderful to live in the desert, where it was always warm? Wouldn't it be great to take care of people who needed him?

Szimi, who was twenty-nine years old, looked at her forty-two-year-old husband as incredulously as if he'd told her about his new imaginary friend.

"Arizona is not what I had in mind." She became more specific about her objections. "I don't want to go to an Indian reservation. It's too far, and it's too isolated."

Then she asked, "What are they offering?"

When he told her—an inconsequential salary, in her opinion—she finally understood what she would describe not as an annoyance—though clearly it was to her—but as a charming defect in her husband's character. He really didn't understand the value of money, though he liked to spend it when he had it. Where had he developed this patrician disregard?

She began studying the want ads in the *Journal of the American Medical Association* with him. At first he looked mainly in the New York area. He drove to Lake Placid to answer the ad of a widow selling her husband's practice, only to find she wanted a fortune for it.

There were other false leads. Months passed. He began writing to medical boards in other states, to find out what he needed to begin practice there. He had been corresponding with the officials in Ohio for almost a year when he saw an ad in the *JAMA* that felt different from the others.

A *town* was advertising for a doctor. No wages were mentioned, but Sanyi was attracted by the language of the ad. "We really need a doctor," it said.

When Szimi saw Sanyi's response, she was reminded of the knowledge that had struck her the night she had been in labor with Suzy. Again she realized that the fragility she had always sensed in him came from an invisible and improbable insecurity that made no sense to her at all. She realized that Sanyi, who had always been adored, felt like a failure when that adoration was missing. She realized that money alone could never satisfy him, but a town that needed him might.

As they wrote to the Ohio address listed in the *JAMA*, she had other reasons for attaching a special urgency to her hopes for this town. She was pregnant with a second child, and she was starting to see unwanted limits encroaching on her vision of life. Even the larger apartment on Parsons Boulevard was feeling cramped, and that would become worse when the baby came. She found herself staring with longing at the spot on the map they'd identified as Hamersville, a dot somewhere near the Ohio River.

It was already winter, late 1952, when Sanyi took the overnight train to Cincinnati, where the men from Hamersville said they would meet him.

He returned from Ohio invigorated, though to Szimi his trip sounded like yet another quixotic trail leading to yet another dead end.

He told her the drive to Hamersville had taken about an hour by car. Though it had been cold and gray, Sanyi had liked the roll of the land, the wide stretches of farmland that separated the tiny towns. The landscape didn't exactly mirror the Carpathian foothills, but something about it, sparse but not desolate, had felt familiar to him. He could imagine how beautiful it would be in springtime, how exhilarating to fly across those country roads in his own car.

His enthusiasm had waned when they had reached Hamersville. The town's main street was being widened; there were only stumps where the trees lining the road had been cut down. It was the kind of charmless village encountered throughout middle America, offering no concessions to history, no special promise for the future. It was especially bare in winter. He hadn't been heartened when his hosts showed him where his office would be—a bleak little apartment above the barber shop.

He didn't elaborate on his conversation with the men from Hamersville except to say they seemed eager to please him. When he had asked if he could visit Georgetown, the larger town nearby whose hospital he would use, they had been happy to oblige. This was a miscalculation.

At the Georgetown Hospital Sanyi had asked to speak with members of the medical staff. They, too, had been happy to oblige. "Don't come here," they had told him. "There are plenty of doctors in the area for Hamersville. It would be a mistake."

Sanyi hadn't repeated this conversation to the Hamersville people. He had simply said he would tell them his decision later, after he had had a chance to discuss it with his wife.

On the way back to Cincinnati he had asked them to drop him at a medical building downtown so he could try to locate a radiologist related to a colleague in New York. Having been told the doctor wasn't in, Sanyi just stood there by the receptionist, holding his hat, not sure what to do. His train wasn't leaving for a few hours, and he had no more business in Ohio, he was sure of that.

His disappointment must have been obvious. A man came up to him and asked him if he needed help.

Sanyi wasn't the kind of person to open his heart to a stranger. But circumstances can provoke unusual intimacies.

Szimi would put it another way, later. "It was *b'shert*," she would say—fate.

The man said to Sanyi, "Why would you go to Hamersville? If you want to settle somewhere around here, go to Adams County. They really need a doctor."

This time Sanyi wasn't seduced by the idea of "they really need."

"How do you know?" he asked.

"I just came back from there," said the man, explaining that he was the representative for a medical supply company. "I swear to you I met with a doctor in West Union, one of the towns there, and he asked me if I knew of anybody that would like to settle in Adams County. You don't believe me? I'll write down his name and address, and you can find out for yourself."

───

▪ Three months later he returned to Ohio, this time by car. Just as he had so many years before, he took a nephew with him, also named Pityu, Louis's son (the other Pityu, the fastidious one who had accompanied him on his first foray into the Carpathian country, a lifetime before, had died in the war).

They booked a room in a motel outside Cincinnati and then drove to Hamersville to take another look before continuing on to Adams County. By then it was early spring and the air was damp and heavy—with promise, Sanyi would say. Pityu wasn't charmed by the ramshackle barns with ads for Mail Pouch tobacco painted on the side, or by the way the stink of cow manure overwhelmed the soft smell of new grass. He was nauseated, not thrilled, by his uncle's wild driving on the treacherous roads.

Yet he knew Sanyi was lost to him and the relatives in New York not long after they pulled into the gas station in the middle of a town called Seaman. There was nothing to the "downtown"—two rows of one- and two-story brick buildings intersecting at the town's one traffic light. But every street was lined with trees, big thick ones that had obviously been there a long time. Main Street looked peaceful and pretty: Trees were budding and crocuses were emerging from flower beds in front of modest, neat houses, mostly white clapboard, some brick.

When the gas station owner found out who Sanyi was, he told him to wait right there. He called Chip Cooper, the used-car dealer, who had been urging the local Lions Club to find a replacement for old Doc Lawwill since he had retired the year before. A town without a doctor had no respectability, in Chip's opinion. Chip's formal schooling had ended in fifth grade, but he had expansive ambitions for himself and his children. He recognized that things had started happening all over the country after the war and that most of them had bypassed Adams County. He believed in self-improvement, and that included improving the place where he lived.

His wife, Prudie, saw it a little differently. She saw Chip's drive for betterment as part of his compulsion to trade. He bought things just so he could trade them. She would always say that she was glad she "was hooked tight to him" or he would have traded her. He was a shy man, but when it came to trading he could talk to the president of the United States and it wouldn't have bothered him, she would say. In fact, Chip would have been just about perfect if he didn't drink so much and scare her to death, driving those curves so loaded on beer he couldn't see straight.

It was the trader Chip, the sober salesman, who met Sanyi and Pityu that day. They saw a man about forty years old with a thick black mustache and a face that had seen a lot of weather. Their first conversation was held at an angle, all of them cocking their heads in this meeting of hillbilly and Hungarian accents. Sanyi and Pityu didn't catch everything Chip said, but they thought they caught this: He had a warm heart and five children, with another on the way. When he told Sanyi about the children, he winked. "You can see why we need a doc, Doc," he said with a grin. Sanyi laughed appreciatively. He sensed a kindred spirit, someone who knew a good joke when he heard one.

Chip took them for a drive down Main Street, where Sanyi could see the budding branches would almost form an arch when the leaves filled in later in the spring. It was just half a mile to the south end of town, where they stopped by a patch of woods. In the middle of this untamed tangle of trees there was a concrete building that looked like a garage and a half-finished structure made of bricks.

Chip explained that the concrete building had been a bakery started by a bricklayer who was looking for a way to make money in the winter. The bakery business hadn't gone well and he'd gotten out, leaving the building vacant and the house he was building next door uncompleted.

They didn't go inside because Chip didn't have the keys. But as the two men stood there talking, Pityu was worried. He saw danger in the small smile that didn't leave Sanyi's lips. "This is the wilderness," he thought. "What will he do here with two kids?"

———

■ The Promised Land comes in many guises. Moses stared across the desert and declared it the land of milk and honey. Marty Weiss thought it was Miami Beach. Sanyi Salamon decided his land of milk and honey was here, the western outpost of Appalachia.

He knew nothing about this place he had decided to fall in love with. That, for example, this county that at one time had occupied a quarter of the state now wavered between being the poorest and the second poorest of Ohio's eighty-eight counties. That fewer than 5 percent of its high school graduates went on to college or even thought about it. That it was sixty miles from Cincinnati, a two-hour drive on stomach-shaking roads, and the geographic distance was small compared to the cultural distance.

He couldn't see up into the hills, where people still believed in both the Devil and moonshine, though the county was officially "dry," having declined to join the rest of the country's repeal of Prohibition twenty years before—a state of affairs that worked to the mutual satisfaction of both the bootleggers and the preachers. The only industry was farming, mostly small family farms handed down from generation to generation.

He didn't know he'd be the only Jew in town, one of a handful in the entire county—nor that his religion wouldn't matter to most of the townspeople, who were much more suspicious of Catholics (but who would casually use the expression "I jewed him down" as a way of saying they'd gotten something at a cheaper price). Yet the homogeneity of the citizenry—almost entirely white Protestant—didn't alleviate the paranoia that prevailed across the county, where it was said if six people gathered together they'd start a town, build a church, and start gossiping suspiciously about their neighbors.

It was a peculiar place, geographically remote and geologically interesting, the place where Ohio burst out of its northern flatness into hills and ridges. Hundreds of thousands of years before, the glacier out of Canada that had rolled the northern United States flat had stopped in Adams County, forever changing its landscape. The foothills of the Appalachian Mountains began there, and so did the fertile soil of the Kentucky bluegrass region. Its plants and fossils, revealing millions of years of evolution, were periodically studied by scientists from Cincinnati but were of scant interest to the local inhabitants. Indeed, with Baptist fundamentalism as the prevailing religion, evolution was a subject best avoided.

People in Adams County didn't care much about the world outside. Until World War II, it was said, you could count on one hand the number of people who had ever been out of the county. They even spoke a special dialect because people came there, got stuck, and never heard anything else.

They sustained themselves on their homegrown beauty and bigotry. Their accents and prejudices were vaguely southern, but their heritage was northern. A man could use the word "nigger" in the same sentence as he noted with pride that Adams County had been the first stop to freedom on the Underground Railroad. The few black people who lived in the county were not fully accepted, nor were they abused—but that was pretty much the way Adams Countyans treated everyone who hadn't lived there for six generations. Serious disdain was much more insular—saved by Methodists for Presbyterians and by residents of Peebles for residents of Blue Creek.

Sanyi saw none of that, or chose not to see it. What he saw was a sky so clear he felt it was possible to see every star in the galaxy, the end of a rainbow. "It's a nice little town with friendly people," he said when he returned to New York, by way of explaining to Szimi why she should leave her friends and family and move to the middle of nowhere just before their second baby was due.

Before he left, Chip Cooper had promised he would find a way to finance the construction needed to finish the house and to turn the bakery into a doctor's office according to Sanyi's specifications. He understood that Sanyi had no money but seemed to believe him when he said he would pay him back all loans when he started making money.

Szimi told a friend at work where she was moving and told her she was worried they wouldn't be able to understand her Hungarian accent.

"Don't worry," said the woman, a girl from Brooklyn, "my grandparents live in Ohio, and when I visit them the people don't understand me either!"

Thus reassured, Szimi prepared to leave. As she packed she realized how poor they were. They didn't even own their furniture—it belonged to Marty and Anna.

Sanyi loaded their few possessions into the car and drove ahead, to supervise the construction of the office. A few weeks later Szimi and Suzy, then four and a half, were to join him. The family gathered at Pennsylvania Station to see them off. Szimi confided to an older cousin that she was a little scared, leaving everyone behind, still concerned that people wouldn't be able to understand her English.

He gave her the kind of answer she liked to hear: "You're taking yourself with you, so you'll be okay wherever you go."

She and Suzy had an uneasy ride, the two of them stuffed into what was called a "roomette," a cubicle that turned into a bedroom when the porter pulled down a platform and mattress that filled the entire room. This ingenious design made maneuvering difficult for a woman in her eighth month of pregnancy. Suzy spent the night staring at her mother's huge stomach, wondering what that baby inside was thinking. She knew there was a baby in there because Baba had told her so when she'd asked why her mommy was getting so fat.

That night, as the train lulled her to sleep, Suzy curled up next to her, Szimi remembered the date with a little shock. They would arrive in Ohio on May 21, 1953, almost nine years to the day after her arrival in Auschwitz.

Yet she slept easily, without dreams. The next morning Sanyi met them at Union Station in Cincinnati. The railroad station was still grand in those days, its walls decorated with impressive murals commissioned by the Works Progress Administration in the 1930s, depicting the grandeur and hardship of the modern age of transportation.

Outside the sun was shining, just as it had been a decade earlier on her first day at Auschwitz. Only now, with this arrival, the beautiful weather offered only pleasure, not a rebuke. They pulled into a gas station just outside the train station. Szimi was staring idly out the window when she saw a man leading around on a rope a beautiful black-and-white creature with a luxurious tail. She opened the car door and stood up to get a better look.

"Don't make him angry, or he'll let you have it," said the man holding the rope.

She smiled because he was smiling, and he must have seen she didn't know what he was talking about.

"Haven't you ever seen a skunk, ma'am?" he asked, apparently incredulous at her lack of what must have been basic knowledge.

When she told him she hadn't, he explained how skunks let loose a foul smell when they were upset.

"Amazing," Szimi said, as she mentally transformed this encounter with a skunk into yet another symbol of life's extraordinary serendipity. It must be a sign, she was sure of it. What else could explain this introduction to an animal she hadn't known existed just as she arrived in Ohio—especially an animal like that, a soft, furry thing with secret powers of survival. She was prepared to believe, once again, that her new life was beginning.

My father holding me; Suz's on the stump with Pat Cooper, one of Prudie and Chip's children.

16

This Is the Place

■ Years later, Prudie Cooper would remember the arrival of Alexander and Lilly Salamon, as Sanyi and Szimi would then be known, with a sense of drama and portent that clearly indicated why she and Lilly became such good friends.

"It all happened in a sort of peculiar way, the way they came to Seaman, Ohio, Adams County, that I believe the Lord God had a hand in it. By virtue of Doc being there, my husband was saved from death."

Prudie was short and stubby and always seemed to be flying, partly because her little legs had to work twice as hard as a normal-sized person's to get her where she was going as fast as she wanted. Her estimation, that the doctor's arrival was a miracle, wasn't altered by the fact the miracle wouldn't take place until a year after the Salamons came to town.

―――

■ She was baking an angel food cake for a friend's surprise birthday party when Chip came down, waxy faced, saying his arms were hurting.

Prudie called Dr. Salamon, whose office was just down the road from the Coopers'. He came right over to the house, took one look at Chip, and told him to go to bed.

"You go ahead and bake your cake," he told Prudie. "I'll see to it everything's all right." And though Chip had had a heart attack, Doc Salamon did see to it that everything was all right, for the longest time.

Like many people in Adams County, which sat on the Ohio River just north of Kentucky, Prudie had been born in Kentucky and spoke with a twang that was part southern, part country. Her family had ended up in Adams County when her father had traded some homes he'd built in Dayton, Ohio, for a farm someone had owned in Adams County. This was also a common sort of phenomenon in Adams County, which was a place people usually didn't head toward but landed in.

Prudie married young and started having babies with the boy everyone called Chip. Prudie, however, always referred to her husband as Charles. She, too, had an irrepressible bent for self-improvement that eventually would lead her to a political career trying to convince state officials that Adams County was not just a backwater full of poor, ignorant people.

She would never forget Dr. Salamon's arrival in town. "It happened that the Lions Club was really interested in getting a doctor in town, but truthfully, no one wanted to put out the money for the building and the house. I got a call from Socks Roush, the president of the Lions Club, who said the doctor from New York was in Hamersville and would like to come down but he needed to know he'd have a permanent place. Socks wanted to know if Chip would put up the money.

"I called every automobile agency in Dayton where I thought he might be, and finally I found him. He said, 'We can't afford all ten thousand dollars, but I'll put in five if the building and loan will put up the rest. If they will,' he said, 'call Socks and tell him we'll do it. Say yes.' "

In a later age it would be said that anyone can reach anyone in just six calls. In reality this would hold true mainly for rich and powerful people. In Seaman, however, whose population in 1953 was 714, it didn't take six calls. Everyone knew everyone else. Prudie called the banker and Socks Roush the hardware store owner, and they all waited for the doctor to arrive. When he did, Socks sent him over to Prudie's house and she told him to come back for supper.

"The Lions Club agreed to put up money to renovate the building because they knew he was coming here with practically nothing," she recalled. "I think that's what they wanted. I think they wanted someone who didn't have."

Prudie began to think about what to make for dinner. She realized she didn't know what nationality Dr. Salamon was, but she thought he might be Jewish. She served on the Ladies' Auxiliary at the hospital, and when they had regional meetings they made sure not to serve ham because they understood it was against the religion of the Jewish doctors. Just to be safe, she decided to make chicken.

That evening she had the kids scrubbed and waiting on the porch when he drove up in a light blue Oldsmobile with a dark green roof. The children couldn't stop staring at this big, dark man wearing a jacket and tie and a white shirt.

They followed the adults into the kitchen and sat in their chairs barely breathing, they were so quiet. The doctor didn't seem to notice them at all until suddenly each of them, one by one, felt him reaching across their shoulders, leaving something on the table by every plate. They stared at these little round contraptions dumbfounded, just the way they'd been staring at him.

"Do you have milk in your glasses?" the doctor asked.

They nodded, eyes wide.

He reached over and turned over one of the boxes.

"Moooo," it went.

The children looked at him, then at the box, their tense little mouths now smiling.

"I brought you the cows!" he said.

Their fascination with this stranger escalated during dinner. While they picked up their fried chicken to get at the meat near the bone, the doctor dissected his neatly with his knife and fork. They left half their meal, they were so absorbed in the doctor's technique, the way he managed to pick off every last shred without getting a drop of grease on his hands.

After dinner the children were excused from the table and Dr. Salamon began to talk, very fast, until he must have noticed from the expression on Prudie and Chip's faces that they were only catching every third word.

He slowed down and told them what he thought they needed to know. He told them about his wife.

"She's no bigger than you," he said to Prudie, smiling, putting his hand low in the air. "She's pregnant like you"—he held his hand way out in front of his stomach—"only bigger. I told her she ate so much watermelon she must have swallowed a seed and was growing one inside."

He told them that he was from Czechoslovakia and that during the war he had been in a concentration camp. Prudie remembered distinctly that when her face tightened in sorrow for him he was quick to assure her that he had got more privileges than he might have because he was a doctor. He told her that "they" had come one night and taken his father and mother—or so he understood—but he had never learned exactly what had happened.

It became clear to her as he talked that he wasn't asking for pity but was trying to emphasize his credentials. "When I went back to where I lived, there was an ash pile behind the house," he told them. "On top of that ash pile was a long cardboard tube, and in it was my medical diploma, unharmed. I was fortunate that it lay there and refused to burn because it gave me distinct proof that I had a diploma."

That was all he had to say about his past, except to mention that he had once played the violin. When he finished talking, he looked at Chip and said, "Shall we go take a look?"

As they drove up the road toward the house, Dr. Salamon said, "They really wanted me in Hamersville, but I couldn't go there. They were widening the roads and cutting down the big trees. I thought to myself, 'You know, I could not live in a place where the big trees were destroyed.'"

He didn't mention the unenthusiastic reception he'd gotten at the Georgetown Hospital, near Hamersville.

When they got to the lot, the trees around the buildings, which had been bare on his first visit, were bursting with leaves. Dr. Salamon spent a few minutes inside the house, then wandered out back. After some time he joined Prudie and Chip by the car.

"Aren't they gorgeous?" he asked, gesturing vaguely at the woods.

They felt the words weren't directed at them. He looked up at the sky, lit by a last golden burst before nightfall, and repeated, "I just couldn't live somewhere where they would cut down the big trees."

Back at the house they were sitting outside talking, watching the sun go down, when a skinny little old man came running up, panting.

"Someone said they's a doctor here. That right?" he said.

Prudie and Chip weren't surprised to see him. In a town like Seaman news of a stranger's arrival at one end of town would reach the other end of town before he did. They introduced Dr. Salamon to the agitated old man.

"Come with me," he said to the doctor. "I got a friend up the road who's really sick. Needs help bad."

The doctor got up to follow the old man without asking him a thing. As he left he thanked Prudie for supper, and the evening was over. They didn't know where he stayed that night.

Prudie and Chip, who had spent most of their lives in Adams County, didn't take unusual appearances and disappearances of strangers lightly. They had the feeling that they'd witnessed something momentous. Prudie would say of that night, "It reminded me of Brigham Young when he got to Utah and said, 'This is the place.' "

———

▪ Suzy, age four and a half, sitting in the backseat, was disgusted as she listened to her parents exclaiming about everything: how beautiful the trees were, how fine the house would be when the walls were up and when the mess in the backyard was put into order. Couldn't they see what she saw? That there was nothing but huge piles of dirt because the town didn't have a sewage system and a septic tank had to be installed for indoor plumbing?

She hated this place. At home in New York she'd had friends to play with in the daytime and so many grown-ups who loved her around at night. She missed Baba, more patient than her mother, who would let her sit in the bath as long as she wanted and read stories to her.

Here, she and Mommy spent all day just sitting outside watching men pounding and digging while her father went off to work somewhere. Once in a while they would walk uptown, about a half a mile, and sit on a bench in front of the dry goods store in the unbearable heat. They were always thirsty. She heard her mother complain to her father one night that when she had asked one of their neighbors where she could get a drink the woman had told her there was a soda machine in the little knife factory across the street. What kind of people were these?

Suzy didn't care to find out. It was too hot and the air was too thick. She wanted to go home.

For three days she refused to eat anything but a spoonful of ice cream. When her father asked her what was wrong she looked at him angrily and asked, precociously, "How could you just drag me away to a strange land? Why are you breaking my heart?"

Szimi could see Sanyi was wounded by Suzy's words, unreasonably so, though she didn't tell him that. She was concerned, too, but not *unreasonably* so. It never occurred to her to connect his responses to his children to the child he never discussed.

"Sure enough," she would say triumphantly, "on the fourth day Suzy's hunger strike ended."

People emerged from the house in the middle of the woods next door, specifically a woman who seemed to have something pulling on her skirts. A face surrounded by a head of curls emerged to stare shyly at the newcomers. The two little girls appraised each other warily while their mothers introduced themselves. Belva Beery, the Baptist missionary's wife, chatted with Lilly Salamon, the Jewish doctor's wife, as their daughters bridged the gap between city and country and ran off into the woods. At lunchtime Mrs. Beery invited Suzy to have lunch with her new friend Annette. That evening Suzy declared to her parents that apple dumplings were the best thing she'd ever eaten.

———

▪ Szimi would eventually learn to make apple dumplings, though her menus would remain primarily Czech and Hungarian. Her children would grow up eating navy beans and ham, mashed potatoes and gravy, and tuna casserole at their friends' houses and food with mysterious names at home—dishes like chicken *paprikás, lecsó, knedle, shliskele.*

Eventually she would accept her position as the town exotic, but in those early days she was concentrating on ordinariness. This would have been the biggest stretch of all for her powers of adaptation even if she hadn't always seen herself as extremely . . . unusual. It seemed to her that ordinariness required a working knowledge of predictability, and it had been a long time since she'd counted predictability among her standards of measure. It was difficult to plan ahead when you didn't know where you would be tomorrow.

Yet when she drove down Main Street in Seaman for the first time with her husband and child, she saw that this was a place where people knew where they'd been and could predict where they were going. She suspected she had reached a place where the striking of lightning was an exception, not the rule. Yet at that moment this insularity seemed not confining but exhilarating. It felt safe, for example, to buy furniture.

For the first few weeks, while the house was being finished, the family lived in an apartment in Winchester, five miles from Seaman. Sanyi would drop Szimi and Suzy off in Seaman, then drive on another fifteen miles to the river, to Manchester, the county's biggest town. He was filling in for Dr. Sam Gendelman who had had a heart attack not long before. The first day Szimi and Suzy were in Ohio, the Gendelmans invited the Salamons for dinner with the Levys, the other Jewish family in Manchester, owners of a clothing store.

That evening Dr. Gendelman explained that when he recovered he would be leaving Adams County for Cincinnati. He had three young sons and didn't want to raise them so isolated from other Jews. It was agreed that Sanyi would take over his office.

Szimi and Sanyi didn't consider much about Dr. Gendelman's decision to leave, except for the opportunity it provided them. Though Szimi always lit the candles on Friday night to celebrate the Sabbath and made matzoh ball soup, religion had dropped out of their lives after the war. They weren't hostile to their religion like some of their relatives, who had no use for a God who experimented with cruelty. They had become indifferent. Prudie Cooper's sensitivity to Sanyi's eating habits had been unnecessary. By the time they got to Seaman they had tasted both shrimp and ham, and Szimi would soon be serving her *knedle* with pork chops grilled on a rotisserie.

Many years later, Sanyi would feel the urge to follow Dr. Gendelman's example, to move to Cincinnati. It was partly the work: His practice would be busier than he would have ever dreamed, he would be more adored than he would have thought possible. But there was a part of him that was always somewhere else. That uneasy corner of his soul expressed itself more and more as a growing desire to see his children grow up among Jews. Perhaps he wondered if he hadn't succeeded too well in creating a perfect isolation for his family.

He floated his plan to move to Cincinnati with his older daughter, Suzy, who was then eleven or twelve but whose opinions were taken as seriously as if she were an adult, as though her status as an American-born child gave her special wisdom. (Sanyi would often laugh and say to his girls, "Do you know how smart you are? You just open your mouth and speak English *perfectly*. Mommy and I have to study and study.")

When the prospect of moving was raised, Suzy looked at her father solemnly and repeated what she'd said when she first came to Ohio: "Why are you breaking my heart?"

For Sanyi that was enough. The discussion was ended. Instead of moving, he would find a partner to help take care of his patients and he would find his own way of teaching his children where they had come from.

In the summer of 1953, all that was in the future. Szimi and Sanyi were consumed by an unfamiliar feeling, the feeling that they had arrived, a strange sense of certainty. Szimi remembered the slight of the neighbor lady who hadn't offered her a glass of water so vividly in part because acceptance came so readily from every other quarter. Glenn Lewis, the local undertaker, whose family also ran the lumber business, sent his son with her to Kentucky to show her where she could buy good furniture at reasonable prices. George and Edna Hannah across the street had the Salamons over for dinner—fried chicken, green beans and bacon, mashed potatoes and gravy, and apple pie. One day Reatha Wickerham showed up at the door, after the walls were up and Szimi could start unpacking her new things, asking if she could help. Though she was in her forties at the most, Reatha was prematurely old looking, false toothed and wrinkled, her thin hair tied back with a kerchief. She was always a little breathless from being too fat and a little smelly from being poor and unable to bathe often. Some people in town disapproved of her because her children and her grandchildren were "illegitimate," but Szimi hired her—for fifty cents an hour—without hesitation. Reatha would remain loyal to her until the day she died.

The office wasn't completed before people started showing up—children with broken bones, farmers holding severed fingers in a piece of cloth. Women in their eighth month of pregnancy left doctors in other towns to show their support for the new doctor. Most patients didn't know where he had come from (except someplace "over there"), and they didn't care. Those who did know, who had seen newsreels about concentration camps, saw a divine purpose in Dr. Salamon's arrival. It would be said by some that this humanitarian had been saved from death at the hands of the Nazis to fill a need in Adams County. He would become acutely aware of this interpretation of his appearance there and would come to believe it himself.

The first thing Prudie Cooper noticed about Lilly Salamon was the way she moved, even in her eighth month of pregnancy. Prudie was a month behind Lilly and not as big, but she always tried to keep her stomach tucked in. Yet here was the doctor's wife, strutting like a barnyard hen, not at all embarrassed about her condition. This was regarded as highly unusual behavior in the 1950s, when women in town made a point of differentiating themselves from farm women by dressing prissily and refusing to acknowledge nature's part in matters that weren't discussed, like human reproduction.

"It was kind of peculiar about this baby thing," Prudie would recall. "No matter where she was at, Suzy would pat Lilly's belly and say, 'I've got a little baby in there.' And that was at a time when kids didn't know where babies came from."

Big as she was, Szimi moved like a whirlwind those first few weeks, buying things and unpacking them, trying to get settled in before the baby came. She and Sanyi drove into Cincinnati to meet an obstetrician at Jewish Hospital. It wasn't convenient, but they wanted a rabbi available in case the baby was a boy and would have to be circumcised according to Jewish law. This was characteristic of their attitude toward their religion—strict adherence to some traditions, disregard of others.

Prudie found it natural enough to get caught up in Lilly's shopping frenzy. Lilly needed her to drive, and Prudie needed Lilly for fun. Prudie had taught herself to drive not long before, when she'd asked Chip to teach her and he'd said, "Nah, you're too dumb to learn."

She'd found a 1948 Oldsmobile with automatic transmission out in the used-car lot and took off across Burnt Cabin Road, driving up and down singing "Blueberry Hill"—to Chip's amazement. The next week he sent her off, without a license, to Fairfax to pick up the title for a car.

She loved it when Lilly would waddle up the road to her house and say, "Let's go." They'd get dolled up, wear high heels even though their fat bellies made it a precarious vanity. Then they'd drive into Cincinnati, "the city," with the kids in the backseat. They always took Lilly's suitcase along, just in case the baby came.

Prudie would always say Lilly had taught her how to shop. The former refugee had found her Nirvana in the basement of Shillito's department store, where everything was on sale. One of the first things they bought on their first trip—marked down 30 percent—were American Girl flats so they could move faster. Prudie watched in awe as her new friend filled up bags with anything on sale, even clothes that couldn't possibly fit her or Doc or little Suzy.

"Don't worry," Szimi would tell her. "Someone can use it, and it's too good a deal to pass up."

They'd stop at Frisch's Big Boy on the way home for a piece of pie. Lilly was so frugal she'd eat half of it and store the rest in her purse for later. It became a standing joke; look in Lilly's purse and you'd always find something wrapped in a napkin, usually pecan pie gone moldy green. Prudie gave up trying to figure out this mixture of tightness and expansiveness—her new friend watched every dime, then gave away the bargains she'd bought to Reatha Wickerham or anyone else they'd fit.

Lilly always made her feel as though she could do anything and get away with it. As they barreled along the country roads, she'd pass the time telling Prudie war stories. She told her how she'd had to rip up blankets or steal paper to use when she was menstruating. She told her how they had been turned out like hogs or cattle when they had been liberated but she'd got a good job because she spoke so many languages. She made Prudie laugh, telling her about how she'd found a bunch of Russian soldiers washing in a toilet because they'd never seen indoor plumbing before and thought it was a sink.

On Fourth of July weekend, a month or so after the Salamons had come to town, their niece Baba and one of her cousins from New York came for a visit. Lilly was due anytime, and the cousin, an energetic girl named Jolie, had agreed to stay on after Baba left to help take care of Suzy for the first few days.

Lilly's shopping frenzy accelerated. She was feeling the deadline of the baby coming. That week she got Prudie to drive her to Maysville, Kentucky, just over the Ohio River, forty-five minutes away. She needed drapery rods, and all they had in the hardware store in Seaman were curtain rods. They took along the out-of-town guests to baby-sit while they shopped. Suzy and all five of Prudie's kids went along. The women dropped them off at the municipal swimming pool and told them they'd be back in an hour.

There may be hotter and more humid places than the Ohio River

Valley in the heat of summer, but no one could have convinced Prudie and Lilly's kids of that while they sweltered in the sun, waiting for their mothers. They'd stayed in the pool for an hour, then gotten out, ready for something to eat. Baba had dutifully herded them to the curb to wait for their mothers, but she couldn't buy them anything because Lilly had convinced her to leave her bag in the car.

One thing Prudie learned about Lilly that day was that one thing always led to another. She couldn't keep track of time, and she had the ability to make you forget as well. When the two of them finally showed up, almost an hour late, they found the children, sunburned and sweaty, sitting on the curb, crying, "We're hungry!"

Lilly was indignant. "Why didn't you get them something?" she asked Baba.

"Because you told me not to bring my pocketbook," Baba replied.

Lilly neither apologized nor hesitated. "Wait right here," she said. She waddled over to a store across the street and returned a few minutes later with bologna and cheese and bread and soda. She passed out the stuff to the kids and sat with them on the curb.

"Isn't this fun?" she said. "A picnic."

The miracle of it was, Prudie would say, that after a minute or two the grumpy kids were smiling and talking about their picnic as if the whole thing had been planned.

———

▪ If they had had more children, Szimi might have said there was a pattern developing. Every time she went into labor, Sanyi was off delivering someone else's baby.

At 5:30 A.M., July 10, the phone rang.

Sleepily Szimi picked it up and passed the message on to Sanyi: A woman from Belfast is having pains, and she's started to bleed.

She would grow accustomed to calls like this, early in the morning, in the middle of the night—watching Sanyi snap to, start pulling on his clothes before he was fully awake.

"You know," she said, "I think I'm having pains, too."

Szimi called Dr. Sam, as they called Dr. Gendelman over in Manchester, who had offered to drive Szimi to Cincinnati if Sanyi wasn't able to.

Szimi tried to go back to sleep, but the pains, though infrequent, were too strong. She pulled herself out of bed and took a cool bath. She emerged to find Jolie racing around the kitchen getting coffee. Szimi told her to relax while the two of them sat at the table chatting in Hungarian about what needed to be done in the house.

There was a rapid knock at the door. Jolie got up to see who was there. "Good morning, Dr. Sam," she said, smiling.

He seemed out of breath.

"Is anything wrong?" Jolie asked, knowing it hadn't been that long since his heart attack.

"Where is she? Where is she?" he said, all agitated.

Jolie laughed.

"She's in there having coffee."

Sam Gendelman couldn't believe what he was hearing. Labor pains were awful. He had watched the agony of his own wife, not to mention countless patients.

"Coffee?" he said. "I raced over here without anything!"

Jolie shrugged her shoulders. "Have some coffee."

Dr. Gendelman walked inside and looked strangely at Szimi, who gave him a friendly nod.

"Aren't you having pain?"

"Yes," she said. "Here and there. Let's have breakfast and then go."

So they had breakfast, then drove to Cincinnati, which took more than two hours because Dr. Sam was so careful.

A doctor examined Szimi at the hospital and told her she was about ready.

"Good," said Szimi, and she turned back to a book she was reading about Mrs. Abraham Lincoln.

Later a nurse came and asked her, "How do you feel?"

"Fine," Szimi said.

Nothing happened for hours. Finally someone stuck her with a needle. She woke up to learn that she'd delivered a baby girl and her husband was on his way. The long-stemmed roses were already in place with a card, "Thank you for the beautiful girl. Love, Sanyi and

Suzy." She smiled at the card and went back to sleep until her family arrived.

Yet she wasn't as cavalier about the birth of her second child as she might have seemed. Every year with great satisfaction she would tell this child—named Julia Marlene for her great-grandmothers—the story of how she had made Dr. Sam wait while she had her coffee. It was her favorite kind of scene, a momentous occasion (starring her) reconstructed as an amusing parable with this soothing message: Isn't life a breeze?

———

▪ By the time Baba returned to Seaman a year later, everything was different. On her last visit her aunt and uncle had been in chaos. Nothing had been ready, not the office, not the house. The baby had been on the way, Suzy had still seemed homesick for New York. Baba hadn't expected them to remain long in this country town, the kind of place she could imagine escaping to for a few days of rest.

Now she wasn't so sure about the impermanence of their stay. They showed no signs of remorse, no longing for the weekly card sessions with the family. Something in them had changed. She could see that.

It wasn't the call of luxury. Their house was nice enough but nothing special, a modest brick ranch given extra dimension by the doctor's office attached to it.

The back entryway was almost impassable, there were so many huge wild roses hanging off bushes. The yard, a muddy mess when Baba had last been there, was now a long sprawl of green, bounded, more or less, by hedges on one side, the woods on the other. There was nothing manicured about that yard—not a straight edge anywhere— but it had a kind of ragged beauty, Baba could see that. The trees Sanyi loved so much seemed grander than she remembered—a giant oak in the front yard, the big hickory and several smaller ones out back, including the locust tree by the tool shed next to the shiny new propane tank.

There was another fixture in the yard—the baby's playpen. Every clear day, summer or winter, Szimi would park her under the hickory tree—naked or in a snowsuit, depending on the season—and hand her a big boiled potato to chew on. Szimi delighted in telling people how her baby spent her first sixteen months waiting to walk, clutching a potato and laughing at the sky.

Suzy seemed to have forgotten New York entirely. She handed Baba a note that said "Welcome Bubbles" when she arrived, kissed her, and disappeared with her friends. She came home a while later and presented Baba with a sackful of candy.

"Where did you get that?" Szimi asked her.

Suzy said, "At the store."

"How did you pay for it?" her mother asked.

Suzy smiled. "I charged it."

Baba groaned when she saw how proud her aunt was of her daughter for this bit of mischief. She was also impressed with the child's freedom, five years old and going all the way uptown by herself with her friends. She was even more impressed—startled, actually—when she realized Sanyi knew about it. Then she realized what was holding them there: Her uncle had found someplace where he felt safe.

———

■ Sanyi would hire and train a number of women to act as nurses in his office over the years. They would speak of him with a fierce loyalty and protectiveness.

Helen Brown was nineteen years old in the summer of 1954, home for vacation from college, when her father suggested she apply for a summer job with Dr. Salamon. Mr. Brown had heard that the woman who helped out in the office was leaving.

Mr. Brown was part of a migration of Kentucky farmers to southern Ohio after the war. He'd owned grocery stores and carried the mail, and now he was trying his luck at farming. He'd pushed education with all his children; Helen was hoping to get a nursing degree.

She found the interview with the doctor most peculiar at first. He briefly went over her responsibilities but seemed most interested in knowing whether she could keep a secret or not.

The doctor soon clarified the relevance of this to the job. He'd seen a patient, a women in her late forties, who was expecting a baby but wasn't ready to have this mortifying turn of events made public. Yet it seemed to her that no sooner had she left the doctor's office than everyone in town was calling her up to find out if what they'd heard was true. It turned out that the current nurse couldn't hold back such a juicy piece of gossip, and that didn't sit well with the doctor.

"I can keep a secret," said Helen, a plump girl with small, even features and curly hair.

That summer she learned to give shots and draw blood, to do a urinalysis. She learned to change the dressings on burns and not to flinch when farmers showed up with their fingers almost separated from their hands. She worked mornings and evenings; it was not unusual to see sixty patients a day and sometimes many more. Afternoons the doctor went for hospital rounds and house calls or, twice a week, to Manchester, where he kept the office he'd inherited from Dr. Gendelman.

When she didn't understand something, he would explain it, without condescension. She felt she was learning so much she didn't go back to school that fall.

She was intrigued by the doctor and by his wife and by what went on in the house, separated from the office only by the tiny "drug room." The doctor insisted on keeping a complete supply of medications, which he often included in the three dollars he charged for an office call.

The family never ventured beyond the drug room during office hours. Yet Helen could always sense their presence. For one thing, it was impossible to avoid the smells of cooking—strange odors Helen found very appetizing.

It wasn't unusual for the doctor to disappear for a few minutes every so often. The patients could hear the faint sound of laughter, and they would ask Helen what was going on. She always said she didn't know, but she did know. The doctor periodically checked in with the children. Helen had seen him tickling the baby's stomach with his nose to make her laugh and then laugh heartily himself when he succeeded.

Without meaning to, she studied the Salamons as if they were some rare species. She learned quickly that Mrs. Salamon had a thing about fresh air. Even in the cruelest cold she kept the windows open a crack and never seemed to think twice about putting the baby outside in the middle of winter. Helen almost froze when she baby-sat for the girls on Thursday, the doctor's one day off. He and his wife would go to the city for shopping and the movies, and come back, bags filled with strawberry tarts and gingerbread men from the bakery at Shillito's, just in time for evening office hours.

She learned to make Mrs. Salamon's cabbage rolls and never refused an invitation for dinner. She admitted, though, that she found some of their eating habits too strange. One day a patient brought the doctor some green peppers and she asked him what he was going to do with them.

"Why, I'm going to eat them for breakfast," he told her.

She was startled. At home they fed peppers to the hogs.

When she investigated their eating habits further, she learned that they ate the same thing for breakfast every day: heavy rye bread with fresh butter, peppers and tomatoes, soft-cooked eggs and coffee. The doctor never ate lunch.

"You don't need lunch," he told her. "Your body just gets used to it because you feed it."

That streak of discipline, of Old Testament judgment, ran deeper than keeping his stomach trim and his back straight. He tolerated a lot that other people wouldn't—patients who didn't wash, drunks, hysterical outbursts from husbands who didn't understand why their sick wives had to wait out front with everyone else (the office operated on a first-come, first-served system).

But when someone would come in to talk about putting a parent into a nursing home she would see the doctor's back go up. He'd listen to the reasons—severe illness or senility. Then he would coldly ask the child if he or she had seen what so-called rest homes looked like, the best of them dark and smelly and largely unregulated in those days.

"You know your mother took care of you when you couldn't take care of yourself?" Dr. Salamon would ask, not caring if the mother in

My mother became a leading lady. Here she is (front right) with her "ladies' club."

question was babbling without comprehension while this discussion was taking place between the doctor and her child.

He would deliver this lecture coolly to his patients. But after they left he would let loose. "What kind of people are these, who won't take care of their parents? Their parents took care of them when they were babies. I wish I had that burden."

The outbursts were especially startling because he was usually so deferential to his patients, so willing to hear their complaints and their confidences, which became more and more frequent as his reputation for discretion was established. No matter how many times patients bought him gifts—of cakes, quilts, green peppers—he seemed overcome with gratitude.

He behaved, Helen thought, as though he owed a debt to everyone and that every gift he received set him back a payment. The list of people she wasn't supposed to charge seemed to be longer than the list of people who were allowed to pay.

There was a new Methodist minister in town, for example, whose son ruptured his appendix during a high school basketball game. The doctor rushed him to the hospital for surgery. When the minister and his wife came in to pay the bill, Dr. Salamon asked them if they had insurance.

No, they said, they didn't.

"Don't pay me," he told them. "But do this. If you ever hear that I am having surgery or someone in my family is ill, just pray for us."

Helen knew the freebies irritated Mrs. Salamon, who was the office business manager. Their dining room table was always covered with charts and bills. Once in a while Helen would pop into the house and hear the beginning of a discussion about money. Mrs. Salamon would ask him to explain the latest charity case, and then he'd try to wheedle her out of the bad mood by calling her that name they used for each other—*zolotik*. Usually after that Helen couldn't catch any more of it because they'd start talking in Hungarian, so fast she couldn't have understood even if she could understand.

When she left to get married, the Salamons took her and her new husband to Cincinnati for a fine meal at the Netherland Hilton Hotel. After that they went to a movie. Helen couldn't remember what it was, but she wouldn't forget the way they set the girls down in their seats like grown-ups and didn't budge when the little one's head suddenly appeared way down front, a dot moving against the screen.

"Do you want me to get her?" Helen whispered.

"No, no," said the doctor. "Let her roam free. We can see where she is."

———

■ In the 1950s *The Cincinnati Times-Star* ran an inside feature called "Your Town," acknowledging, perhaps, the fact that the paper's circulation had spread far into the rural outposts of southern Ohio.

In the summer of 1956 Winchester and Seaman made the column under the headline "Small but Ambitious." The two-page spread included brief historical summaries of the two towns and profiles of a woman garage owner in Winchester, an insurance agent in Seaman, and the doctors in both towns. The doctors' stories were combined into a patriotic, anti-Communist article under the headline "Two Who Found Freedom from Fear."

One of the cliches of American folklore is that small towns in this country are very slow to welcome outsiders.

In Seaman and Winchester, at least, two "outsiders" have become an important part of their respective communities.

They are Dr. Kenneth C. Jee, Winchester, and Dr. Alexander Salamon, Seaman. Both, in a coincidence so unusual that it could only be a coincidence, are from iron curtain countries.

And neither Winchester nor Seaman had a town doctor before the two came.

Dr. Alexander Salamon was the first on the scene, coming to Seaman three years ago. He is a native of Czechoslovakia, having left that country in 1947 with his wife, Lilly. His medical degree is from Prague University.

Why did he come to America?

"Well, as you know," says Alexander Salamon, "we were a democratic country then. I wouldn't say there were rumblings, exactly, of the Communism that would come the next year, but someone with a good nose could smell it.

"We had had so much trouble during the war," the dark-eyed black-haired doctor continues, "and we couldn't feel secure. We came to America to find a place free from fear."

They found it.

For a while Dr. Salamon worked in New York hospitals, in 1949 passed his state medical examinations there. In 1953 he came to Ohio at the suggestion of a surgical appliance salesman and looked for a place where "they really needed a doctor."

In Seaman, Dr. Salamon got not only that but what he considers a fine home for his family as well.

He has two children now, three and seven, and he likes the town that they will grow up in.

"I've had no trouble here at all," he says, smiling. "I was born and brought up on a farm in Czechoslovakia, so New York was too big for me. But here the people are pretty much the same. The only difference is the language."

For 46-year-old Dr. Salamon there are many things he is thankful for in his adopted home. "I love it," he insists. "The doctors, the people, are wonderful." And there is another reason.

"It is a very peaceful place."

Our faithful dog Poochie had almost one hundred puppies in her lifetime. My mother, me, and my sister are playing with some of them.

17
———

The Conspiracy
of Happiness

■ For the longest time I was happy to remember it simply as that—a peaceful place. Then I grew up, moved to New York, and discovered that angst was acceptable, even desirable. So I went through a period when I saw only the dark side. After all this shifting of perspective, I'm not sure I trust my own memory.

What do I remember?

Over time, the Norman Rockwell trappings would multiply. There would be a faithful dog named Poochie, who walked my sister and me to school every day and returned promptly at three to pick us up. Every year she presented us with a litter of puppies—close to a hundred puppies in her long lifetime—which we named thematically: flavors of ice cream one year (Butterscotch, Chocolate Chip, Vanilla . . .), animal television idols the next (Rin Tin Tin, Lassie, Mr. Ed . . .) Every year we dressed the pups in doll clothes and entered them (and ourselves) in the Child and Pet Parade at the annual Fall Festival.

There would be a chicken named Penny, who laid a double-yolk egg every day and came running when called by name. (I learned only recently that Penny really wasn't the green Easter chick we'd bought at the five-and-ten-cent store in Hillsboro but a replacement for the chick that died.)

There was a succession of guinea pigs and rabbits and pet geese, most of which ended up buried out by the septic tank. We would belong to 4-H and Girl Scouts and work as candy stripers at the county hospital; compete in spelling bees and play noisy instruments in the local marching band. Our father recorded all of it on film, with cameras that grew more and more sophisticated over the years as new models came out.

We rode our bikes miles out into the country without answering to anyone and learned to drive well before we were sixteen. When our father started making money, he bought farmland. We watched him spend more and more time on the farm, obsessing about whether it would rain or not, whether the corn would grow or not. He loved that farm and kept expanding his vision of what it should be (leaving the details of management to my mother, who began to hate it). Both Suzy and I set tobacco, but she lost interest after that. I, however, learned to bale hay and haul manure—at first, I believe, to endear myself to our father, then because I took great pleasure in the solitude the fields provided me. I suppose, too, that playing farmgirl was a way for me to feel that I really did belong in Adams County, that I was no different from anyone else there.

Of course, we couldn't help but notice that we were different, and not just because of our parents' accents, or because we celebrated the Jewish holidays and always lit the candles on Friday nights (before going to basketball games and gorging ourselves on distinctly nonkosher hot dogs).

While few kids in Seaman ever ventured beyond Cincinnati, we'd visit our cousins in New York every summer. We rode the subway, went to shows on Broadway, and ate in Hungarian restaurants where men walked around playing Gypsy music on violins. Our New York cousins also visited us in Ohio, just as Grandfather Salamon's grandchildren had gathered at his house every summer—though we didn't know we were re-creating history. They spent their days outside, their nights playing hide-and-seek in my father's office, doing gymnastics on the stirrups of the gynecology examining table, playing games of Monopoly that went on for days in rainy weather.

Every winter we'd go to Miami Beach to visit our Great-uncle Marty and Aunt Anna. They never seemed very interested in children, but we'd been told they had been very good to our parents and so had to be treated warmly. We went to nightclubs, watched our Uncle Joe get up on stage to sing with Cab Calloway. Once, at Junior's Delicatessen, we were urged by our parents to say hello to Cassius Clay (later Muhammad Ali), who autographed a napkin for us.

We watched our mother become a minor mogul, especially after the federal government began paying the medical bills for the indigent patients our father had treated free for years. She was always on the telephone, talking with her stockbroker in Cincinnati and Uncle Marty in New York, with whom she became an increasingly significant partner in real estate deals. We pretended we weren't embarrassed when she became head of the PTA mainly to orchestrate the building of a tennis court for the school because she wanted to teach us how to play tennis.

We accepted our mother's eccentricity as casually as we accepted our father's sainthood—willingly following, for example, her method of history instruction. Both of us became avid students of *Gone with the Wind*, which we read when we were quite young and saw in the movies the first time the picture appeared in Cincinnati in revival. On my twelfth birthday, my mother presented me with nine volumes of the Lanny Budd series, Upton Sinclair's pop socialist history of the twentieth century.

We were embarrassed by her only occasionally—when, for example, she wore her fake leopard jacket and a turban to basketball games. We grew accustomed to what seemed like outrageousness to good little girls like us—like the time she parked the car illegally at the airport and told the policeman to wait before he wrote out a ticket. She jumped out of the car and went to the trunk, where she had a basketful of big ripe tomatoes, fresh from the garden. To our wails of "Mommy," she said, "Shhhhh." When the policeman, inevitably, happily accepted the tomatoes, she turned to us and said triumphantly, "See!"

We had Easter egg hunts in the backyard and decorated our father's office every Christmas. We spent hours hanging the hundreds of cards he would receive from his patients and painting elaborate stencils on the windows with Glass Wax. We went to Presbyterian Sunday school all the way through the Old Testament but were yanked out when we came home singing "Jesus Loves Me." At the same time our parents cultivated their private brand of Judaism, a melding of traditional ritual and pop culture—with the reading of the *megillah* at Purim and *Fiddler on the Roof* holding equal sway.

We felt superior to the Jewish kids we met in Cincinnati, whom we regarded as spoiled suburban brats, insufficiently grateful for being American or Jewish. But then, we were unusually grateful for almost everything, though this trait was most pronounced in our relationship with our parents. We expressed this gratitude constantly, especially on birthdays, which were treated in our household like national holidays. My father took pains to assure us of our unique place in his universe. Each of us had special flowers (mine were carnations; Suzy's were cyclamens); each of us would wake up to a special song (mine was "Oh, Julie"; hers was "Wake Up, Little Suzy") followed by Bing Crosby singing "Happy Birthday." In return, we embellished the sentimental cards we bought our parents with outpourings of love that sounded strangely like reassurance.

We understood we were supposed to be humble like our father, who rejected most special privileges he would have been accorded as a doctor (except when he was stopped for speeding, which was often). Whenever my parents traveled overseas, he would identify his profession on the customs card as "farmer." He never even bothered to hang a sign outside the office or put his diplomas up on the wall. He taught us important things—not to throw our Popsicle sticks on the ground, to be careful when we crossed the street, that it was better to give than to receive. He never let us leave the house without kissing good-bye or go to sleep without saying our prayers. After I saw the movie version of *To Kill a Mockingbird* I forever adored Gregory Peck, who played the noble southern lawyer, because he reminded me so much of my father, both physically and spiritually.

We were acutely conscious of the evils of laziness, having never seen our parents idle except when on vacation—and even then they idled feverishly. When we'd drive into Cincinnati, our mother would unwrap a big package of insurance forms and quiz our father about various patients while he drove. (His driving both fascinated and terrified us—the way he'd zoom along at eighty miles an hour on winding roads but never touch the wheel with more than two fingers except on the most terrifying curves.)

Our lives might have seemed lifted from one of the Disney movies we loved so much, if only the grown-ups hadn't had so many secrets— ominous secrets. Our cousins Baba and Aliska both had numbers tattooed on their arms. Another group of cousins had a different last name: They were Salaway instead of Salamon. Most disturbing to us was the moods our father would periodically fall into; he was capable of not talking for days at a time.

Just as we couldn't place an exact date on the moment we learned to walk, or to read, we couldn't pinpoint exactly when we learned about Nazis and concentration camps. But we were aware for as long as we could remember that our parents had experienced terrible things in an earlier life, just as surely as we knew no one had ever sat us down and told us that such things had taken place. We understood there was something deeper than affection for Al Jolson that accounted for our father's melancholy appreciation of "Sonny Boy," a father's ode to his little boy who has gone to join the angels. We would learn about the past haphazardly, shocked by each new discovery and ashamed, finding the normal complaints of children and teenagers—our complaints—so insignificant after all our parents must have suffered. We could only hypothesize about the suffering, because our father spoke of it not at all and our mother could never sit still long enough to finish a story.

———

▪ There was the terrible Yom Kippur of 1960. We hadn't yet joined the synagogue in Cincinnati and used to attend High Holy Day services in Portsmouth, a river town about an hour away that had a small Jewish population. Once a year a local church would be converted into a synagogue headed by a traveling rabbi, usually a rabbinical student from Cincinnati.

The tension in the house would build from the moment we got up. My mother recently told me there had been two sources of her anxiety. She had thought of Huszt only during the Jewish holidays and so associated going to the synagogue with painful memories. But her real concern had been that we wouldn't leave on time and that Daddy would get angry.

We learned to hate the holidays, too, as a time of terror. Inevitably our father would return from hospital rounds so late we ended up racing to Portsmouth around hair-raising curves. We would arrive at the "synagogue" so jittery we spent most of the service thanking God for getting us there alive.

On what would become known as That Terrible Yom Kippur, we were dressed and waiting for Daddy. There was a knock at the back door. Chip Cooper had come to visit with his friend Vernon Young, whose wife, Eileen, was our mother's best friend. The men were drunk and out for a good time.

My father couldn't say no to patients, and my mother couldn't say no to anyone. She couldn't imagine turning away a guest, even an uninvited one. No one needed an invitation to our house. Still, she did tell Chip and Vernon we had to go to Portsmouth and would be leaving as soon as "Doc" got home.

"We'll just stay a few minutes," they said, and came inside to chat.

My mother told us that when Daddy had walked in the door she had been chilled by the look on his face—though Chip and Vernon had happily been oblivious to his silent fury.

He had greeted them politely, then abruptly left the room. My mother had told Chip and Vernon to leave.

When she had gone to tell her husband she was ready, she had been shocked by his response. He had started yelling at her in Hungarian, accusing her of deliberately trying to sabotage Yom Kippur: *You don't want the children to go to services.*

She had tried to interrupt him: "What are you talking about?"

Without answering, he had stormed out of the house and slammed the door.

Our mother had gone to find us. Suzy was sitting in the guest room with the door closed while I huddled in the living room closet, my face pressed to the floor. The three of us had hugged each other and cried.

He had returned later that night and behaved as though nothing had happened.

That Yom Kippur forever infected the atmosphere of the household. From then on we, the family females, were guarded toward our father and husband, unable to understand where these unfathomable attacks came from and afraid to find out. We couldn't hate him, so we pitied him and denounced ourselves for not knowing what to do. We became adept at sidestepping possible conflicts, trying to ensure that nothing would make him sad or angry. We never found out if he was aware of our conspiracy of happiness.

———

▪ I remember something else. I was especially worried about setting off my father because I felt I was on tenuous ground with him. I'd heard the stories of how he hadn't paid much attention to me when I was a baby because he had been worried Suzy would feel rejected. My mother had become my protector, and that was a mixed blessing. As she would put it later, "I just took it for granted that whatever you were doing you were doing fine."

I was a chubby little girl and got chubbier and chubbier until, at age eleven, I had grown quite fat (a fact that was vehemently denied by my mother and sister but acknowledged on the playground, where I was called "Tub-a-lard"). I remember eating large quantities of food quite deliberately, knowing that one of my father's favorite sayings was "Moderation in all things." He disapproved of people who smoked too much, drank too much—and ate too much. I knew he disapproved of me—not just because I was fat but because I wasn't properly respectful. When he came in from the office to see us when we were watching cartoons, for example, I didn't get up to kiss him until a commercial came on. This infraction set off the silent treatment, which wouldn't end until I apologized. I would endure a few days and then write a profuse apology, which was immediately accepted without comment.

When I turned twelve, I resolved to become thin—and a year later I was. After that my relationship with my father improved noticeably. I felt I could talk to him without fear of reprisal.

My mother bore the brunt of the angry silences, though I didn't know this at the time. They intensified when my sister began dating a non-Jew and it occurred to my father that she might marry someone who wasn't Jewish. She promised him she wouldn't, but that wasn't enough, so she agreed to break up with the boy on their next date. When my father came into the house at the end of office hours that night—around 11 P.M.—to find Suzy hadn't come home yet, he got in the car and drove to Cincinnati, where he spent the night in a motel.

On this occasion my mother asked him what was wrong with him, and she got an answer. He blamed himself: "It's my fault we came here and I let her go out with these guys, but I've been through enough."

The bursts of snappishness grew more frequent when I was in high school. Though he had always gone out of his way for the family, he seemed irritated by the presence of my cousin Mark, Béla's son, who came to live with us because he'd gotten into some trouble in high school in New York. We speculated that my father was jealous of the attention Mark was getting from my mother and me—though Mark took pains to stay out of Daddy's way. My mother, too, circled around him as though he had temporarily gone mad, never sure what suggestion might trigger a bout of angry silence.

At the time she didn't confide in anyone and made excuses when any of us questioned his behavior toward her. Only later did she tell us she concluded that he had gone a little crazy after his brothers died—Louis in 1966 and Jani in 1969, both of cancer. I remember when Uncle Louis died we could hear Daddy crying in the bathroom. We had never heard him cry before. When Uncle Jani became ill, my father brought him to Seaman to care for him while he suffered through chemotherapy treatments in Cincinnati. Jani died a few months later, at home in Lima, Peru. My father returned from the funeral in a depression whose repercussions seemed directed mainly at his wife.

They continued to pretend everything was "normal." In the summer we took one of our periodic trips to Israel to visit relatives. My mother posed for pictures in front of Yad Vashem, the Holocaust Museum, looking angry, and I subsequently thought she had used the occasion to express her resentment toward Daddy.

——

■ I suppose it doesn't matter anymore. It doesn't to my mother. When I asked her not long ago about how she looks back on her marriage, she didn't hesitate. "I think we had a very good marriage," she said. "Looking back on the situation, I blame myself. Maybe it would have been better to blow my top instead of trying to keep peace. I didn't have experience and no friends in similar situations, and I wouldn't have told them anyway. I guess that was implanted in me by my mother: 'They should rather envy you than once feel sorry for you.' "

She paused for a minute. "I really loved your daddy and admired him," she said. "Whenever he had these outbursts, I would attribute it to what he lost in the war and that he was working so hard and had so much on his head. I tried to get everything right so he didn't have to worry about anything."

My father loved the farm.

18

A Very Good Life

■ From time to time Szimi would remember the fortune-teller in Auschwitz, the Jewish woman who had learned her magic from Gypsies. Everyone in the barracks had felt protective toward her. Though theirs was designated the "children's barracks," only four little ones lived there and two of them belonged to the fortune-teller.

Szimi took comfort from her recollection of the time the woman had read her hand. The woman seemed to have no doubt about what she saw there. She, Szimi, would survive, and when she "came out" she would meet somebody whom she would marry and have a very good life.

As the years went by, she would think with satisfaction: that woman really knew what she was talking about. She might pause a minute, to wonder if the woman herself had survived (Szimi was fairly sure she hadn't; she had had two small children with her, and mothers of young children hadn't been likely to survive).

Her memory of this occurrence was vivid and precise, and it gave her particular pleasure because it suited her own prognostication (*Everything will turn out fine*).

In fact, however, her memory was faulty—or, as she herself would put it, "selective." Her memory of the fortune-teller was only half a memory.

On a cold day in the spring of 1971, the image of the fortune-teller appeared in her head, as it had many times before. Only this time the vision was untouched by Szimi's editing pencil.

There she was, holding the hand of the young Szimi, both of them dressed in rags, heads shaved.

The fortune-teller was smiling, happy to tell her subject what she wanted to hear: "You will meet somebody you will marry and have a very good life—"

Then she paused.

In the past Szimi had taken that pause as a cue. Time for the image to fade into a burst of sunlight, leaving her to wonder at fate's kindness to her.

Now, however, Szimi lost her power to stop the scene from moving ahead to its unsettling conclusion.

"What's wrong?" the young Szimi asked the fortune-teller, whose face had become quite grim.

The woman pushed Szimi's hand away and said abruptly, "I don't know what will happen."

Szimi put her hand back into the woman's and asked again, "What is it?"

Again the woman refused to look. She shrugged. "That's all. I really don't know."

The woman might have been telling the truth, or she might have been covering up. As usual, given two possible interpretations, Szimi chose the one that conformed most closely to her own desire. From then on, whenever she told the story of the "Jewish Gypsy" woman, she deleted the ambiguous ending.

She was satisfied to declare the shortened version a historical fact. It had served her well for years. She had survived, she had met someone when she came out, and she was having a very happy life. There seemed no need to speculate on the possibilities in the fortune-teller's pause, to experience again the cold fear she'd felt in Auschwitz when the gentle woman had refused to reexamine her hand. She was willing to remember only the fortune-teller's smile, her obvious delight in being able to offer hope to allay Szimi's misery. She successfully erased the sorrowful contortion on the woman's face when she set Szimi's hand aside and refused to elaborate on what she saw there when Szimi asked her. She was willing to forget her own eagerness to let it go at that, to accept what the fortune-teller had said and not think about what she hadn't.

Yet she could no longer let it go at that. Sanyi was going to die, and not even she could conjure a miracle—or even pretend that she had.

———

▪ Less than four months before, Szimi and Sanyi had been lying with the girls by the side of Marty and Anna's swimming pool in Miami Beach.

A tall, handsome young man with bushy black hair was with them. He was Peter Danes, one of the two boys Suzy had been dating for some time. She had her doubts about Peter, but Sanyi didn't. He seemed to adore this young medical student, whom he had invited to work with him the summer before. Peter came from the "right" background. His parents were Czech Jews who had lived in Israel before settling in Cleveland. He was familiar in a way that the other boy—also a medical student but from a wealthy German Jewish family in Scarsdale—was not.

There had been much discussion in the family about whether Suzy, who had just turned twenty-two, would ever make up her mind, as though she were being seriously threatened in some way by the prospect of spinsterhood. The urgency seemed especially odd since Sanyi had lectured his daughters since birth about the importance of having a profession and economic independence. He always made sure they had money before they went on dates, urging them to pay their own way so they wouldn't feel any obligation.

That Florida trip was dominated by the drama of Suzy and Peter.

Two days before New Year's Eve, Peter presented Suzy with a large diamond ring picked out by his mother. She accepted it, then immediately flew to New York, where she had plans to spend New Year's with her other beau, whose feelings she didn't want to hurt.

Peter, an agreeable fellow who mainly wanted to avoid confrontation, flew back to Ohio with his fiancée's family. His acquiescence in this farce gives some indication about his lack of seriousness about the engagement.

Throughout all of this, Szimi thought Sanyi was putting undue pressure on Suzy to reach a decision. He had always had a special concern about her marriage plans, a concern that had begun early, when she was sixteen and had started dating the boy from Seaman with what Sanyi thought was too much ardor.

He had never discussed his concerns with Suzy, but once he said to her in passing, "You have hot blood like me."

Szimi felt there was something out of the ordinary in the way he insisted that Suzy reach a decision. Sanyi rarely issued ultimatums for his children. If anything, he was too oblique, scattering hints and riddles like tea leaves for the family to attempt to read.

Yet there was nothing obviously amiss. They spent their days sunbathing and went out to a dinner or a show almost every evening, either alone or with other relatives who were spending Christmas vacation in Florida. The only small thing, barely noticeable, was Sanyi's persistent cough.

When they returned he tried cough syrup, then antibiotics, but nothing relieved the subdued but steady hacking.

On February 7, Szimi planned a big party to celebrate Sanyi's sixty-second birthday.

She had much to celebrate. Months had passed since the end of the period of estrangement that had begun two years earlier, when Sanyi had returned from his brother Jani's funeral. Sanyi's hostility toward Szimi had vanished as mysteriously as it had arrived. The change hadn't appeared to be triggered by any specific event. Of course, any close examination of the rift is impossible. Szimi didn't acknowledge the end of this period of estrangement because she hadn't acknowledged the beginning. Hard to celebrate armistice when no war was declared.

Yet she did want to celebrate, and she was given the perfect opportunity. Her book club was scheduled to meet on the Sunday evening that was Sanyi's birthday. It was men's night, the one time a year the women invited their husbands to join them at a potluck supper. Szimi decided to turn the event into a party for Sanyi. She wasn't certain how he would react. He rarely socialized with his patients, which meant most of the town was off limits. But that night he was lit up, fully engaged in his dual role as host and honoree, obviously enjoying the food and warm feelings, which were abundant.

His buoyant spirits continued into the bedroom that night. There was every sign that their life had returned to normal; life had progressed so that normalcy was something Szimi had come to count on.

She was unprepared for what Sanyi told her as he was finishing breakfast the next morning: "I'm going to Columbus this afternoon after office hours."

Szimi immediately detected the false casualness. Sanyi kept to a rigorous schedule—office hours, hospital rounds, house calls, home, office hours. Even his departure from routine was scheduled; on Thursday afternoons they had kept up the tradition of going to Cincinnati together, to shop and go to the movies.

"What for?" she asked.

"Ohio State has a very good lung department," he said. "I want them to take an X ray."

Szimi nodded. This seemed reasonable to her. After years of referrals Sanyi knew all the specialists at the various city hospitals. She saw no cause for alarm, certainly not in his words or his manner. Still, when he came to say good-bye after office hours, she said, "I'm going with you."

Szimi gladly accepted the findings of the Columbus doctors: nothing wrong. But Sanyi was sober on the way home. He carried a curse she did not. He was a gifted diagnostician, and he knew that "nothing" was not the correct diagnosis.

The cough persisted. Two weeks later Sanyi checked into Jewish

Hospital in Cincinnati for three days of tests, administered by Dr. Goodman, an internist Sanyi liked and trusted.

Szimi also liked Dr. Goodman, whom she had never met. He was about her age, forty-eight, a slightly built man with fine features and the aura of a caring person, without cant.

On the third day, Dr. Goodman joined the two of them in Sanyi's room. Very quietly he said, "Everything looks perfect, but there is a metastasis in the fluid in his upper chest. Since everything else was eliminated, they assume it was from the lung." He recommended a dye test.

Sanyi nodded and thanked Dr. Goodman. Szimi, however, was bewildered. "Metastasis" meant secondary cancer, she thought, suddenly forgetting all the medical terminology she'd picked up from conversations with Sanyi and from handling all the paperwork for him all these years. *They assume it was from the lung.* She reviewed Louis's cancer (bone) and Jani's (colon). Sanyi had never been more than a light smoker—a few cigarettes a day when he was a student, not more than one a day for years, at night, while they watched the evening news, and he had stopped even that after Louis had died.

Sanyi drove in silence, fast as always, two fingers on the wheel. After a long while he spoke, though she wasn't sure if he was talking to her or not. Matter-of-factly, as if he were musing over whether to buy some new piece of farm equipment, he said, "If this is the story, we'll go to Columbus and I'll have the dye test there. I know the people there, and they have a much better lung division."

She didn't realize it then, but she was embarking on a journey no less devastating to her than her trip to Auschwitz all those years before. This time there would be no lice and filth and cruelty. The horror would unfold in ultrasanitary conditions, in sterilized hospital rooms where the scientific experiments would be conducted on her husband by colleagues who respected him and wanted only the best for him. It would be a gentle torture, no less horrible because it was cloaked in the best of intentions.

This time she couldn't call on fate to be her benefactor, the intervention between good and evil. This time there were no Nazis, no human forces who saw the elimination of her loved ones as a necessary step toward their master plan. This time there was no blaming the fragile idiocy of fallen humans. Fate itself was the enemy, and she would helplessly watch her husband fight it valiantly, with the same determination that had helped keep him alive before. She assumed he would win, long past the moment indicated by rationality. But rationality, except for her own special brand of it, had never appealed to Szimi, and so she willingly complied with Sanyi's decision to be cured.

The oncologist in Columbus who conducted the dye test was a big, stout young fellow whose sympathetic tone, unlike Dr. Goodman's, seemed like something he'd acquired as part of his professional training.

"There's nothing much that can be done" was his conclusion after the dye test revealed a tumor on one of Sanyi's lungs.

Sanyi asked him about mustard irradiation, a debilitating cancer treatment.

"It's very painful and not much use for lung cancer," said the doctor.

When Sanyi insisted, the doctor shrugged. "We can try."

The treatment took twenty-four hours. Szimi checked into a nearby boarding house and stayed with Sanyi in the hospital until eleven that night. They listened to the news on the radio (a leftover from the war years; they never missed an opportunity to hear the news). During a commercial break a man came on the radio, speaking from somewhere near Tijuana, Mexico: "Lung cancer? I have the only cure available in the world."

Usually Szimi was susceptible to this kind of prophetic coincidence. Not this time. When Sanyi murmured, "We'll have to write to them," she didn't take down the address.

She hated to leave him that night, burning with fever, so fragile she was afraid a light touch would break him.

As the doctor had predicted, the treatment had no effect other than to leave Sanyi terribly weakened. Yet when they returned home the next day, he saw patients as usual, pretending nothing was wrong.

He was a man obsessed, not denying himself the diligence he would show any other patient. That evening he showed Szimi an article in a medical journal about a Japanese doctor in Buffalo, New York, who was using chemotherapy on cancer patients. He had already called the doctor and made an appointment for a consultation the following day.

They flew to Buffalo. While Sanyi saw the doctor, Szimi talked with a patient in the waiting room, a young woman, about twenty, her hair wrapped in a turban. Szimi's spirits lifted as the young woman praised the doctor, told Szimi how she had leukemia and now was in remission, what a miracle worker this doctor was.

Sanyi's appointment lasted about half an hour. When he emerged, she saw from his face that they would not be in this waiting room a year later, cheering on some new patient with tales of the miracle-worker doctor.

The doctor told Sanyi they'd had limited success with melanoma tumors but never with lung tumors. A few hospitals were conducting experiments, and Ohio State was one of them.

They had flown out of the Columbus airport, so Sanyi called the Ohio State oncologist and told him he'd like to stop by on the way home and begin chemotherapy injections. "Not for lung cancer," the doctor told him, but he relented when Sanyi insisted that he wanted to try. Sanyi told him he would pick up the injections and take them to Dr. Goodman in Cincinnati, an easier drive.

Szimi was with him when the doctor tried to discourage him: "It makes you deathly sick. Vomiting, nausea, fever. It is very dangerous, very painful."

Sanyi responded patiently, as though trying to explain a simple procedure to a patient who was unnecessarily complicating it. "I have no choice," he said simply. "If I don't take it, I have no hope. At least this way I can keep track of what's going on."

The doctor handed over the injections reluctantly. Szimi sensed he was chalking up this insanity to professional courtesy.

On the way home Szimi asked him, "How shall we tell the girls?"

He shook his head vehemently. "No one should know," he said. "We'll tell them I have a fungus on my lung and the treatment is for that."

The conversation went no further. Szimi didn't like lying to the girls. She never did so deliberately, not when she was asked something directly, and she wasn't sure she could do so now. But her daughters never pressed her to elaborate on this mysterious fungus. They had learned well from their parents, to look for the happy ending.

———

▪ "If you have a patient with lung cancer that has metastasized, don't do anything. You will just put him through misery for nothing. Let him enjoy himself, encourage him to do what he can do, because the most he has is six months."

That was the unequivocal prescription for lung cancer according to the wisdom of the day. The message arrived in the mail the day after Szimi and Sanyi arrived home from Columbus with a bag full of chemical injections. It wasn't a message from God, or, if it was, the messenger was one of the drug companies that periodically sent instructional records to doctors, offering diagnostic and treatment advice. Every time Szimi listened to Sanyi retching in the bathroom after an injection, she replayed the record in her mind: "If you have a patient with lung cancer that has metastasized, don't do anything. You will just put him through misery for nothing."

Sanyi, however, wouldn't relent. He wouldn't believe the misery would be "for nothing." But the treatments were to remain a secret, and the secrecy was to include everyone, even the nurses, though they would have to give him the injections. Dr. Goodman laid it out plainly for Sanyi: If he insisted on seeing patients, he couldn't drive to Cincinnati, take the shots, recuperate, then drive home in time. It took only one injection for Sanyi to capitulate (though later he began calming the vile effects of the chemotherapy with large doses of Compazine, an antinausea drug). He told the nurses the shots were for treatment of a rare fungus, serious but not lethal (none of these exact words were used; it was all implied). Sanyi kept careful notes on his reaction to the injections, which he regularly passed along to the doctor in Columbus.

Szimi asked him, more than once, "Do these shots make any sense?"

He didn't respond directly to the question. "You have to try everything," he said.

She decided to have hope because he did. She allowed herself to be convinced that his strength and determination would defeat the odds against him.

Then came the cold day in April when the fortune-teller from Lager C appeared in her dreams.

The vision didn't arise from out of the blue. Szimi's memory was triggered by an event whose meaning was so clear she was at a loss to provide any interpretation but the obvious.

There was a bond drive for Israel at the Netherland Hilton Hotel in Cincinnati. In recent years Sanyi had felt a deep connection with Israel or, perhaps, the idea of Israel. He invested large sums of money in the country, usually in the form of bonds for his children. He and Szimi found they enjoyed the large formal dinners that went along with these appeals. They took the speeches seriously, fully accepting and reveling in the concept of Israel as the defiant legacy of the Holocaust. And they liked dressing up, modeling their understated finery in the living room for the children's approval before they left for the evening.

They arrived just as the cocktail hour was beginning. Sanyi told Szimi to go ahead while he rested in their hotel room and to come get him when the dinner was about to begin.

Szimi knew she looked elegant that evening in a long-sleeved black dress and pearls—no big jewelry for her. She liked the excitement in the air at gatherings like this, the growing murmur of anticipation. Joining in the flirtatious conversation over cocktails followed by a heady discussion of geopolitics was like visiting another planet, nothing like their world in Seaman, rooted in the passing of seasons, the immediacy of the earth and its earthly demands.

"Hello, Lilly," said a familiar voice.

She turned to find Dr. Goodman, unfamiliar at first in his evening clothes.

"Where's Alex?" he asked.

Szimi put on her best party smile. "He's lying down because he wants to be fit for the dinner," she said.

Before she realized what she was doing, she put the question to him. "What *is* the prognosis? He's taking these shots and they're making him so sick."

Szimi never went out of her way to find answers she didn't want to hear. So it must be concluded from her bluntness that she wanted to hear the truth, perhaps hoping that Dr. Goodman would put to rest her unspoken fear.

"My dear," said Dr. Goodman.

That was enough. She didn't want him to go any further. There was too much solicitude for comfort in that *my dear.* The words came at her like a spray of ice, fastening her to the moment like a glacier overtaking a helpless deer.

"I'm very sorry to tell you. He doesn't have too long. My own brother just passed away six months after we discovered the disease."

Szimi thought, He doesn't know what he's talking about. She must have sounded angry as she said, "That's impossible!"

The sympathetic Dr. Goodman shrugged. "I'm really sorry," he said.

Szimi had to leave. She walked away, trying to find respite from the cocktail party chatter. She found the traditional women's refuge in situations like this—the ladies' room.

In Auschwitz she hadn't felt it. Not this consuming terror. Her parents had been torn from her so abruptly, she had had no time to think. As for herself, she had never doubted her own future, that she would have one. A quarter century had passed. She was no longer twenty-two, immersed in death but certain she had her life ahead of her. Now she was forty-eight, in the middle of a complex and variegated existence, every strand of which was tied up with Sanyi. Now she was shaking with sobs in a bathroom whose modest luxury would have seemed an impossible fantasy then, beyond even Szimi's improbably hopeful outlook. She cried not so much from sorrow—she had been consumed by sorrow since all this had begun—as from fear.

She could feel her face swelling from all the tears and tried to pat herself back into place. She found herself doing what women always did in movies—staring at herself in a bathroom mirror, overcome by grief but stopping to carefully apply lipstick, finding strange solace in that small vanity.

When she got to their room, she was relieved to see it was dark. She put on a light far from the bed so Sanyi wouldn't see her eyes when she woke him. As he got dressed, she thought how well he looked. He often recuperated from the treatments by lying on the floor next to the sliding doors in the den. The sun shone fiercely in the afternoon; she used to pull the curtains to keep the carpet from bleaching out. Lately, however, she'd taken to leaving the curtains open, letting the sun pour onto her and Sanyi, lying side by side on the floor while she read the

They liked to catch the rays that came through the windows of our family room.

newspaper to him. All that indoor tanning had given his broad face a deceptively healthy glow; his weight loss was hidden under his dinner jacket. The thought crossed her mind, as she looked at their image in the mirror by the elevator, that they were still, at their age, an exceedingly handsome couple.

Only the jacket he was wearing on a hot July day gave it away: He was dying.

19
─────

Nem Tudom

■ By the end of May Sanyi was forced to acknowledge his physical limits. He more or less stopped making his afternoon hospital rounds. During one of his checkups in Cincinnati he hired a young doctor, who was about to complete his residency at the University Hospital, to work in Seaman that summer.

He wasn't capitulating to death, however—not openly. He and Szimi passed many of their afternoons sunbathing on the floor discussing where they might travel when the new doctor was able to take over for a few weeks. Szimi would later realize that these were no ordinary vacation plans. Sanyi seemed more and more intent on a prolonged visit to Israel. It would occur to her that his itinerary wasn't as open ended as he made it seem, that—perhaps—he was formulating a scheme to die in Israel.

She could only guess because mention of the actual possibility of his dying was carefully avoided by both of them. They had taken care of their wills years before, so weren't forced by legal considerations to bring up the subject. She did ask him, one day, whether they should postpone Julie's graduation present. They had given her a trip to Australia, to give her a chance to meet the boy she'd been writing to for four years. He was no ordinary pen pal but the son of Zeldi, the sister of Baszi, Szimi's concentration camp friend who now lived in Cleveland. Though no one openly made the suggestion, the thought occurred to all the adults that it would be nice if the friendship became something else.

Sanyi wouldn't hear of it. Their daughter, he said, was number one in her class, and this was her reward. He behaved as though there were no plausible reason to delay the trip.

Szimi didn't argue with Sanyi's decision about Australia. She thought, "Who knows what will be after?"

She was shocked at having the thought. She refused to think of "after." Sanyi referred to "after" only once. He told her if he should become incapacitated he wanted to be taken to Cincinnati, not West Union Hospital. He didn't want his colleagues to see him like that or his patients to pity him.

One day in June an emergency arose at the hospital. An obstetrics patient of another doctor arrived bleeding, and the doctor on call didn't do C-sections. The nurses on duty realized the woman had a placenta previa—her cervix was blocked by a low-lying placenta, leaving no room for the baby to emerge. If the baby wasn't taken out soon, the placenta might rupture—a disaster, sure to lead to massive bleeding. They'd seen it happen, blood splashing on the walls. They might lose both mother and child.

One of the nurses on duty was Annette Beery, Suzy's dearest friend, the little girl who had "rescued" Suzy that fourth day in Seaman. They were so close that when the Beerys had moved across town—a five-minute bike ride—Annette had begun having a recurring dream. She'd wake up in the middle of the night sweating, just thinking about it. She'd remember it as the worst fear she had growing up.

This was her dream: The Berlin Wall had been built right across Seaman. She didn't understand why they'd done it or who "they" were. All she knew was that her town had been cut in half and she would never see her best friend, Suzy, again. How would she live? For the longest time this dream had haunted her, but she had never told anyone.

After graduating from high school, Annette had gone on to become a registered nurse. Now she heard one of her colleagues tell another, "Maybe Dr. Salamon could come in. I bet if you call Dr. Salamon he'll be here in ten minutes."

Annette had to laugh when she heard that. It was only ten miles from Seaman to West Union. But Route 247 faithfully followed the dips and the curves that made southern Ohio so beautiful. She remembered all the times the doctor had given her and Suzy a ride to the hospital when they were candy stripers. That blue Oldsmobile used to fly from the top of one hill to the other, landing hard on the humps. *Whump. Whump.* Each *whump* had heightened her disbelief. Could this maniac be the same gentle man who had taken care of their family so often, who was so subtle with a needle that he could effortlessly hit a vein no one else could penetrate?

As predicted, he arrived at the hospital ten minutes after the call. Annette didn't have a chance to look at him when he got there. He'd swooped in, put on his scrubs, and raced into surgery, swiftly as he ever had.

It wasn't until afterward that she got her shock. When he pulled off his cap she could see his dark hair, now salt-and-pepper, was wringing wet, and the air-conditioning was working overtime. His green operating shirt was sticking to him, completely wet, too. She saw him struggle to get to North Station, the nurse's station a few feet out of surgery, and get up onto one of the stools. His face was ghostly white.

She couldn't believe her eyes. She had just seen him less than a month earlier, at the high school graduation, and he'd seemed fine.

She couldn't stop staring at him, sitting there looking as though he'd never be able to get up. How many times had she seen him stopping at North Station early in the morning on weekends? As a young nurse she was stuck with the night shift, so she'd just be getting off when he'd get there at 7 or 7:15 in the morning, always natty in a sport jacket or a suit, a tie, those white shirts. He used to march down the hallway with his big shoulders pulled back, looking exactly the way Annette thought a doctor should look.

Without fail he'd stop at the desk and just stand there, waiting like a kid trying to attract the grown-ups' attention. When the nurses noticed him, he'd tell his joke. Sometimes it was funny and sometimes it wasn't, but they always laughed. They weren't just being polite. His little routine made them feel special, as though the day couldn't get going until they'd had a laugh together. The jokes were beside the point.

She'd always liked Suzy's dad. He'd always made the kids feel important. When she and Suzy would double-date, they'd come back to Suzy's house at 10:30 at night and Dr. Salamon would still be working. At 11:00 he'd come in no matter what and sit down with them while they all watched the news. He'd ask them what they'd been doing, what they thought about what was going on. When the main headlines were over, at 11:15, he'd jump up and say, "I've got three more patients I've got to see."

After she'd got her nurse's training in Cincinnati and had come back to the county hospital, Annette had felt as if he was watching over her. Once she was handling the emergency room when he was on call. When he came in for rounds, she explained what the various patients' complaints were.

She handed him the workup sheet on a young man who was complaining of a discharge from the penis, which Annette had diagnosed as gonorrhea. The man was waiting on the examining table while the doctor looked over the paperwork. When the doctor saw what the problem was, he glanced over at Annette.

"Git, git, git!" he said.

"Excuse me?" she replied, thinking she was misunderstanding him because of his accent.

He repeated, "Git, git, git," waving his hand as though the gonorrhea were going to jump off and land on Annette.

She didn't realize what was going on at first, thinking she, the novice, had screwed up. She had the jitters as she waited by the door outside the room while the doctor examined the man and wrote him a prescription.

What had she done?

Only after the doctor came out and was especially jovial did she get it. She wasn't quite a nurse yet, not to him. She was still Suzy's friend, and he wasn't ready for her to see the nastier side of life (though of course she'd seen far worse in the emergency room in Cincinnati).

She wasn't angry with him. How could she be? She'd loved watching him with the patients, his congeniality. She'd never seen a better bedside manner. Sometimes she thought his patients would stick with him even if he weren't any good because no one would treat them the way he did. He'd sit down by the side of the bed and explain what was wrong with them and how long he thought they'd have to be there and why he was giving them medicine. He always had time to go through

My father's nurses (from left): Nola Ryan, Alice Michael, Anna Marie Foster

everything with them, always treated the poorest of them with respect.

She figured she could learn a lot from him. But that day he came in for the C-section she realized she might have learned all she ever would.

———

▪ Alice Michael was a soft woman. Though she was physically strong, raised on a farm, there was a delicacy about her. Her curly hair, her large sad eyes, and especially her voice—all soft, as though she didn't want to impose on anybody in any way as she made her way through life. Her father was a hard man off a farm in Kentucky who had remained a loner all his life. When his daughter had graduated from high school—class valedictorian—he had stayed home and she hadn't cared. He'd embarrassed her, the way he had worn old, ragged clothes, even when he'd had money, because he hadn't wanted anybody to think he was worth anything. He'd died when he was eighty-four and Alice couldn't remember him kissing her once. But she had a picture of him hugging her. She really liked that picture because it was the only time she remembered him touching her.

She grew up remembering kindness the way most people hang on to grudges. So she would never forget how Dr. Salamon had saved her life and her baby's. She'd miscarried with her first baby, and they had been expecting problems the next time: pelvis too narrow. When it was time for the baby to be pulled from her by cesarean section, she was deathly sick with pneumonia. The doctor came in and stayed with her the whole night, helping her overcome her fear that she and her baby were going to die. He was right. They both lived, and five years later Dr. Salamon delivered her second son.

She would have done anything for him, and when her younger boy was three she had her chance. Mrs. Salamon called her and asked her if she'd like to come work for the doctor. The workload had gotten to be too much for one nurse to handle, even Nola Belle Ryan, the big, capable woman who had taken care of the office for four years. They needed help.

Alice was hesitant. She'd never held a job. But she felt she couldn't say no. She knew it was something outsiders might not understand, but she loved Dr. Salamon. She owed him her life. Her kids, her mother, whenever anything happened to anybody he was there to take care of it. He made them feel that everything would be okay.

Once she started working, her reasons for doing so changed. She discovered the excitement of becoming extremely competent at something. Over time she and Nola and the doctor worked out a great routine that allowed them the efficiency they needed to take care of everyone who came and gave the doctor time with patients who needed it. They saw anywhere from sixty to a hundred patients a day, often working past eleven at night. Eventually a third "girl" joined the group.

The atmosphere was relaxed, despite the grueling pace. The doctor never seemed rushed, chitchatting with the farmers about problems he was having on the farm, telling his famously bad jokes. The only way they could tell he was annoyed with a patient—for taking the wrong dose of medicine, for example—was to look at his hands. He'd stand at the sink by the window and squeeze the edge so hard his knuckles turned bright white under the fine black hair that covered his hands. They'd catch him sometimes standing alone at that window, staring out at a bird in the parking lot, or a squirrel. If he caught them looking at him, he'd wave them over and point at whatever he'd been watching, pleased as if he'd hit the jackpot.

His patience seemed endless to them, even for habitual pains in the neck. There was the old lady they called Panties-in-Booties, who was always showing up with some woman's problem that would require a gynecological exam. The doctor always asked the nurses to stay in the room during these exams. They'd given her her nickname the first time she'd arrived wearing high-heeled boots trimmed with fur. While she was undressing, she had asked the nurses if it was all right for her to stuff her panties into her boots. They'd assured her it would be fine, then groaned as they heard her thin, high voice ask the doctor why she didn't enjoy sex as much as she used to.

There was the man who used to come to the office when he'd drink too much and get a fit of delirium tremens. They'd stick him into one of the examining rooms and the doctor would calm him down while they waited for the ambulance to come. Nola and Alice would say, "Oh, if only we had a psychiatrist in that back room." But there wasn't, just Dr. Salamon, who became surgeon, obstetrician, internist, and, when need be, psychiatrist. They eavesdropped on the patients in the waiting room, and it was obvious to them: These people felt proprietary toward the doctor. They felt as though they owned him.

The nurses sometimes wondered how Mrs. Salamon took it: her husband jumping up from dinner a half hour after he'd sat down, to run back to his patients. And the women! The nurses were sometimes amused, sometimes disgusted at how they doted on the doctor, trusting him with their problems, medical and otherwise. When certain women came in, Nola and Alice would look at each other and whisper with feigned seductiveness, "Oh, Doctor."

But they never worried about him acting improperly, the way they knew some of the other doctors were said to. No one ever reported his car parked out in front of some woman's house on a regular basis, for example.

They knew sometimes he'd get testy with "the missus." They could tell because he'd be extra jokey in the office. Mostly, however, he seemed to dote on his family, never seemed to mind the blasts of saxophone and piano that came out of the house when the girls practiced their duets. They knew they'd never have to miss a band performance during Friday-night basketball breaks once Suzy got to high school. The doctor never missed a show his daughters were in. Same for the school parades: He'd always be out there on Main Street, his movie camera stuck to his face, waiting for his kids to march past. That was one time the patients had to wait.

Alice admitted it: She had no perspective on him. She'd try to think of something bad. The worst thing she could say about him was that sometimes he didn't notice that he had holes in his nice wing-tip shoes and that he was no help at all with the billing. They saw the difference during the couple of years the young doctor from New York came to help out, before he was drafted into the Army. He'd chart and chart and chart; they had to tear him away from the paperwork to get to the patients.

Dr. Salamon couldn't seem to tolerate even the mention of money. The nurses learned never to question the list of people he gave courtesy to—the teachers, old family friends, the preachers (in a county where the ministry called a wide variety of people, both with training and without). The nurses thought he was often taken advantage of, but they knew better than to suggest this to the doctor.

Of course these "negatives" only heightened Alice's admiration and affection for the man. So it isn't surprising that when Dr. Salamon got sick the softhearted Alice let Nola give him the IV treatments. She couldn't bear to look at him when he took his shirt off. He was burnt from radiation treatments; his arms were so clotted from needle holes Nola had to swab his arms with Burow's solution.

They didn't question the lie they knew he was telling them. This was no fungus. They could see how sick he was getting, having to sit and rest after every patient, his breath so short they wanted to breathe for him. He never turned anyone away, just stretched things out so he could take a break.

The patients saw the change, too, the thinness, the shortness of breath. They'd whisper out front, to the nurses, "How is he?"

"A little better," they always said, though they knew he wasn't better at all.

That winter the flu had hit worse than any time Alice could remember. They had them sprawled on the floor in the hallway. The office looked like a hospital ward, there were so many sick people.

One afternoon they got a call around 1:30 from a patient of Dr. Jee, over in Winchester. She would never forget that voice, whining on the phone: "I'm really sick and Dr. Jee is out of town. Can I come over?"

Reluctantly Alice asked the doctor what to tell him. They'd had a long, difficult morning, and office hours were over. It was too much for the doctor.

"Don't do it," said Nola.

"Yes, we will," said the doctor. "We'll see him. We'll wait. We have to take care of our competitor's patients. It's the right thing to do."

By the time the patient arrived it was past two o'clock. No sooner had he walked into the examining room than he began to vomit explosively.

For a moment the three of them just stared at the mess. Then the doctor spoke. "You girls go," he said. "Just leave."

When they tried to argue with him, he nodded toward the door. He cleaned up the mess and treated the patient.

Alice would never forget that man, whose name she had long forgotten. She convinced herself that the doctor had been brought down sooner than he should have been because of exposure to that man's flu. For some reason it made her feel better, blaming it on that patient. She often thought, "Who knows what would have happened if we hadn't had that man in there? Maybe the doctor would have survived awhile longer."

———

▪ Szimi spent hours each afternoon with Sanyi, sunbathing indoors on the pale green wall-to-wall carpet in the back room. The repose was fake. She was always on guard, ready to jump if Sanyi only hinted he wanted something. She was halfway to her feet one day when he grabbed onto her arm to hold her down.

He looked at her, tears in his eyes. "You were a much better wife than I was a husband."

Jarring, that use of the past tense. You *were* a much better wife.

She assured him that wasn't so, but silently she agreed with him. His sainthood had taken a toll on her. Though words like "neurotic" weren't part of her vocabulary, she felt something was "not right" about his extreme devotion to his patients, his deep insecurity when one of them didn't respond to him.

She remembered one of his early obstetrics patients, a nervous woman petrified about childbirth. Her due date was on a Thursday, and she knew that was Dr. Salamon's afternoon off. He'd called her that morning to find out if she'd had any labor pains yet. None. "Don't worry, then," he'd said, "I'll be home in plenty of time—five hours. But just in case, here's the doctor on call, don't hesitate."

All afternoon he'd worried, even though the only unusual aspect of the case was the mother's extreme anxiety. As soon as they'd returned from Cincinnati, he'd telephoned. She was in the hospital. No pains yet, but she'd called the other doctor almost immediately after they'd left. That was it. She never came back, and Sanyi never stopped blaming himself for failing to make her comfortable.

Maybe it wouldn't have bothered Szimi so much if Sanyi hadn't exposed that other side of himself to her, that . . . *irrationality*. The events were few, scattered over a period of years, but they had left a deep imprint, perhaps because he'd always made it clear that nothing mattered in the world except her and the girls. This devotion only accentuated the horror of his outbursts, which might have been less inexplicable in a household where kindness and love weren't an absolute requirement.

——

■ Miki Hermel, Sanyi's nephew, remembered the summer of 1971 as exceedingly hot. Miki would always be the relative to whom Sanyi felt the closest. Miki was the nephew who tried to follow in his uncle's footsteps by going to medical school. The war had kept him from finishing, but he had become a laboratory technician. Sanyi appreciated Miki's sly sense of humor and admired, perhaps, his impetuousness. In the postwar Prague years Miki had dabbled in smuggling, married his girlfriend six weeks after they met. Miki would push a joke farther than Sanyi dared, to the edge of meanness. Miki, on the other hand, spared Sanyi his caustic wit. He loved his uncle, who was generally regarded as the family patriarch even when he wasn't the oldest living Salamon.

When Szimi called him to come to Seaman for a visit, Miki had been relieved to hear that Sanyi wanted to see him. He'd sensed that something "was up" with his uncle, who had neglected to call to congratulate Miki that spring, when he'd finally completed his doctorate in London. Miki, hurt by this uncharacteristic lapse in encouragement, loved Sanyi too well to harbor a grudge, his usual response to this kind of slight (a characteristic, everyone agreed, that came from the Hermel, not the Salamon, side of the family despite the Salamon tendency to nurse old wounds).

They settled on July Fourth weekend for a visit. The date was still up in the air until a few days before. When Miki called Szimi and said maybe it would be better if they came in the fall, when it was cooler, she made it clear that later wouldn't be better: "Sanyi would like you to come."

Miki spent the weekend with his wife, Erzsi, in a daze. The surface signs were normal. They arrived to a house in chaos. Szimi was painting the dining room and had transferred her mountain of papers into the kitchen. Sanyi spent most of their first day occupied with the young doctor who had been hired, Miki was told, to give him more free time to travel and to be with the family.

On the second day, which Sanyi had reserved for Miki, the two men spent the afternoon on the farm. Sanyi proudly showed his nephew the trees he'd planted, loaded with little *nem tudom szilva*, "I-don't-know plums," just a little bigger than cherries. Miki hadn't seen them since he'd left home. They pruned the trees and kept the conversation to simple, homey subjects, such as the various delicacies that could be made from Sanyi's plums when they ripened. When the trees were manicured to Sanyi's satisfaction, they went for a walk. Sanyi laid various travel plans before Miki and urged his nephew to consider coming along, they'd had so much fun together the summer before on their trip to California and Las Vegas—remember Szimi asking Sammy Davis, Jr., to put his arms around her and the kids for a picture by the pool at Caesars Palace? By then this fungus would be cleared up (the story was maintained even for Miki, no stranger to disease, a professional).

Miki agreed that another trip would be great, let's make plans. But, he said, let's have a cold drink first. This sun is getting to me.

"That was it," he told the family when he got back to New York. "That was when I knew that Sali [he always called Sanyi "Sali"] doesn't have too many days to go. The sun was shining, and it was hot. Let me tell you, it was so hot. You know how hot it gets in Seaman. It was really hot.

"But there was Sali, sitting on a lounge chair in the backyard—wearing a jacket!—and he was shivering from the cold."

———

■ Tommy Schlanger was eight and a half that summer, a skinny little boy allergic to everything, it seemed. He ate almost nothing, used to hide the bologna sandwiches his father made him eat "for strength" inside the pull-out couch in the living room. His mother was Baba Schlanger, *née* Feierstein, and *her* mother was one of his Great-uncle Sanyi's sisters who had died a long time ago in "the war." That was pretty much the extent of his knowledge of the family's history. When he asked his mother about the tattoo on her arm she never managed to find an answer that matched the sad look in her eyes.

Baba had married after Sanyi and Szimi had moved to Ohio and had herself ended up in the Midwest. Her husband was a tempestuous man who had not emerged gently from spending part of his teenage years in Auschwitz. They had lived for several years in Cincinnati, which allowed them to see her uncle often. They had two sons. Tommy was in Seaman because they were moving to Roanoke, Virginia, and had gone ahead to find a new house. David, the older one, a Little League star, had stayed with friends in Cincinnati so he could finish the season.

If Tommy had to describe the way he felt about his great-uncle, he would say he felt "warmly uncomfortable." He wasn't sure why he felt uncomfortable, really. He was sure he saw Uncle Sanyi's eyes light up every time he saw him, and he loved the way he'd throw him up in the air. Some of it must have been the allergy shots, he felt. Whenever his uncle walked in the door, Tommy would scoot under a chair to escape the needle he knew would follow.

But there was more to it than that. Tommy was a shy kid, and his uncle was always asking him questions—what he was doing at school, stuff like that. It wasn't the accent that threw the boy off but the way

Uncle Sanyi talked to him, respectfully, as if his uncle really wanted to know what he thought, something he wasn't used to from adults.

Tommy understood the "warmly" part better. There was something very comforting about Uncle Sanyi. He didn't fly off the handle the way Aunt Lilly did. She was more inclined to get upset over small things, but not for long. She'd yell and completely forget about whatever it was and never mention it again. Tommy felt as if nothing could bother his uncle. In fact, he noticed that he seemed to enjoy the smallest things, like a really pretty day. He went fishing with him a few times on the farm. They didn't catch any fish and Uncle Sanyi didn't say much, but he seemed to be having a good time just taking in the sun and looking around, even though the pond was out in a field that seemed pretty scraggly to Tommy. When he was grown up and reflecting back, he would say that his uncle seemed like someone who was at peace with himself.

Tommy liked spending time out in Seaman. His great-uncle and -aunt didn't seem scared of anything. He remembered one time speeding along and a policeman stopped them. Aunt Szimi didn't blink as she told the policeman Tommy was sick and they were rushing him to the hospital. It was a believable story. Tommy was so pale and thin, he always looked a little sick. The boy didn't understand what was going on and was surprised to hear of his illness. He began worrying that he was sick and didn't know it.

The truth was, he didn't get to spend all that much time with Uncle Sanyi because Uncle Sanyi was always working. Lately, however, he'd spent the afternoons hanging around the house—a bad case of the flu, Aunt Lilly explained—and Tommy would keep him company.

Even so, the little boy was surprised on Monday morning, July 12, to come in the hall and see his uncle still lying in bed wearing a pair of pale blue pajamas that looked thin, as though they'd been washed too many times.

Aunt Lilly came out of the room and screamed at him to go get the nurse—well, she didn't scream, exactly, just talked in a really serious voice, as if something emergencylike was happening.

Tommy went to the office. As he walked down the hallway, not seeing anyone, he got more and more nervous. When he did see someone, his shyness overcame him. He didn't do what Aunt Lilly told him. He didn't tell her to get there in a hurry. He didn't say a word.

It took him a long while to stop blaming himself, at least partly, for not getting the nurse.

My father's last birthday, February 7, 1971. There's Baba (standing on the left) and her sons Tommy (left) and David; my mother; me kissing Daddy; and Uncle Joe.

20

Absence

- I wasn't there.

For years I was haunted by my absence—not just at the moment he died, but in the months before. I condemned myself for my insensitivity, my preoccupation with . . . with what?

I have clues, those detailed diaries. I know the following: I listened to Moody Blues albums with my cousin Mark. I did yoga. I worried about the pimples on my chin and physics. I played Ping-Pong and fed old people Jell-O at the hospital and sneaked out of the house to speed around country roads with my friends, me driving the old Triumph Spitfire convertible my sister's boyfriend, Peter, left at our house that spring. I fought with my mother about whether I was eating enough or not, and I wondered if it was hypocritical to cook fried chicken for the family since I had become a vegetarian. I spent hours exploring the farm with my best friend, Ginger, the only black kid in school. I tasted cherry vodka, and I practiced my saxophone and the piano. I went on dates that invariably ended in a car parked on a deserted country road where nice boys and I groped passionately but never went all the way. I read incessantly if not analytically: "Yesterday finished 'Dr. Spock on

Vietnam' and today 'The Ugly American,' " I noted on February 1, 1971. "Both good and both thinkers."

On February 22 I let my hair dry without a blow-dryer. "Mistake. Wavy frizzies." That same day I recorded the following: "D is going to a Medical Convention in Columbus for three days. It'll be weird without him."

I began scrutinizing the diary entries for more clues, tucked in among the catalogue of the day's events. Until now I hadn't wanted to know anything about that spring I'd wiped from memory in a vain effort to reestablish a link between spring and life, not death. This is what I found, a line here or there, sometimes a paragraph, surrounded by voluminous text on what I had done at school, who had said what to whom, my continuing dilemma about whether to wash my hair or not.

February 23: Today we joined the ranks of convention families. D went to a three day Med. convention in Columbus. It's strange not having him here. I miss him. We don't really see each other so much but supper is strange with just girls and M seems more vulnerable without him. He called this evening—he said he loves me just like me and if I'd be quiet and sit still for half-hour he wouldn't know me. So I guess he's a little homesick. I hope he enjoys it.

I massaged M's back (D told her I do his all the time) and rubbed junk in it and we talked. She's a nice lady and we're friends. I really love M & D.

February 26: I found out D's been not at a convention but in the hospital at Cincinnati for a test series. Thank God all is O.K. I love him so much.

February 27: Whew am I tired. Gin and me talked until 4:30 this morning and woke up at 8 so I've been functioning on a big $3^1/2$ hours of sleep. Ginger left around 9:30 and M & I left for the city at 10. Was a gorgeous sunny windy day. I drove. We first picked up Tommy and David (Mike and Baba are in Virginia to check a job offer). They are such dolls and we went to Zayre's and then down to Jewish Hospital. I had fun driving in the city. We went to D's room (M & I), it was so weird to see him as a patient.

Knock wood he looks great only tired. I hope all the tests come out right—so far they have, Thank God or whoever. I love D so much. We finally got him checked out (it was funny—D makes a lousy patient) & I drove with D while M took the boys. I was in a happy mood. When Mark got home we had a talk. In the end we're the best buddies. I am so tired. I feel irrational.

March 1: M & D went to Columbus. After school I had sax sectional rehearsal til 4:15. No one was home so I practiced piano and did yoga and M & D still weren't here. Finally at 5:30 M came. D stayed at the University hospital for more tests that didn't get done at Cincinnati. I'll be glad when he ever gets home for good. He was in a very good mood on the phone.

March 2: D called. Nothing was done today & M got really upset. She cried after he hung up. I hadn't realized what a strain this is on her. I love her so much and D, too. I'll be so glad when he's home again.

March 3: Snow. Mark has been having a beer every night since D isn't here. It's funny. D called. He sounds tired—he got tested all day. I hope the roads clear up so M can go to him tomorrow.

March 5: When I got back from piano lessons I felt like being alone. (M went to Columbus for D—they called and won't be home til tomorrow) & Mark was here so I kind of resented it inside I guess.

March 6: Mrs. Gray's starting a girls volleyball team. Hope I make it. D was here after school with M. He looks so tired & thin & weak—those tests knocked him out. I feel so bad for him but M said he should be OK in a couple of days.

April 3: Rog and I decided to go to Maysville to see "The Great White Hope." Was very good and very depressing. Rog & me talked a lot about bigotry and got depressed. At 12 we passed the bowling alley and decided to bowl & did. Was really fun. Got home after 1.

Then . . . College acceptances, preparation for graduation, my friends—these were the subjects that filled the pages of my diary. "It is very difficult to concentrate on classes when Spring is in my body," I observed on April 13. I did note, on April 21, that "Miki called—he got his PHD! I really admire him. He's got determination, anyhow. D is much better (knock on wood)."

May 4: D took me in the office and the nurses filled my physical out for college. I'm so scared of growing up. It surrounds me & I can't help but think of it. I don't want to leave my friends, I want to stay home with M & D.

May 12: Tried on my cap and gown for M & D & read them the speech. They like it. We just sat around and talked. I love them so much. After supper I practiced piano and did yoga. Stood on my head 6¼ minutes. M had a club meeting and D & I were alone (Mark worked late). We had a nice time—I read to him from "The Prophet" and we talked. I hope so much he's better soon.

June 14: D was in a very very crap mood. I'm worried—he must feel bad. We called Uncle Bela for his birthday and D wouldn't even say h'lo.

June 15: Got up, took a shower, said bye to M & D, got in my baby car & headed toward Blue Creek and Head Start. My job is really like a kindergarten teacher. I like it a lot. The kids are adorable but it's tiring. I finished at 1 and had a sleepy afternoon. Poor D was sickish from the shot. We talked awhile. D went to sleep early and M told me about right after the war and for the first time mentioned D's first wife. I feel so weird.

June 16: Suzy called from N.Y. She returns tomorrow. Gin called and we talked 45 minutes.

June 17: Roger called. He and his Dad are back from Canada and he was going to disk a field out by the river and wanted me to come. We disked a whole field. We always have such a good time. I got home at 8, showered, ate, talked with M, watered the flowers. D is so sick. It is awful. Suzy called. She's in Cincinnati at Peter's. I got a tan (burn).

June 18: D felt better and I massaged his back and we three watched a good movie.

June 19: Read to D, played piano, massaged D's back and listened to records and read. At 5 M & D left to meet Suzy and Ginger came over. She told me Benny likes me! We took a drive and then M & D & Suzy & the boys came. Watched a good movie on the T.V. Everyone went to sleep but Suz and me fixed D's presents for father's day. Am glad she's home.

June 23: I took six of my Head Start kids to the dentist. After lunch the class got up and sang the good-bye song to me. Jerry my pouter said, "I don't want you to go" and before they left he called me over and gave me a kiss. I came very close to crying. I will miss Head Start. For once I was responsible, kind of. Talked with M & D. Brooded over growing up, leaving. I can't find my class ring. After supper, cleaning. I cleaned the kitchen, D cleaned my ears, M cleaned my clothes, I cleaned the Spitfire. I packed. It makes the trip seem real. My stomach is queasy.

June 27: I lost yesterday. Crossed the International Date Line. Changed clothes before we landed at Sydney, went through customs and went through the gate. And there was Michael with beautiful flowers and Zeldi and Harry. Was a beautiful day. It's winter but not too cool at all and green. Zeldi & Harry are so nice and Michael is a doll. I feel right at home and am happy I came.

July 9: I was just reading over this year—what a year it was. Started in Israel, ended in Australia and in between passed the very best year of my entire life. . . .

July 10: My 18th birthday! The phone rang and Michael said it was for me. I picked it up and couldn't believe my ears! It was M, D, & S. I (for once) was speechless. I could only stammer. And kick myself for not asking and talking. Am very happy. I love them so very very much.

July 11: I'm having a very good time. But I kind of miss M & D & S.

July 13: I am on my way home. At 3:30 A.M. Suzy called & said, "D is very bad & you should come home" & I threw the phone down and screamed and ran to Zeldi. My God I still don't know what to do or think. I was hysterical. David got me sedatives. Finally I fell asleep with Michael and Zeldi. The whole day has been hell. Daddy . . . I can't express my feelings. Harry and I went to the city and got my flight booked. 5:30 was the earliest. I stayed on the balcony with Michael all afternoon. Zeldi and Harry and Michael have been wonderful. I love them. I dread going home. How can we live without Sanyi. Now I feel numb. As long as I don't think it's O.K. I love you Daddy. All I can think of is my strong handsome father. I wish I were asleep and then I could wake up. Oh God. What will Mom do? And us. . . . I just was in Honolulu for an hour. Beautiful airport. Switched from 707 to 747. Until now have been numb. Think sedatives wearing off. Will take another or I keep crying. Dread going home. Keep hoping D's all right. Even tho . . . Just saw a movie "Cromwell." Had cry in bathroom. Outside I've got to look alright. Daddy doesn't like public tears. I wish Mommy and Suzy were here. Los Angeles will be in less than an hour. Must call home.

Called home. Mark was there and told me. I love him. Called Baba's and talked to Suzy and M. All N.Y. is here. Uncle Fritz came to see me at L.A. airport. Waited in L.A. from 5 to 10. Now on a 747 to Atlanta.

July 14: Suzy and Mommy got me at 8 A.M. at the airport. They are both doing well. Suzy has done so many of the arrangements. Daddy had lung cancer and he & M knew it all this time. I still can't believe how brave they both were. So many things make me think of him. I guess I loved him more than anyone could love a father. Or anyone. The day mixes together. All the relatives came. People have been so great. Mark stayed all Tues. in Seaman with D at Lewis's [the funeral home]. Hundreds of people went. There were a lot of people at the funeral. Suzy and me saw D but we closed it [the coffin] for the funeral. I am so tired.

"I want to tell you exactly what happened," my mother said to me conspiratorially. "But I'll call you when Arthur isn't in the room."

Was it possible we had never had this discussion?

"Call me," I said.

She called me. First she set the stage for the story she was about to tell.

Suzy had come home that weekend, along with her college roommate and her boyfriend and Jim, the medical student from Scarsdale.

She told our parents she'd finally made up her mind. She had given the engagement ring back to Peter and was going to continue seeing Jim, though they had no plans to marry.

If my father was upset, he hid it. That evening—it was a Saturday—he joined Suzy's friends for dinner and put on his company charm, though he was noticeably subdued.

Sunday morning it was raining when they got up.

"Daddy said to me that he doesn't feel like getting up and maybe Suzy should take her friends into Cincinnati to see a movie. Jim had an early plane Monday and they could sleep at Baba's. She was in Roanoke anyway.

"That was the first time that Daddy didn't get dressed. He stayed in bed during the day, then got up for dinner. Then he lay on the couch in the living room to watch the news. I sat next to him and he put my hand on his loin and said, 'You feel that?'

"There was a knot.

"He said, 'That's a blood clot, if it goes into my brain I become a vegetable. If that happens, I don't want you to take me to the hospital here. Call Lewis's and get an ambulance to take me to Dr. Goodman. I hope it will hit my heart and that will be that.' "

I put my hand over the phone so my mother couldn't hear my jagged breathing. No use.

"Are you all right?" she asked me. "Are you sure you want to hear this?"

I nodded. "Fine," I said. "Go on."

"After the news we went to bed and went to sleep. In the morning he embraced me and pulled me toward him. He couldn't move too much, so I got on top."

I felt as though I were twelve years old again, experiencing the shock of knowing my parents had sex. This lusty finish didn't correspond to my own naïvely sentimental vision of the death scene.

"You had sex!" I said incredulously.

"We'd always had sex, even when he was sick," said my mother matter-of-factly.

"Well, how was it?" I said, embarrassed by my own prurience.

"It was as usual," she said. "Good."

"Oh," I said, thinking my father's final moments had been so finely calibrated they might have been orchestrated by a hopelessly romantic director. "Then what?"

"He put his shoes and socks on to go to work and he started breathing hard. He couldn't catch his breath. He said I should get some aminophylline. That expands the airways.

"I ran into the office. The nurses were already there, they came in at eight. I got the pill and gave it to Daddy. He swallowed the pill, and that was it. He just died. That's when I yelled to Tommy, 'Go get the nurse.'

"Poor Tommy didn't know. I ran into the office and yelled, 'Dr. Fisher, please come in and come in right away.' All three girls and he came in right away and put Daddy on the floor. He started to hit Daddy on the chest and told me to give him mouth-to-mouth resuscitation.

"John Fisher kept saying, 'Please, please, don't do this to me. Don't die on me.' "

She paused. "Poor thing. He had started to work the Monday before.

"He said, 'Call the ambulance to take him to the hospital.'

"I said, 'Is he dead?'

" 'Yes,' he said.

" 'Then,' I said, 'we are not taking him anyplace.'

"I called Lewis's—not I, one of the girls called. He came right away. Not only he came. It spread like fire. Within ten minutes Eileen was over, Marie Roush, Prudie."

Her voice was trembling.

"Are you okay, Mommy?" I asked her, now openly crying.

"Yes, Juliska, I'm fine," she said. "I was standing there trying to think. First of all I have to call Suzy, that she has to come home right away. Then I was thinking, What to do with you? To call you or not to call you? That it will be horrible news to you. We talked to you on Saturday, your birthday.

"Suzy came home right away. Your sister is remarkable. She just took over. She came. She said, 'Did you call Julie?'

"I said, 'I don't know what to do.'

"She said, 'She'll never forgive you if you don't.'

"While Suzy was talking to you, I got everything ready to go to Cincinnati. I gave Glenn the suit and everything but told him Daddy will be buried in Cincinnati. I realized I didn't know what kind of casket to buy. Funny, this was only my second Jewish funeral. The only one I'd been to was Uncle Louis's."

———

■ Later, another conversation. She told me this:

"People are always inquiring. What do you do when you find out your husband is going to die? What do you feel? What do you do?

"Usually you don't do too much different. Death is hanging over your head, you know that it will come. Once in a while fear comes over you: How and what will you do? Then when it happens you do whatever you have to do.

"I look at myself through your eyes. I would expect these emotions to overwhelm me when I tell you about all that has happened to me. When we went back to Auschwitz, I was a little apprehensive about what my reaction would be. I was surprised at it, that I didn't feel like I'd been there. But with your daddy I didn't have a doubt. I knew I'd been there."

The road home

"Is It So, Suzy?"

■ My journey seemed finished, yet I felt something was missing. I decided to talk to Suzy, my sister.

For most of my childhood I had verified everything with her. I had understood that she alone constituted my peer group. We weren't like our friends, but we certainly weren't like Mommy and Daddy, either. She was my teacher, my friend, and my protector.

The summer our parents sent us to a Jewish camp—a failed experiment—I left my bunk every night and sneaked over to Suzy's. Though she was four and a half years older than me, a huge chasm when you are twelve, as she was, and eight, as I was, she always welcomed me. The other girls taunted her, and one night they issued an ultimatum: "You have to choose your sister or us." She chose me.

When she saw I was about to say something that would inevitably result in a spanking (by my mother), Suzy would clap her hand over my mouth and drag me from the room.

She was my touchstone for matters large and small. If our mother told me the big hand on twelve and the little hand on nine meant it was nine o'clock, I checked with my sister: "Is it so, Suzy?"

When our cousin Barbara told me that girls bled every month and this was called their period I asked Suzy in horror, "Is it so, Suzy?"

When I heard my cousins discussing my father's first family, of course it was my sister I turned to: "It isn't so, is it, Suzy?"

———

■ Arranging a time to talk was both easier and more difficult than it may sound. We are in touch frequently, at least once or twice a week. But the talks are always brief these days: We are busy with jobs, husbands, young children. After teaching emotionally disturbed children for several years, Suzy enrolled in medical school; she now runs the geriatric care unit at a large Boston hospital.

She has watched my adventures develop into this book with some trepidation. She had already endured the publication of a fictionalized account of our childhood, friends wondering what was true and what wasn't. "I worry about the intrusion into our privacy," she told me. "But Mommy has an interesting story, and it would be a shame not to have it written down."

When I told her I needed her, she responded as she always has. We made arrangements for our two families to take a weekend trip together to New Hampshire, with our mother and Arthur. On Sunday morning Suzy and I broke away from the family and climbed to the top of a hill near North Conway. From our perch we had a panoramic view of brilliant fall foliage—the peak of the season, according to *The New York Times*. As we sat there talking, in jeans and sweaters, I felt—incorrectly—that we were the same girls who used to take peanut butter milk shakes to the little bridge on Burnt Cabin Road and talk about whatever it was that came into our heads.

I was pregnant with my second child. Except for a few lines, more noticeable in the bright autumn sun than indoors, Suzy looked remarkably as she always has—slender, with large brown eyes and arching black eyebrows, a beautiful girlish mouth, and delicate hands and feet.

I was happy sitting alone again with my sister, poking about the past, though I was struck by how different her memories were from mine. I didn't realize that my sister had always felt displaced, no matter how well adjusted and popular she had seemed to me. I learned how hard it had been for her, moving to Seaman from New York, away from the relatives who had doted on her. She had carried her own secret fear, that being Jewish would prove disastrous for us as it had for our family in Europe.

She had toyed briefly with the idea of "curing" herself by becoming Christian. For a few Wednesdays she had gone to revival meetings with a friend who belonged to a fundamentalist church. It was common at these meetings for various members of the congregation to be seized with the spirit—though Suzy, already clinically minded, interpreted their wild gyrations as fits. Occasionally parishioners were so stirred they would leap from their seats and run around the small cement building that housed the church. Suzy longed to be similarly overtaken but retained full possession of her reason throughout her first visit and her second. However, she was sufficiently affected to weep for our parents because, as Jews, they would never be saved.

Finally she decided it was time to rescue herself. On her third visit she went up to the minister and knelt, waiting to be moved. She was trembling as he placed his hands on her shoulders and appealed loudly to heaven. But Suzy felt only the weight of his heavy hands.

I, too, went to a revival meeting or two, but I remembered only what I wore—a starchy white dress with purple flowers—and the excitement of watching adults run around calling to Jesus. Even then Suzy responded to life's contrariness by grappling with it while I stepped back and watched. No wonder that she became a teacher, then a doctor, while I became a film critic and journalist, a professional spectator.

———

▪ After we'd talked for a couple of hours, Suzy said it was time to go. The others would be waiting. As we began walking down the hill to the condominium where we were staying, I felt discouraged. Not even Suzy had an answer for me this time. She wasn't able to tell me why I had been working so hard to find out who our parents were, why I

A family get-together in New Hampshire in the fall of 1994. *From left:* **My mother; Arthur; my sister's husband, Alan Einhorn; Suzy; me, almost eight months pregnant with Eli; my husband, Bill Abrams; and the kids (from left): Alexandra, David, and Roxie.**

needed so badly to put it all together—the death camps, our mother, Ohio, the laughs, the great weight our father carried inside him. I wished we didn't have to rush back, especially when we found that no one was looking for us. The children were noisily entertaining themselves while the adults were lolling contentedly, reading the newspaper, watching TV.

Only later did it occur to me that perhaps my search had culminated in that placid scene. Wasn't this ordinariness, this *miraculous* ordinariness, what my parents had struggled so hard for? All my father had seemed to want was a wife and children and to do some good. Achieving this deceptively modest ambition—so much can go wrong!—must have taken heroic effort for this man who had lost everything.

Yet instead of locking his heart he had opened it—as much as he had dared. He had tried again in a new country, with a new family and a new life. He told my mother before he died that he had no regrets about anything he did *after the war.* I like to think of this parting gift as assurance that, although part of him died with his first family, he still loved his second.

I feel more grateful than ever for that love but no longer as burdened by it. I now believe my mother when she tells me, "Don't you know that all your Daddy and I ever wanted for you girls is for you to be happy?"

I am overwhelmed by the love and courage my mother put forth by taking this trip with me. She has so carefully kept a distance from the hard facts of her life, wearing blitheness like a protective shield against the specter of evil. Yet to help me she forced herself to remember, in piercing detail, the terrible betrayals she had chosen to suppress.

This revelation came to me not at the top of a mountain, as I had planned, but during a minor argument I was having with my daughter, Roxie. She was angry at me because, trying to get her to eat a green vegetable, I'd said, in an excessively cheery voice, "Look, sweetie, *I* love broccoli!"

She looked at me with the sweeping dismissiveness of a four-year-old. "I'm me and you're you, and we're not the same," she announced.

At first I felt wounded. "How could you say that?" I thought. "When I look at you, I see myself." But of course she was right. She could love me and learn from me, but she would decide when and if she wanted to eat broccoli just as she would decide what dreams to dream.

"Mommy?"

I saw Roxie staring up at me, looking worried as she tried to figure out what was on my mind.

I hugged her and said, "You're right. You're you and I'm me."

Still, Roxie is learning to belt out the Old Testament to my scratchy old Bible records, and she has already explained to her new brother, Eli, that he—like his Aunt Suzy's daughter—had a grandfather named Alex who died a long time ago. My husband and I haven't yet figured out how to tell our children about Hitler, but we have taken Roxie to Seaman. She is convinced, for now, that the stars are more abundant there than anywhere, and brighter. We're already planning to take Eli for a visit, as soon as we can.

One day I suspect my children will discover for themselves what has taken me so long to learn—that we are bound together by our family stories, which are written and revised every day. They will understand why, every night before they go to bed, we say the prayer my father said with Suzy and me:

> *Now I lay me down to sleep,*
> *I pray the Lord my soul to keep.*
> *Guard me through the starry night*
> *And wake me safe with sunshine bright.*

Amen.

Roxie's first trip to Seaman

Acknowledgments

■ My mother says fate dictated the writing of this book.

That may be the case, but then fate enlisted a lot of assistants, people whose generosity of spirit and time helped me so very much.

Kathy Robbins and Noelle Hannon nurtured the idea at inception, then turned me over to Ann Godoff, who became my catalyst and muse.

I received valuable aid of various kinds from David Blum, Megan Barnett, Trish Hall, Barry Kramer, Sara Krulwich, Russlyn Ransome, and Steven Spielberg.

I am grateful to my friends in Adams County who helped me in the research of this book—and another book that has yet to be written— especially Diane and Bill Lewis, Candee and Gary Basford, Vernon and Eileen Young, Betty Hoop, Prudie Snider, Herb Lax, Stephen Kelley, Annette Glasgow, Alice Michael, Nola Ryan, and Mary White.

Many people offered insight into my parents' past and I thank all of them, with special gratitude for Joseph Rapaport, Ella Schlanger, Stephen Salamon, Alice Greenberg, Michael Hermel, Elizabeth Roth, Ilana Siman-Tov, Tommy Schlanger, and Tibor Mermelstein.

None of it could have been done, of course, without the participants in this journey. My stepfather, Arthur Salcman, was a wonderful traveling companion and a great help all around. As for my sister, Suzy Salamon, and our amazing mother, Lilly Salcman, the soul of this book belongs to you.

Above all I want to thank my husband, Bill Abrams, who watched over me during the writing of this book as he has since we were teenagers—with good sense, good jokes, and a most tender heart.

ABOUT THE AUTHOR

JULIE SALAMON grew up in Seaman, Ohio, and now lives in New York City with her husband, Bill Abrams, and their children, Roxie and Eli. She worked for *The Wall Street Journal* for sixteen years as a reporter and film critic. Her writing has appeared in *The New York Times, Harper's Bazaar, Vogue, Vanity Fair,* and *The New Republic.* She is the author of a novel, *White Lies,* and of *The Devil's Candy: "The Bonfire of the Vanities" Goes to Hollywood.*

ABOUT THE TYPE

This book was set in Galliard, a typeface designed by Matthew Carter for the Merganthaler Linotype Company in 1978. Galliard is based on the sixteenth-century typefaces of Robert Granjon.

9 780812 991697

Printed in the United States
by Baker & Taylor Publisher Services